Boatbuilding Down East

Boatbuilding Down East

How Lobsterboats are Built

by
Royal Lowell

WoodenBoat Publications

Brooklin, Maine

Published by
WoodenBoat Books
Naskeag Road, PO Box 78
84 Great Cove Drive
Brooklin, Maine 04616 USA
www.woodenboatbooks.com

ISBN 10: 0-937822-73-6
ISBN 13: 978-0-937822-73-9

Previously published by International Marine, and Simonton Cove Publishing

Cover design: Olga Lange

Front and back cover paintings by:
R.B. Dance
2107 St. George Place
Kinston, North Carolina 28504
www.robertbdance.com

Printed in the USA by Versa Press

10 9 8 7 6 5 4 3 2

Dedication

This book is dedicated to two people who were very close to me:

William Frost, my grandfather, who taught me how to design and build boats, both commercial and pleasure. When I was a young boy, I couldn't stay away from his shop; everything about boatbuilding fascinated me.

Riley Lowell, my father, who had hands like baseball gloves with which he could "hoss" heavy oak timbers around. Yet he could also make fancy moldings and other wooden items that required a delicate touch. He was second to none as a boatbuilder.

Contents

(Above) Royal Lowell, the author.
(Below) The crew of the Even Keel Boatshop in Yarmouth, Maine, where many of Royal Lowell's boats are built. The choice of this yard is not surprising; his two brothers are at the left of the picture and that's his son on the right. (Photo by Brooks Townes)

Foreword

The Maine lobsterboat is known and admired all over the country. This is a book on how to build one of these beautiful boats from start to finish. Over the years many hundreds of these craft have been built, so that the methods and construction details have been worked out and refined to an unusual degree. For their size, these lobsterboats withstand some of the harshest possible use, as most of them fish all winter off the stormy coast of Maine. Such a boat has to be good to survive.

There are differences in the boats from one part of the coast to another and from one boat to another within an area, but the boats from Beals Island and Jonesport have always been highly regarded, especially for their graceful good looks and high speed. The late Will Frost's boats were always advanced for their day, and it was not at all strange that during Prohibition his shops on Beals Island and Jonesport were engaged to build some fast, high-powered rumrunners. His influence has had much to do with the modern Maine lobsterboat as we know it today.

Not a little of Will Frost's thinking about lobsterboats was passed on to his grandson Royal Lowell, the author of this book. He is a gifted designer, and, like his grandfather before him, he has an eye for a boat. Whatever else his boats may be, they never fail to please the eye. Since Will Frost's day, boats have become wider and higher powered. Royal Lowell is out among the leaders in modelling and designing these present-day lobsterboats, and his designs are a nice blend of the best features from boats all along the coast—and of course contain some of his own original thinking. Although he is a traditionalist and prefers wooden hulls, Royal has kept up with the times by designing a number of production fiberglass boats ranging in length from 21 feet to 55 feet. The series of 35-, 42-, and 55-footers manufactured by Bruno and Stillman have become quite popular.

The author has a wonderful talent for expressing himself by drawing or sketching, as the illustrations in this book indicate. The perspective sketches were just "laid out" by eye until they looked right. But the important thing is that Lowell is not only a designer, but also a boatbuilder—he has many times performed all of the operations which he describes, making this book a first-person account of how to build a boat. There is no better kind of "how to" book.

The emphasis here is on how things are done and why, rather than on what the completed structure looks like—a weakness of many books on the subject. Fortunately, he tells only about how to build one of his boats the way he has always done it. There are no vague generalities because the scope is too broad or the knowledge too shallow, yet much of the information so carefully explained and so well illustrated is directly applicable to building other types of boats.

The book is laid out and written as though the author were explaining to his apprentice just how to go about building the boat from start of construction to finish. Experts may know of other ways to put a boat together, some of which may be quicker and others perhaps even better. There is absolutely no doubt in my mind, however, that if one were to follow this text to the letter, he would end up with an exceptionally fine boat without much wasted time in the building of her. The sketches and photos are proof enough of this.

The designing and lofting aspects of boatbuilding would, in themselves, fill a book, and rather than to treat them superficially, the author has chosen to begin his instruction after the plans for the boat have been drawn and her lines have been laid down on the mold loft floor. If he needs to, the reader should refer to any one of a number of good books on boat design and lofting.

This is not a book for the rank beginner.

The reader is expected to be familiar with normal woodworking operations and with the terms used in a boatshop. Some of these terms do vary, however, from place to place, and, because of this, a glossary of the more unusual ones has been provided in the appendix.

As I have always been an admirer of Royal Lowell boats, it gave me great pleasure to work with him on certain aspects of this book. There have been few such works that have taught me so much about boatbuilding as this, and it is my hope that the reader will feel the same way. Here is an entire approach to boatbuilding written by a professional, and we can all benefit from studying it well. We should also feel grateful that Royal Lowell chose to take the time to prepare such a book. It is rare indeed to find a good boatbuilder who wants to do anything but build boats. After reading his book, it's not hard to understand why.

As this is written in 1976, it appears that fiberglass may be replacing a good many of the wooden lobsterboats, as it has already in most other craft. However, Royal is still designing several new custom wooden lobsterboats each year, and he feels that there will always be wooden lobsterboats "abuilding." But in any event, the information in this book will ensure that the technology of building them from wood will not vanish completely.

Maynard Bray
Brooklin, Maine

Prologue

I was born on Beals Island, Maine, in 1926, into a boatbuilding family. Call it luck or not, but boatbuilding and boat design are all I know. When other boys were playing as boys usually do, I was hanging around Gramp's boatshop watching the crew turn raw timber into a handsome, finished product.

I built my first boat, a kayak, when I was ten. I swiped my mother's bedsheets to use for a skin. After sewing and tacking the sheets on the frame, my brother and I had a launching, and I mean a wet launching. Her waterline "warn't too far from the sheer." To have such a disaster after all that work was just too much. A fellow who worked for Gramps saw our predicament and offered us a couple of well-treated canvas tarpaulins. You can imagine our utter delight. We tore the sheets off and "smacked" the tarps to her and had a great day, and a few more to come. Funny thing, every once in a while we would hear a roar of laughter coming from the shop. We were having a good time and figured that those boys in the shop had found some fun of their own, too.

A little later on, I guess I was twelve or so, I helped my father build a couple of "pods," and Gramp, seeing that I was genuinely interested not only in building but also in design, taught me what he knew, which was a tremendous amount. It didn't matter what it was to be, powerboat or sailboat, he designed and built many beauties.

From then on, I have been involved in boat design and boatbuilding except for a "stint" in the Merchant Marine late in World War II. I was educated in Maine and Massachusetts schools (just about all of my relatives worked at the Boston Navy Yard boatshop or nearby Massachusetts yards doing war work during World War II).

After the war, I settled back into boat-building and studied every book on boat design that I could find, but my actual design work was confined to after work hours and Sundays. In the last five or six years, my design work has increased substantially and has treated me well. I have even turned to designing fiberglass boats also. I suppose we have to follow the trends, but how can you help falling in love with a well-designed wooden boat? After all, they are the closest material thing that is built like your own body.

There are those who say that wooden boat-building is through. Cheer up, people, there will always be a wooden boat. If you don't believe me, go to a launching at an old wood boatshop, take a "gander" at the sparkling lady, smell the fresh bottom paint, and you tell me if wood boats are a thing of the past.

Royal Lowell
Pownal, Maine

Acknowledgments

First of all I would like to express my deep appreciation to the fellows at International Marine Publishing Company, Roger Taylor and Peter Spectre, for publishing this book. I would also like to thank:

Maynard Bray of Brooklin, Maine, for his fine efforts in helping to edit and organize the material.

Charles Broun, Yarmouth, Maine, who has allowed me to use his excellent photographs.

Even Keel Marine, Yarmouth, Maine, for their contribution of photographs.

My family for helping to provide time for this project.

And last, but not least, my son, William Lowell, who has helped me tremendously.

Boatbuilding Down East

Chapter 1

Mold and Pattern Making

The first task in any boatbuilding project is to lay down the lines of the boat full size. This is done by taking the drawings prepared by the naval architect, which are drafted to scale, and re-drawing them on the floor to the actual size of the boat. From these full-size lines the molds and patterns for building the boat are taken. Since lofting, as laying down lines full size is termed, is covered adequately in other books (see, for instance, *Boatbuilding* by Howard I. Chapelle, W.W. Norton Company, N.Y.), I will assume from the beginning that the lines for the boat to be built have already been lofted full size. If you do not know how to lay down lines, study up on the subject by reading books and getting advice from someone who does, or have an experienced loftsman lay down the lines for you. An accurate lofting job is absolutely essential to the building of a lobsterboat, or any boat for that matter.

The building instructions I provide here are applicable in general to all lobsterboats as a type, but I provide at the back of this book the plans for a 36-footer designed by me. This boat can serve as our building example. However, since it is a custom design for one of my clients, it differs in a few ways from the drawings and explanations used in the text. Here are some features of my 36-footer that are different from the corresponding features of the example of a lobsterboat I'll be talking about throughout the book.

1. The hull is semi-built down, in that the garboard doesn't run all the way to the stern and the keel is less deep in molding.

2. Double bolts on either side of the shaft log go all the way through the keel.

3. Floor timbers are placed on, rather than between, the timbers.

4. The cockpit is ceiled with plywood covered with fiberglass and there is ceiling running across the inboard face of the transom.

5. Scuppers go out through the transom, rather than through the sides of the hull.

6. The engine beds run much farther aft than in the text and drawings.

7. There are no quarter knees as the deck is laminated of two layers of plywood. The layers are glued together and then fiberglassed.

8. No beams are used in the cabin and pilothouse roofs as they are cold-molded over forms. They are made up of four or five sheets of plywood glued together.

9. The front of the trunk cabin is V-shaped rather than straight.

10. The pilothouse runs beyond the trunk cabin on the port side.

11. A visor is worked into the pilothouse roof.

12. Deck plates are shown in the cockpit in addition to the engine hatch.

13. A single thickness, rather than double, bilge stringer is shown, which is okay as long as the wood is of good quality and comes in adequate lengths.

14. The companionway hatch coaming rabbets over the cabin roof instead of resting completely on it. This allows the coaming to form its own frame. The hatch cover sets into the coaming rather than overlapping it. This type of construction is used on cold-molded cabin tops only.

As you read my instructions and look at my plans and drawings, keep these differences in mind, and you will realize soon enough why wooden lobsterboats downeast aren't built on a production line.

STEM PATTERN

Once the lines have been laid down on the floor, you have to make the molds as well as the patterns for pieces such as the stem, keel, and transom. Start by making the stem pattern. First, mill out two green (unseasoned) oak fairing battens about ¼ inch by 1¼ inches. These will be bent together as one and will give a truer bend than will a single piece, especially if there is a slightly weak spot in one batten, which will be evened out with two of them working together. Make the battens long enough to go a bit above the top of the stem and to run a couple of feet aft of the keel splice. Take a handful of 6d common nails and drive them about one-half an inch into the floor along the stem profile line. Now bend your battens together around these nails, holding them along the outside with more 6d nails. Lay a piece of ½-inch pine pattern stock on the floor close to the battens and with your pencil mark a line on it that roughly matches the shape of the stem profile. Saw to this line on the bandsaw and lay the pattern back on the floor against the battens. Rough saw the pattern again if necessary to get it within one inch of the battens along its entire length. Then, using your dividers, scribe the pattern, cut it out again on your bandsaw, and go back to the floor and finish fitting it to the battens with a smooth or jack plane. Make the patterns for the forefoot and stem knee in the very same manner. Now, using the method shown in Figure 1-3, mark off and cut all three patterns on their inboard and joining edges.

With all of your cutting and fitting done, tack the patterns into place on the lay-down with 5d box nails. Using your two-foot square, mark off the sheer line, waterlines, and station lines on the patterns. Take the patterns up and measure from the outboard profile line on the floor along the sheer, waterlines, and station lines to the rabbet and bearding lines, and transfer these measurements to your patterns. Now tack your patterns back into place on the floor, and, using your battens and 5d box nails, mark off the rabbet and bearding lines. Label all station lines and waterlines on the pattern, and bore ¹⁄₁₆-inch holes along both the rabbet and bearding lines so these lines can be transferred to the building stock. The stem, knee, and forefoot patterns are now completed.

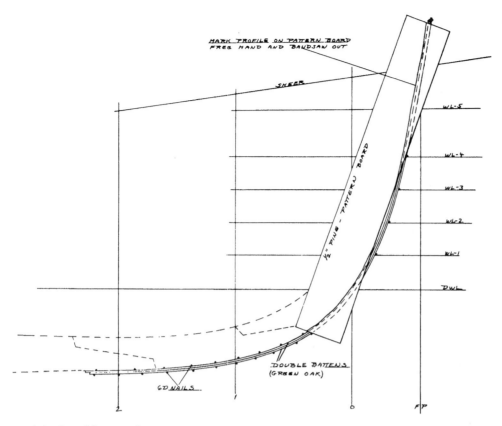

1-1   Roughing out the stem pattern.

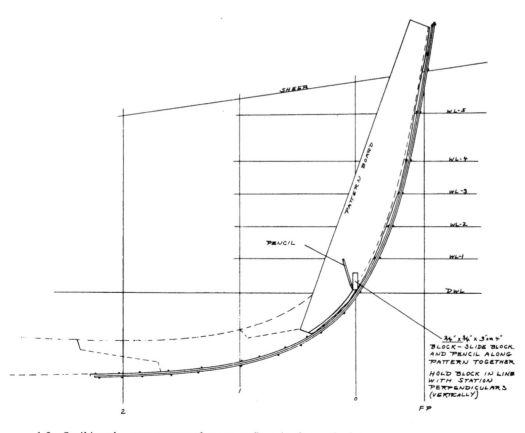

1-2   Scribing the stem pattern for a neat fit at its forward edge.

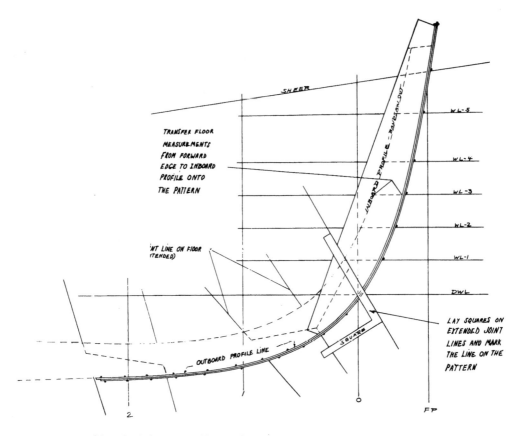

1-3   Marking the inboard profile and joints on the pattern.

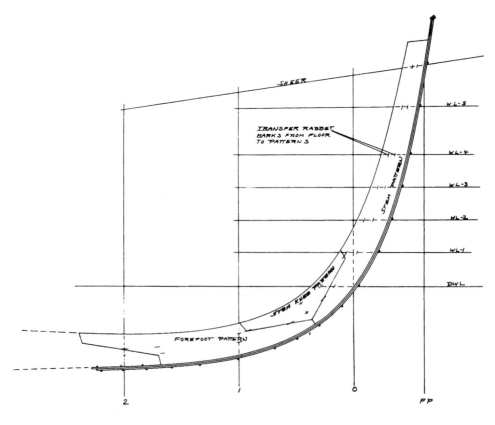

1-4   Transferring the rabbet spots to the patterns.

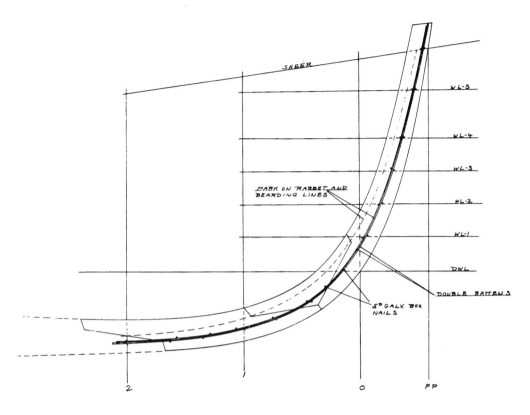

1-5 *Marking the rabbet lines on the patterns.*

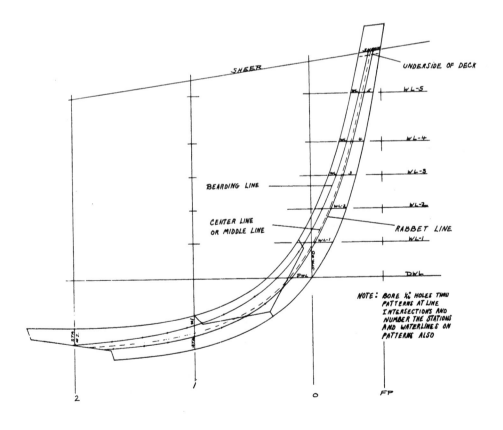

1-6 *The completed stem pattern.*

ADDITIONAL PATTERNS

The profile or bottom edge of the keel pattern can be made as was the stem. Once this is done, make a batten about 1½ inches wide from pattern stock and tack it on the laydown along the inboard or top profile of the keel. Now make a straightedge from your pattern stock and tack it along the lower edge of the shaft log. Then make your stern post pattern and temporarily tack it into place. Mark and cut out for the scarf forward and the skeg and sternpost aft. You now have the profile pattern of the entire keel.

At the stations on the laydown, nail uprights of 4-inch pattern stock, keeping one edge against the station line. Threepenny box nails are best for this because they don't go into the floor too far, making it easier to lift the pattern from the floor. Once the pattern has been fastened together, it is a good idea to nail on some diagonal struts from top to bottom, made from pattern stock that is about 3 inches wide. Now transfer the rabbet and bearding lines from the floor to the keel pattern and lift it from the floor, turn it over, and clinch the nails.

The horn timber is usually straight or nearly so, and you will only need to make a pattern of its forward end where it fits against the shaft log.

It is not necessary to make a pattern of the jib piece or wedge, which goes between the upper edge of the shaft log and the horn timber, as you can transfer its measurements directly to the oak from which this piece will be made.

You next make the stern knee pattern. This is done by taking its bevel between the horn timber and transom, laying the bevel onto the pattern stock, marking the knee pattern to the measured length, and drawing in the inner edge of the knee freehand.

The transom patterns are made from the body plan, rather than the profile, and are fitted to the inside of the planking. Nail your double oak battens around the outline of the transom as it appears in the body plan of your laydown. Make the sill pattern first by laying in a piece of the pattern and rough fitting it to within an inch or so of the battens. Then take a small block of wood the same thickness as your planking, hold it against the battens and with your pencil at its inboard edge, slide the block and pencil along the battens. This will automatically deduct the planking thickness and give you the actual bottom of the sill pattern. Now draw in the top edge of the sill piece with your straightedge, and this pattern is finished.

Follow this same procedure in making the cheek piece pattern and *be sure to mark* the sheer line on it. Make your pattern of the corner knee and the transom radius pattern, which can be made directly from the transom half breadth on your lofting. This will complete the transom patterns, as you don't have to make the top header pattern—you will use your deck beam mold and transom radius pattern to mark from.

You will need a 12-foot straightedge, which is best made from a ¾-inch or 1-inch clear pine or mahogany board about 6 inches wide. Use a string stretched tightly between two nails to establish the straight line and mark along the string on the board every 24 inches or so. Remove the string and use a batten against the tick marks to line off the edge. Cut and joint the straightedge to this line and finish it.

A cabin beam mold is needed. Make this as shown in Figures 1-8 and 1-9.

To mark out the deck beams and cut down the sheer, a deck beam mold will be needed. Make it from a ¾-inch or 1-inch clear pine board about 12 feet long and wide enough for the crown of the deck plus the molded height of the deck beams. A board 6 inches to 8 inches wide will usually be about right. Lay out the curve the same way as for the cabin beam mold, changing the crown to suit.

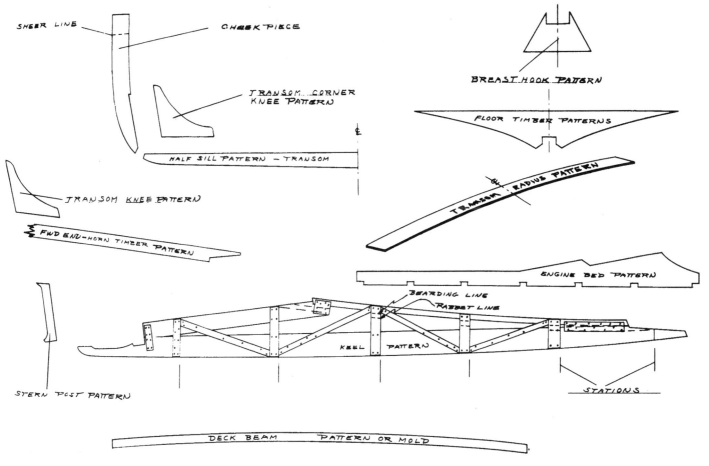

1-7   Other patterns needed in hull construction.

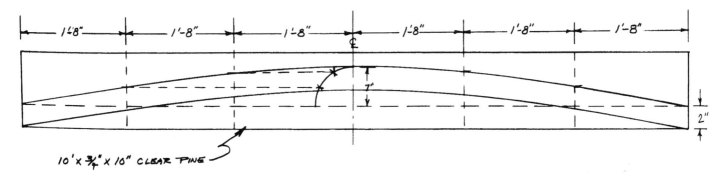

1-8   The trunk cabin beam mold with a 7-inch crown. The deck beam mold is made in the same manner but with a 3½-inch crown.

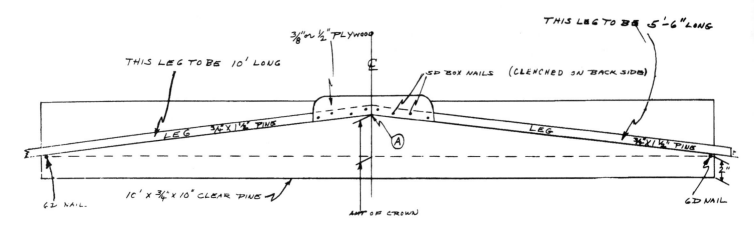

1-9 *A marking rig, an alternate method of marking beam molds. Hold a pencil point at A and slide the rig to starboard, marking the crown on this half of the pattern. Then turn the marking rig over and draw in the port side in the same manner.*

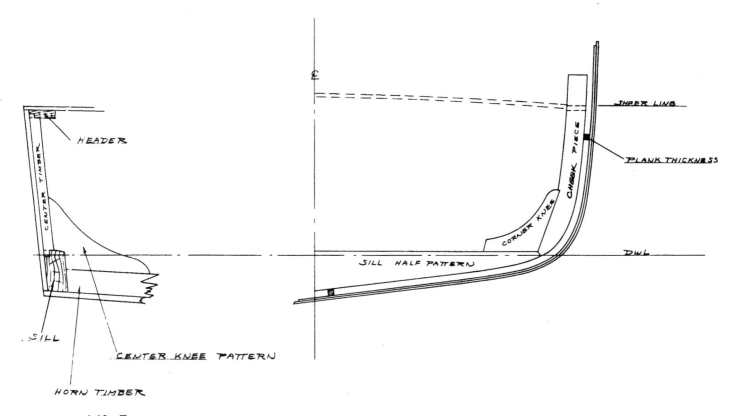

1-10 *Transom patterns.*

HULL MOLDS

If your double battens are still in good shape, they will be all right for mold work. If not, then make new ones. I feel that molds should be made fairly heavy, so I wouldn't use any stock thinner than a full 1 inch, and 1¼ inches is even better. Number 3 pine is the most common wood used for this purpose.

Mill out the cross spalls first and lay them to one side. These should be about 7 or 8

10

inches wide and should be run over the jointer so their edges are perfectly straight. *These are important parts of the molds, as they will be your levelling points, both lengthwise and athwartship.* You will need one for each mold, and the length of each can be picked off the body plan.

To make the boundary pieces for a typical mold, tack 6d nails around the inside edge of the station line in the body plan on the floor, and bend your battens around these nails, holding them in place with more nails along the outside edge, the same as you did with your stem and transom battens.

From the amidship mold, which is to be our example, to the transom, the molds will have a joint near the turn of the bilge. Forward of amidship you can usually get each side of the molds out of one piece of wide stock. The bandsaw, if portable, should be moved close by, because of the amount of cutting. Cut a piece of mold stock long enough to extend from about a foot above the sheer down to 3 or 4 inches below the bilge joint. Look down at the lines, get an idea of the shape, and rough saw this piece. Then check it for fit, and, if it is within roughly ¾ inch of the true shape, it will be good enough to tack down. Then take your marking block (the same one you used in making the transom patterns), hold it against the battens, and, with your pencil at its inside edge, slide it along the batten, marking the mold piece as you go. With your two-foot square, mark the sheer line and waterlines across the mold piece. Also, *mark the joint line at the bilge.* Take up the mold piece, tack it to another piece of mold stock of the same size, bandsaw them both to your line, and cut the bilge joint. *At this point,* you should transfer the sheer (top of the sheer strake in this case) and waterlines around to the other piece of mold stock, which will be for the other side of the boat, using a combination square and your two-foot square. *Be careful*

not to forget this or you will have to put both sides of the mold back together to do it. Now take the pieces apart and label them as #5 port and #5 starboard top pieces.

Take another piece of mold stock and cut it *a few inches longer* than what it takes to go from the center of the keel to the bilge joint. Again, look at your lines, rough-cut this mold piece, and go through the same procedure as you did in marking the top piece—*except that you must mark the center joint over the keel.* Lay the top piece of mold into position and transfer the bilge joint on the bottom piece, then tack this bottom piece to another piece of mold stock and bandsaw them both to your line. There are usually no waterlines to transfer around on these pieces; they are just labelled as port and starboard bottom pieces for mold #5.

Lay the top and bottom pieces on the floor, using your marking block as a spacer between their outboard edges and the battens to position them. When they are in position, tack them to the floor. Look down at your mold at the bilge and by eye cut a gusset as close to two feet long as you can get it. Saw another one like it for the other side. This gusset connects the top and bottom pieces of one side of the mold and is fastened with 2-inch #12 flat-head galvanized screws. Pull the nails holding this half of the mold to the floor and turn it over. Now tack the mold pieces for the opposite side to this half mold, being careful that the sheer and waterline marks line up square with each other, and screw the gusset on to join these pieces together.

Separate the half molds and tack the original half mold back into place on the floor. Place the opposite half mold on the floor next to it, with your center joint at the keel lined up. Adjust the opposite half mold until the waterlines on it correspond with those on the floor, then tack it into place. Using your tape measure, check that both halves of the mold are the same distance from the centerline at the sheer. If there is a slight difference, adjust the opposite side half mold.

The bottom of the mold halves are joined by a saddle, milled from your mold stock and screwed on with 2-inch #12 flat-head galvanized screws. Mark the centerline on the saddle after it is fastened. (The saddles and your cross spalls are the only single pieces on the molds; all the others are cut in pairs.)

Get one of your cross spalls and lay it across the mold, with its top edge lying on the uppermost waterline below the sheer that runs the length of the boat. Transfer the centerline from the floor to the cross spall with your square, then mark the ends

of the cross spalls so they are about 1½ inches inside the outer edge of the mold. Cut off the ends and fasten the cross spall back in place, again using 2-inch #12 screws.

If you haven't already done so, put the mold number and "port" or "starboard" on each side of the mold tops with a crayon or felt-tipped marking pen. Pull the temporary nails and lift the mold off the floor and stand it against the wall. You are now ready for the next one.

A final word: Be sure to keep the outboard edges of the gussets and saddle, as well as the cross spalls already mentioned, about 1½ inches shy of the mold line to allow room for a timber in case it comes close to the mold.

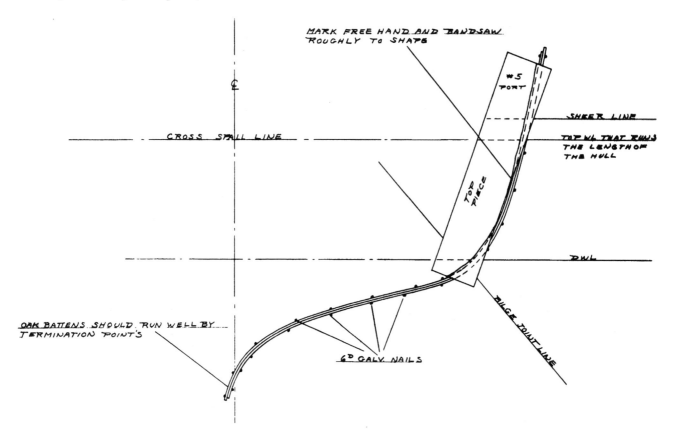

1-11 *Rough marking of a mold piece.*

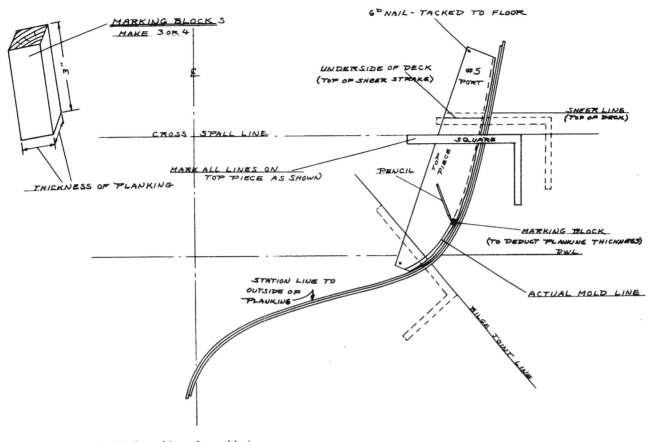

MARKING BLOCKS
MAKE 3 OR 4

3"

THICKNESS OF PLANKING

6ᴰ NAIL - TACKED TO FLOOR

UNDERSIDE OF DECK
(TOP OF SHEER STRAKE)

#5
PORT

SHEER LINE
(TOP OF DECK)

CROSS SPALL LINE

SQUARE

MARK ALL LINES ON
TOP PIECE AS SHOWN

PENCIL

TOP PIECE

MARKING BLOCK
(TO DEDUCT PLANKING THICKNESS)
DWL

ACTUAL MOLD LINE

STATION LINE TO
OUTSIDE OF
PLANKING

BILGE JOINT LINE

1-12   *Final marking of a mold piece.*

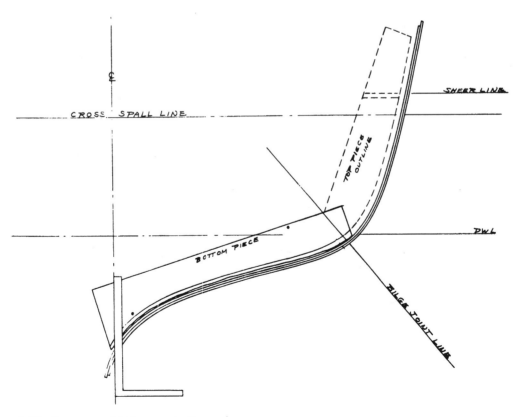

℄

CROSS SPALL LINE

SHEER LINE

TOP PIECE OUTLINE

DWL

BOTTOM PIECE

BILGE JOINT LINE

1-13   *Bottom mold piece ready for sawing.*

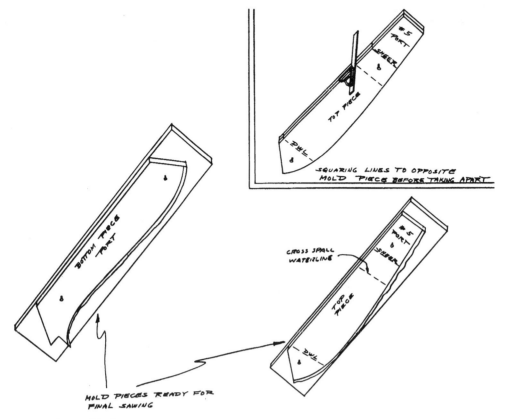

SQUARING LINES TO OPPOSITE
MOLD PIECE BEFORE TAKING APART

CROSS SPALL
WATERLINE

MOLD PIECES READY FOR
FINAL SAWING

1-14   Sawing mold pieces.

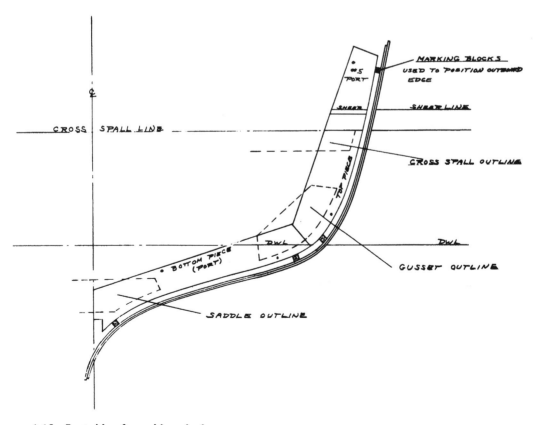

MARKING BLOCKS
USED TO POSITION OUTBOARD
EDGE

SHEAR LINE

CROSS SPALL LINE

CROSS SPALL OUTLINE

DWL

GUSSET OUTLINE

SADDLE OUTLINE

1-15   Port side of a mold ready for a gusset.

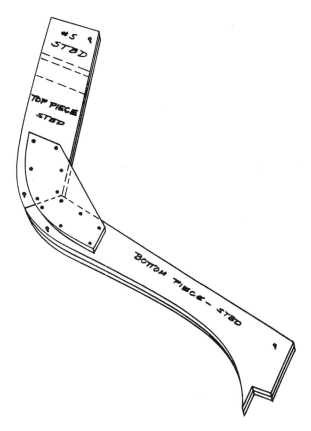

1-16   Tack both sides of the same mold together and fasten on the gusset.

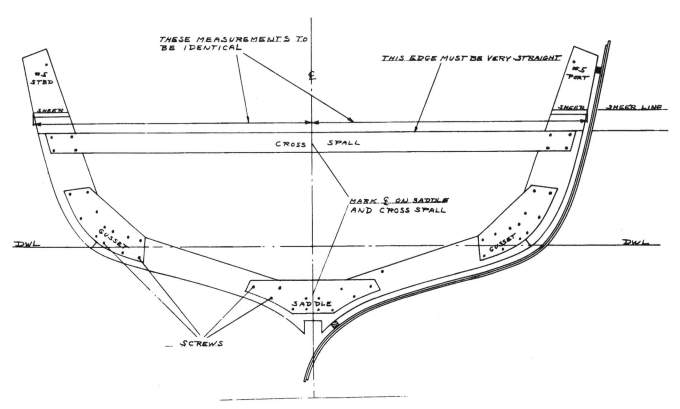

1-17   Completed mold.

Chapter 2

The Foundation

SOME NOTES ON OAK

The foundation will be made from oak. White oak is probably best if you can get it, but most Maine builders use a type of native red oak called gray oak because of its color. It is quite fine grained and can be worked and bent easily. What we call red oak, as opposed to gray, is very pink in color and has a coarse, open grain. Its smell is distinctive, like urine, which gives it its obvious nickname.

Oak is ordered from the mill rough-sawn to the desired thickness but with the bark left on the edges. Live edge, flitch sawn, round edge, or through and through are terms commonly used when ordering lumber with bark on the edges.

The heart or center of an oak tree is porous, and rot spreads quickly in it. We ask the sawyer for the pieces on either side of the heart for our stem and transom stock. But the keel, because of its larger size, usually contains the heart, although much of it can be eliminated (or it can be boxed entirely if desired) by careful placement of the keel pattern. Other pieces, such as those for the shaft log, horn timber, and sternpost, are small enough so the heart can be avoided.

Heart (the center of the tree) and heartwood (the usable wood inside the sapwood) are two different things. Heartwood is the most durable part of the tree, and, where possible, foundation pieces should be made from it. This means not using the sapwood, i.e., the light-colored wood just inside the bark, in any of your work.

For use above the waterline, seasoned oak is desirable, but for the pieces described in this chapter, newly cut wood is usually used.

All oak should be liberally coated with preservative after it is fashioned to its final shape. End grain, particularly, should be well saturated.

STEM

Begin your foundation by making up the stem. Choose a select piece of oak, preferably with a sweeping grain. This piece would probably be from a clear butt log, which as a rule has some sweep at its bottom end. Lay your stem pattern on the oak and mark around it. Be sure to mark the joints with a square or straightedge. Pick out another piece of oak for your forefoot and stem knee. Lay on your patterns and mark these pieces also.

With your helper, bandsaw these pieces out, being careful to leave the pencil line. After sawing, work the outside edges down to the line with your jack and smooth plane, all the while keeping the edges square. In jointing the surfaces of the scarfs or splices, you will need your 1½-inch chisel to trim out the inside corners. All surfaces of the joints should be squared in from the marked side of the pieces. Now plane the saw marks off the inboard edge of these pieces to give them a finished look and you are ready to fit the joints and bolt them off.

Clamp the stem in a vise with its lower end angled up to clear your bench and set the stem knee in place. I should mention at this point that these parts should be marked only on one side so they don't accidentally get turned around. With a sliding bar clamp or a C clamp, if you have a large one, clamp the knee to the stem. Tack angle blocks under the clamp to keep it from slipping.

Run your 10-point crosscut handsaw through joint *A* in Figure 2-2, being very careful not to run down by the end of the joint. Tap end *C* with your hammer and a block of wood, and tighten the clamp to close the joint. It may take two or three saw cuts for a tight fit, depending on how well the pieces were sawn out originally.

The stem and stern knee can now be bolted up. Turn the assembly over in your vise so that the face of the stem is up. Using your combination square and a pencil, line off the centerline and width of the finished stem face. The face of the stem is usually made a strong ¾ inch to allow for a ¾-inch half-round or half-oval metal stem band. Now mark the angle of the bolts on one side of the stem and square them across its face. Using a bit large enough to counterbore for the head of the bolt makes a mess of the job, as you must use an enormous plug to fill the hole that overlaps the finished stem face. So *forget* about counterboring, and,

with your ½-inch auger, bore through the stem and the knee for the shank of the bolt. It is good to have someone sight your auger for a proper line-up. When both holes have been bored, take your ¼-inch and ½-inch chisels and cut an oblong recess (½ inch by 2 inches) for your bolt head in the face of the stem. Using your two-pound hammer, beat the bolt heads to a ½-inch width on your anvil, then thread the bolts if required and cut them off to the proper length.

It is now time for the final fastening. Take off the clamp and treat the joint with Cuprinol; reclamp the pieces after tapping them firmly together again. Now drive the bolts home, holding an adjustable wrench on each bolt head to keep it lined up with its head recess until it is down flush, after which you can set it in with a heavy punch. Put washers and nuts on the bolts and tighten them up. Then saw off the protruding end of each bolt, leaving about ⅛ inch, which is peened over. Take off your clamp and fit and bolt on the forefoot to the other end of the knee, using this same method. The only difference is that you now have two joints to saw cut, *B* and *C* in Figure 2-2, in order to fit the forefoot to both the knee and the stem. After bolting, cut out four plugs of oak with a slight taper on their ends and sides, drive these in over the bolt heads, and chisel off the excess. Set these plugs in Cuprinol or bottom paint.

With the stem, stem knee, and forefoot all bolted up as a unit, you can lay out and cut the rabbet. Tack your patterns in place and, using a 6d common or 5d box nail, drive through the pattern along the rabbet and bearding lines, where you bored pilot holes earlier. Drive only until you feel the nail fetch against the oak. Now square all waterlines, station lines, and the sheer line from the pattern across the face of the stem assembly and its inboard edge. Lift off your patterns and, with your two-foot square, carry these lines back onto both sides of the assembly. With your double battens, line off your rabbet and bearding lines also on both sides.

You are now ready to start cutting in the rabbet, and to guide in this operation make yourself a planking block about 3 inches by 6 inches, and the thickness of your planking. Put identifying marks on both sides of this block, as you will use it for all of your rabbet cutting and the marks make the block easy to spot when you are looking for it. I usually start cutting at the top of the stem. From your laydown, take bevels of the angles of the sheer line, waterlines, and station lines at the stem and mark them on a short board. This is called a *bevel board*, and you will later make another one for the keel bevels. But, getting back to the stem, set the bevel gauge for the sheer angle and position it on the side of the stem at the sheer, lay the planking block against the bevel gauge blade, and from this get a mental picture of where the middle line of the rabbet would be. With your 1½-inch chisel, rough a section of rabbet about 6 inches long, then, using your chisel as a paring tool, shave down the surfaces until the block fits in the rabbet at the correct angle. Repeat this procedure at intervals along the length of the rabbet, always using your bevel board to obtain the correct bevel gauge setting for each location. Stop the rabbet about 8 inches from the aft joint on the forefoot, so that when you join the forefoot to the keel, you have a little room to connect and fair in the rabbet lines of each piece. Otherwise, you may end up with a quick place or kink in the rabbet.

Now go back and finish cutting the rabbet between the spots, fairing the change between bevels. When one side is completed, turn the assembly over and do the other side. After the rabbet cutting is completed, you have to cut the excess wood off each side of the assembly from the rabbet line to the face, which as you recall is a strong ¾ of an inch. If you feel hale and hearty and want to do it the way we used to, use a lipped adze. If you should do this, lay the unit on the floor or lean it against a bench, clamped if necessary to hold it steady. Now, holding the end of your adze handle in one hand, close against your hip or belly, use the other hand to swing the adze with. Cut a little at a time, and be extremely careful not to chop over the line. These days, we have the electric hand jointer, which in this case can be used in place of an adze; I would not be without this tool, as it does the same job as an adze, but is much easier to use and lessens the risk of cutting over the line.

Plane or adze these surfaces down to within 1/16 inch or so of the lines, then finish them with your jack and smooth planes, using a spoke shave at the joint intersections where the grain runs in different directions. Be sure your tools are very sharp and *do not* leave them on the oak when not in use. The acid in the oak will rust and pit them in only a few hours.

There is no need to sand the assembly at this point, because you will be sanding it along with the hull after planking. Apply a liberal coat of Cuprinol or a similar preservative *now*, and *a day or so later put another* coat on the end grain of the stem and on that of the forefoot joint. The stem assembly is completed.

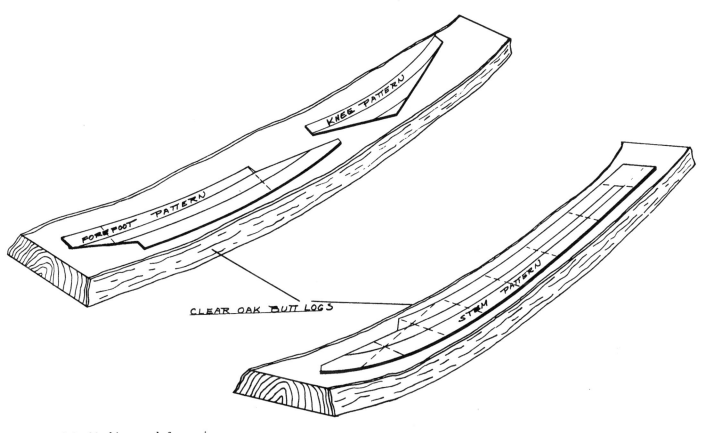

2-1 *Marking stock for sawing*

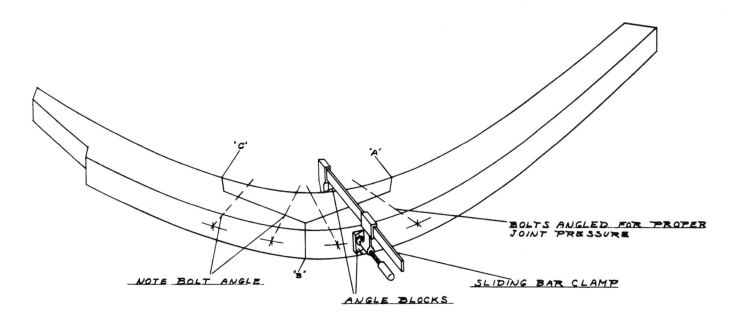

2-2 *Fitting stem joints.*

19

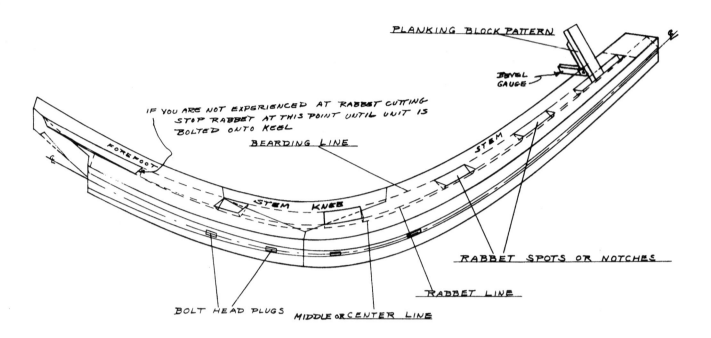

IF YOU ARE NOT EXPERIENCED AT RABBET CUTTING STOP RABBET AT THIS POINT UNTIL UNIT IS BOLTED ONTO KEEL

PLANKING BLOCK PATTERN

BEVEL GAUGE

BEARDING LINE

FOREFOOT

STEM

STEM KNEE

RABBET SPOTS OR NOTCHES

RABBET LINE

BOLT HEAD PLUGS

MIDDLE OR CENTER LINE

BEVEL BOARD

2-3 Spotting the rabbet.

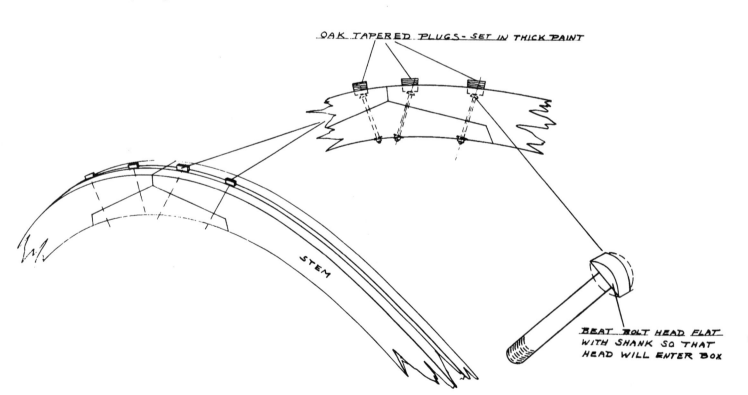

OAK TAPERED PLUGS - SET IN THICK PAINT

STEM

BEAT BOLT HEAD FLAT WITH SHANK SO THAT HEAD WILL ENTER BOX

2-4 Stem bolt and plug detail.

20

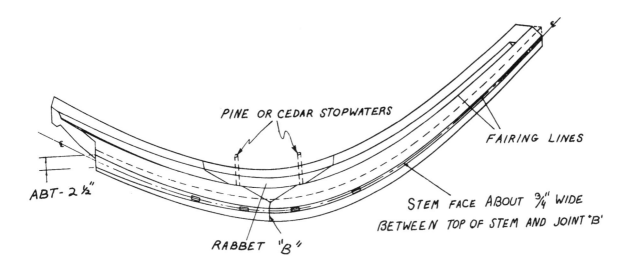

PINE OR CEDAR STOPWATERS

FAIRING LINES

ABT - 2½"

STEM FACE ABOUT ¾" WIDE
BETWEEN TOP OF STEM AND JOINT "B"

RABBET "B"

2-5   *The rabbet complete and one side faired.*

KEEL

In making the keel, which is usually in two pieces, you will need a heavy-duty portable saw. This saw should be able to cut through 2¼-inch oak without strain, as the sided thickness of the keel is 4½ inches. The main piece of the keel (bottom piece) will usually need an additional piece fastened to it to make up the needed width. If this piece is used, it is a good practice to use a joint stop at its forward end rather than letting it run out to a sliver. Then, if the boat should hit a ledge, the joint stop will help prevent the keel from shifting.

Once the two pieces of keel stock are nicely fitted together as shown in Figure 2-6, take your keel pattern and mark off one side of the keel, marking the shaft log line with a straightedge and marking the forefoot splice with a two-foot square. Saw around this side of the keel with a portable saw, just leaving your pencil line. With the two pieces of keel stock clamped together with door clamps staggered from one side to the other, stand the assembly up on its bottom edge. Make a transfer gauge as

shown in the drawing, and transfer the top line to the other side at three locations along its length.

Turn the keel over, remove the door clamps from this side, and lay the pattern against your index marks, making sure its fore and aft position matches the other side as well. Mark around the pattern and saw through this side with your portable saw. You will have to use your handsaw at the stop joint and at the forefoot to finish cutting before the keel will come free.

In jointing your keel pieces, use an electric jointer and finish squaring and fine planing with your hand jointer. Plane out the forefoot splice and shaft log joint and check for squareness and straightness continually as you go. Cut out and fair the lower stern post recess and the skeg. Bore off the keel with your ½-inch auger, first counterboring the bottom edge for the nuts and washers and allowing room for a ¾-inch-deep bung. Bolts should be placed every 16 to 20 inches. Take off the clamps and remove the top piece of the keel. Apply Cuprinol to the surfaces to be joined and clamp them back together.

21

Make up bolts from a ½-inch bronze rod and thread their bottom ends for the nuts and washers. Their upper ends should be left about ½ inch longer than you think you need and threaded for about 1½ inches, as it is especially difficult to back them out to cut more thread once they have been driven. With the keel lying on its side on saw horses and the lower washers and nuts in place, drive the bolts up from the bottom. Put on and tighten the upper washers and nuts, cut off the excess thread, and peen the ends over. *Do not bolt in way of your shaft logs*, as the bolts from the bottom half of the log will be used for this purpose. However, it is essential to bore through the top piece of the keel at this point down into the lower keel piece about 4 inches or 5 inches and drive in a few ½-inch pine dowels just to hold the keel pieces in line until you bolt on the shaft log. Now get out some bungs and bung the counterbores in the bottom of the keel.

The shaft logs are made in two halves, top and bottom. These pieces are usually 1 inch wider than the sided thickness of the keel to allow for the splines and bolts on either side of the shaft hole. A square shaft hole may be used if you don't have a narrow hollowing plane for this job. For this, use your table saw with dado cutters to cut half the hole out of each log half. If you do have a narrow, hollowing plane, make the center cuts with your dado and keep lowering the cutters as you shift toward the outer edges of the shaft hole. Then plane this out with the hollowing plane to form a semicircular trough.

The spline grooves are also cut out with your dado cutters. The grooves are usually ⅜ inch wide and ⁷⁄₁₆ inch deep, as the splines are ⅜ inch by ¾ inch, made from pine or cedar. The splines are to be at least ¼ inch from the shaft hole.

There will be a double row of ½-inch bolts driven up from the bottom half of the shaft log through the top half, and the after ones will be driven through the jib piece and horn timber as well. Clamp and bore both pieces of the shaft log for the double bolting now, placing the holes so the bolts will pass through the splines and their heads will be inside the edge of the keel when everything is bolted together and faired up. There should be *five* pairs of double bolts.

The bottom log will have five or six single bolts driven downward through it and the keel, spaced about as shown in Figure 2-7. To bore for them, clamp the bottom log in place on top of the keel, being careful to get it centered. Counterbore 1½-inch holes in the center of the shaft groove, just deep enough so that the nuts and washers, which form the head of the bolt in this case, will be flush, or nearly so, with the bottom of the shaft hole. Now, with someone sighting your auger, bore a ½-inch hole down through the lower log and the keel at each bolt location. Plug the ½-inch holes in the bottom of the keel to make a center for the worm of your 1½-inch bit, and with the bit counterbore back up into the bottom of the keel about 2 inches. The reason for a deeper bore here is that both ends of these bolts will be recessed, and there is no way to cut off any extra bolt length. So I make the bolts a bit shorter and the lower counterbore a bit deeper than normal to make certain there is room for the bung. Cut the bolts to the exact length required, as it is miserable when you get one of them a little longer and have to bore a hole in the bung so it will go on over the bolt end. So be careful!

Now make up the double bolts to go through the upper assembly. These should be *an inch longer than measured for,* as you can always cut them off, but with this assembly all together, it would be a most difficult job to replace a bolt that was too short. Also *be sure that these bolts have extra threads on their top ends* to go with the extra length. *The lower ends should be threaded just enough to take the nuts*, as a longer thread here would allow the bolt to turn, maybe holding the shaft log joint apart. The lower end nuts will have no washers and must be a lock fit in the wood so they can't turn when the bolt is being tightened. To lock in the nuts, plug the bolt holes bored earlier in the underside of the bottom log piece and counterbore just deep enough for the nuts, using a smaller bit than the nuts' width. This will lock the nuts into the wood after the bolts have been driven up through, and the nuts will look as if they had been let in with a chisel.

Once these double bolts have been driven up through the bottom shaft log piece, the shaft log will be ready to be attached to the keel. Add Cuprinol to the surfaces of the joints and clamp the bottom log piece back onto the keel. Drive the single bolts down through the keel, put on the washers and nuts, and tighten them up. Remove the clamps and, with a helper holding and aligning the upper log piece, drive it on over the double bolts. But first be sure that the splines are in place and that the bolts and shaft hole are well smeared with water pump grease.

Mill out the jib piece, bore it, and drive it on over the double bolts. Take the two-foot square, lay it on the jib piece, and slide it forward alongside the top of the shaft log to the point where the bottom corner of the square is one inch, or the planking thickness, below the top of the log. Mark this notch and cut it out as shown in Figure 2-8, smoothing it up with a jack plane and chisel so it is square. This makes the rabbet notch for the horn timber.

Mill out the horn timber and cut out its rabbet. If the deadrise is fairly flat, you can do this on a table saw. Leave the lines plus

1/16 inch so that you will have enough wood to fair in with your rabbet plane. If the deadrise is excessive, the rabbet may have to be cut entirely by hand, using your hammer and a 1½-inch to 2-inch chisel and then fairing it in with your rabbet plane. Cut a notch in the horn timber's after end for the transom sill.

If you haven't already done so, make a pattern of the horn timber by setting a piece of the pattern stock on its edge on the jib piece and letting it run by the horn timber rabbet notch about 8 or 10 inches. Mark it by running your pencil up the notch and along the top of the log going forward. Cut out the pattern and use it to mark out the forward end of the horn timber. The pattern can also be used to transfer the bolt locations to the horn timber so it can be accurately bored. Once the horn timber has been cut and bored, have your helper steady it, and drive it over the bolts and into place on the jib piece and shaft log, using a block of wood and top maul (sledge hammer). Put on the washers and nuts and tighten them, cut off the excess bolt lengths, and peen over the ends.

Use your pattern for the stern post to mark and bandsaw that piece out, then square it and fit it into place. Fasten it by angling by about 45 degrees one ½-inch bolt up through the horn timber and one down through the bottom of the keel. Plug and counterbore back into the bottom of the keel as you did with the single bolts of the shaft log. Don't use washers under the nuts in the stern post, as washers will interfere with streamlining it. Drive two ½-inch drift bolts about 10 inches long and without washers through the stern post into the keel. In boring for drift bolts, use a ½-inch bit through the stern post, then use a 7/16-inch bit into the keel. Bore about ½ inch longer than needed. Be sure to peen a head on one end of the drift. The keel assembly is now

23

all bolted together. So much for that job.

Mark and bore the sternpost somewhat smaller than the stern bearing, being careful to get good alignment with your bit. (This hole will later be line bored for an exact fit, see chapter 7). Fair the shaft logs into the keel with your electric jointer, hollowing plane, and spoke shave. Scoop out or streamline the stern post and fair in the end of the shaft log to it as shown in Figure 2-9.

The bottom corners of the keel look very neat if they are chamfered off. To do this, mark a line up 3½ inches on the sides and in ½ inch along the bottom. Plane the corners off to these lines, then sand up the entire keel assembly with a flexback pad on a disc sander, and you are ready to cut the keel rabbet.

Use your keel pattern to transfer the rabbet and bearding lines to both sides of the keel assembly. Fair them in with your batten. Make a bevel board to indicate the keel rabbets at the stations, and using the planking block and the bevel gauge as you did in rabbeting the stem, cut your 6-inch rabbet notches at each station along the keel. Proceed to cut the rough rabbet the full length of the keel, fairing it nicely between the notches, and stopping 8 or 10 inches from the forefoot splice. Make sure that your rabbet plane is *very sharp*, then plane out the rough-cut rabbet, sliding your planking block along and checking the fit as you go. It is very easy to cut a rabbet too deep—so be very careful! With this side of the keel all finished, you can turn it over and cut in the station rabbet notches on the other side. I always like to cut in the station rabbet notches on each side because it doesn't take long and it gives a good guide for cutting the rest of the rabbet. Do your fairing, and the keel is ready for the timber heel boxes.

Lay the boxes off at their correct spacing along the top of the bearding line. Make a

test piece of timber about a foot long, having the same cross section as the actual timber, and cut out the boxes neatly to fit the test piece, which should have to be tapped in if the fit is good. A 1-inch Forstner bit, which has no lead screw and only a short spur, works well in roughing out the timber heel boxes. Use a very sharp chisel to finish cleaning them out. When the timber boxes are all cut in on one side, clean off the keel and give it a healthy coat of Cuprinol on the finished side. Turn the keel assembly over, cut in the timber heel boxes, and give a liberal application of Cuprinol to that side.

Water holes should be bored now in the shaft log to ensure good water flow to the stern bearing. One should be on each side, about 16 to 18 inches forward of the aft edge of the stern post. Bore at about a 45-degree angle aft with a 1-inch bit and fair the hole away on its forward edge to give it a tear-drop shape when looking at it from the side of the keel. Sand it smooth with 50-grit production sandpaper.

Now fit the stem assembly to that of the keel and clamp the forefoot splice together with a bar clamp and wedge blocks. Run your handsaw through the stop joints, and, when a good fit is obtained, counterbore and bore for the bolts, being careful to angle them so they will draw the joint together when tightened. Treat the joint with Cuprinol and bolt it off. Fair and finish the uncut section of the rabbet on each side and coat the whole thing with Cuprinol. Except for the pine, cedar, or mahogany stopwaters in the rabbet, the keel assembly is completed.

The ½-inch or ⅝-inch diameter stopwaters are driven wherever a stem or keel joint intersects the rabbet and should be positioned between the rabbet line and the middle or apex line so that when the rabbet is caulked the cotton will reach them. Their purpose, of course, is to stop leakage between adjoining surfaces which are unlikely to swell and which cannot be caulked. Being of soft wood the stopwater swells up when water soaked and prevents water from passing by it.

You can save some time making stopwaters if you make up a sizing die of oak or steel plate and drive squared stock through it.

Boring the keel or stem for a stopwater is sometimes a problem as the bit doesn't start easily on the rabbeted surface. A block of wood having the same thickness as the planking, if tacked in the rabbet will give the bit a flat surface to start on.

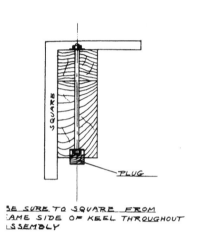

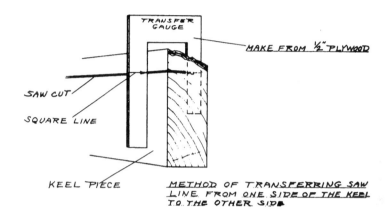

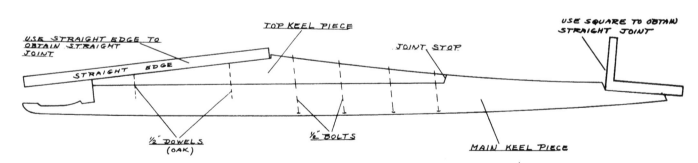

2-6 The main keel.

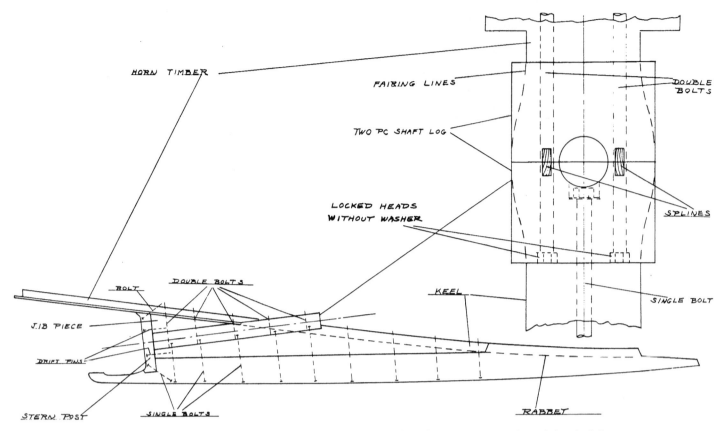

HORN TIMBER

FAIRING LINES

TWO PC SHAFT LOG

DOUBLE BOLTS

LOCKED HEADS
WITHOUT WASHER

SPLINES

SINGLE BOLT

BOLT

DOUBLE BOLTS

JIB PIECE

KEEL

DRIFT PINS

STERN POST

SINGLE BOLTS

RABBET

2-7   The keel all assembled. The detail drawing at the upper right shows a cross-section of the shaft log.

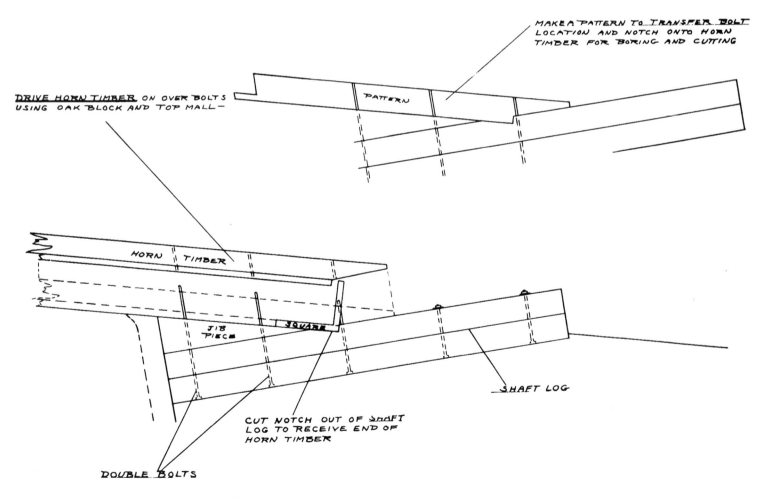

MAKE A PATTERN TO TRANSFER BOLT
LOCATION AND NOTCH ONTO HORN
TIMBER FOR BORING AND CUTTING

DRIVE HORN TIMBER ON OVER BOLTS
USING OAK BLOCK AND TOP MALL—

PATTERN

HORN   TIMBER

JIB
PIECE

SQUARE

SHAFT LOG

CUT NOTCH OUT OF SHAFT
LOG TO RECEIVE END OF
HORN TIMBER

DOUBLE BOLTS

2-8   Horn timber detail.

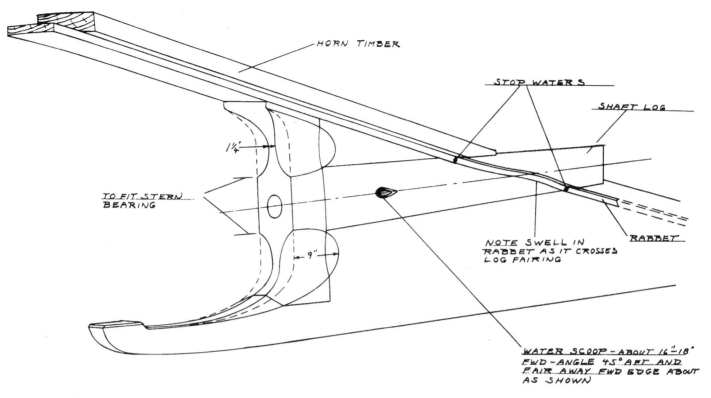

Labels in figure:
HORN TIMBER
STOP WATERS
SHAFT LOG
1¼"
TO FIT STERN BEARING
9"
NOTE SWELL IN RABBET AS IT CROSSES LOG FAIRING
RABBET
WATER SCOOP - ABOUT 16"-18" FWD - ANGLE 45° AFT AND FAIR AWAY FWD EDGE ABOUT AS SHOWN

2-9 *Fairing of the stern post.*

TRANSOM

We will start by making the transom header and the bottom sill. Both are milled from 4-inch oak sweeps. Bandsaw the header to the transom radius using your radius pattern. Its fore and aft width is usually about 4 inches. Joint its edges and mark the crown on its aft edge with your beam mold and bandsaw it out. Clean up the top surface with your jack plane and run the piece through the thickness planer to clean up its bottom. The header's thickness should finish 1¾ to 2 inches. Bevel the aft edge for the transom rake.

The sill is also about 4 inches wide fore and aft. After marking the oak with your radius pattern, bandsaw your radius cuts with the saw set at the angle of the transom rake. Plane the edges and mark a centerline

on the aft edge of the sill. Lay your half pattern on this edge, even with the top of the sill (which is straight), and mark around it. Turn the pattern over and mark the opposite side. After taking the bevels from your buttock lines, cut and fair the bottom of the sill and cut off its ends with your handsaw, squaring these joints in from the aft edge. Bevel off the top at both ends for the corner knees. Now saw out the cheek pieces and corner knees from 2-inch oak, marking them out with your patterns. To saw the outside edges of the cheek pieces, take your extreme waterline bevel and set your bandsaw to it. Your pattern is for the aft surface, so be careful to saw the bevel the right way. The inside edges may be sawn square. The corner knees are not bevelled, so you can also saw their edges square.

Fit the corner knee to the cheek piece

27

and bolt them together with two ⅜-inch bolts, heads countersunk. Remember to angle the bolts so they will bring the joint together as they are tightened, as in the stem and the keel joints. Fit and bolt the opposite corner knee to its cheek piece. Now, clamping the sill in a vise, set the starboard cheek piece assembly on the starboard end of the sill, clamp it there, and handsaw the stop joint for a good fit. Afterward, bore it off and bolt it with two ⅜-inch bolts, heads also countersunk. Do the same thing on the port side.

Lay the sill and cheek piece assembly on saw horses, inside up, and you are ready to fit the header. Get the length of the header by laying it in place and marking it at both the inner and outer edges of the cheek pieces. Measure in on the header from the aft edge at these marks, the thickness of the cheek pieces. Mark and notch this out on each end of the header. Clamp the header to the cheek pieces and bolt it off with one ⅜-inch bolt per side.

Mill out a center timber of 2-inch by 4-inch oak and 8 or 10 side timbers of 2-inch by 1½-inch oak. Lay off these timbers on the outer side of the transom frame. Fit the 2-inch by 4-inch center timber in first by cutting half boxes out of the header and the sill with your 1-inch and ½-inch chisels. Notch the ends of the timber to fit, drive it into the half boxes, and screw it to the sill and header with 2-inch flat-head screws. Lay off side timbers about 10 inches apart and go through this same procedure.

Trim the aft surface of the frame with your jack plane, apply Cuprinol to it generously, and you are ready to plank it up.

The planking for the transom is usually about 1⅛-inch cedar for a lobsterboat of this size. Some builders prefer oak, but cedar holds the paint better. To start planking, clamp on the bottom plank, which should be about 7 or 8 inches wide. Locate its top edge by measuring down from the sheer at each side of the transom an equal distance. Mark the under side of the plank around the frame, take it off, and saw it out. Now clamp the plank back in place and fasten it to the frame with 1¾-inch #12 flat-head screws with holes counterbored for bungs. Lay off the rest of the planks about 4 to 4½ inches wide, plane a caulking seam on one side of each, and fasten them on, using door clamps to draw them together as you work toward the top of the transom. Be sure to stagger the fastenings as you go. After the planking is completed, trim the plank edges to match the transom frame bevel. The caulking seam on these edges should not be planed now but done as the boat is planked up when a final fairing of the transom frame will assure that each plank lays well against it. Now bung the screw holes and joint the outside of the planking with your jack plane and roll cotton caulking into each seam. (See Chapter 8 for more on caulking.) Smooth the surface by sanding with a dual-action vibrator sander and prime-paint it. Another job is done!

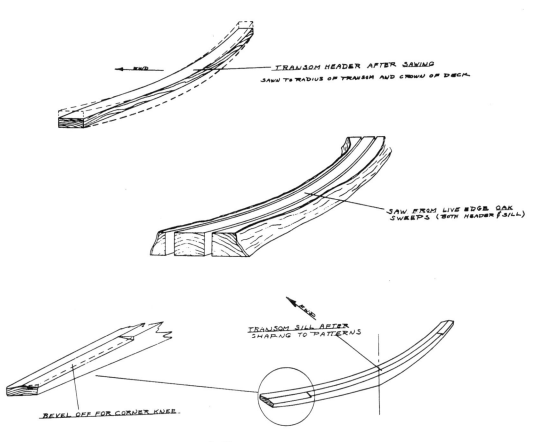

TRANSOM HEADER AFTER SAWING

SAWN TO RADIUS OF TRANSOM AND CROWN OF DECK

SAW FROM LIVE EDGE OAK SWEEPS (BOTH HEADER & SILL)

TRANSOM SILL AFTER SHAPING TO PATTERNS

BEVEL OFF FOR CORNER KNEE.

2-10   Milling the transom header and sill.

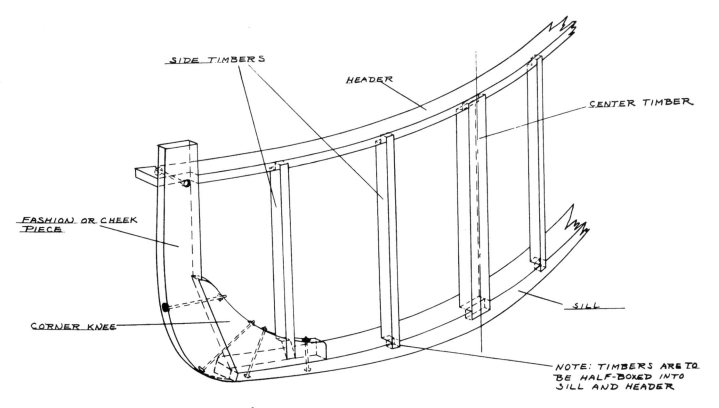

SIDE TIMBERS

HEADER

CENTER TIMBER

FASHION OR CHEEK PIECE

CORNER KNEE

SILL

NOTE: TIMBERS ARE TO BE HALF-BOXED INTO SILL AND HEADER

2-11   Details of the transom frame.

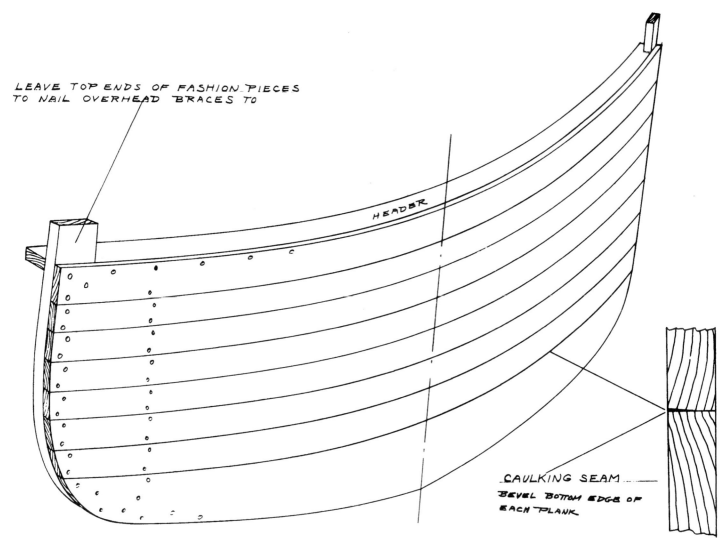

LEAVE TOP ENDS OF FASHION PIECES
TO NAIL OVERHEAD BRACES TO

HEADER

CAULKING SEAM
BEVEL BOTTOM EDGE OF
EACH PLANK

2-12 *The finished transom.*

Chapter 3

Setting Up

The first stages of setting up will be blocking the keel, fore and aft, so the waterline is level, plumbing the upright members, and bracing this assembly from both the floor and overhead. From your laydown at Stations 2 and 8, measure from the bottom of the keel down to a point that will give you an 8-inch-high block at Station 8. Transfer this point forward to Station 2 and measure up to the bottom of the keel. On a level floor, this will give you the height of the forward block and its bevel. Add 1 inch extra height to both the forward and aft blockings for the keel recess. Allowances will of course have to be made for boats set up on uneven surfaces.

The forward blocking can be sawn from a piece of the keel scrap. As an example, if the keel were sided 4½ inches, the block might taper from 8 inches in width at the top to 12 inches in width at the bottom. Brace the forward block to the floor on all four sides, using 5/4 (1¼-inch) rough spruce or transom planking scraps.

For the aft blocking, two pieces of scrap from the keel will do. Make the lower one about 3 feet long and toe nail it solidly to the floor at the ends. Try to make this piece 6 inches wide, if possible. The top piece should be about 4½ inches by 6 inches and 2 feet long. Cut out a 1-inch deep recess to fit the bottom of the keel, then spike it to the bottom piece with 16d or 20d nails.

You will need help at this point to set the keel assembly onto the blocking and brace it off temporarily. Station 8 will be close to the stern post, so on the bottom of the horn timber, just behind the stern post, mark a centerline and tack a 5d box nail in it. Wrap the plumb bob string around this nail and bend it over to hold the string tight, with the point of the plumb bob just clearing the skeg. Now mark the centerline onto the skeg. Cut a pair of braces to run about 45 degrees from the keel rabbet to the floor. Nail the top ends into the rabbet with 6d nails. With your helper steadying the keel, remove the temporary brace and have him move the top of the keel back or forth until the plumb bob point is standing right over the centerline on the skeg. Nail the brace to the floor on one side and check the plumb bob to see if it has moved. If not, nail off the opposite brace into the floor, using 8d nails.

Move your plumb bob to the stem. Mark a centerline at the top of the stem at its face and attach the string the same way as you did at the horn timber, leaving enough length so that the plumb bob is swinging just below the keel. Rig two overhead braces to run diagonally at about 45 degrees from the overhead to the top of the stem. With your helper moving the stem back or forth, sight the plumb line from about 6 or 8 feet ahead of the bow. With the string sighting in the center of the stem face at the designed waterline, have a second helper nail one brace to the back of the stem, assuming that the top of the brace is already nailed to the overhead. (You should nail the lower ends into the excess stem wood above the sheer.) After nailing the brace, sight again to see if anything shifted while you nailed. If not, nail the other brace into position at the top of the stem.

Now rig a chalkline from the center of the stem (back edge) at the designed waterline to the center of the horn timber at the stern. Be sure that this line is very taut. You sometimes have to use a block at the stern in order for the string to clear the forward end of the shaft log.

With this done, cut a couple more braces for the forward end of the shaft log and nail their top ends into the rabbet. Mark a centerline on the top of the shaft log at this point. Using a spirit level, with its lower corner set on the centerline, have your helper move the keel until the level just touches the chalkline. Nail the bottom of the brace to the floor on one side. Recheck with the level. If it stayed put, nail off the other brace to the floor.

Cut a 2-inch by 4-inch prop or punchin, whichever you prefer to call it, to fit under and support the horn timber at the stern, and nail it into place with 6d nails at the top and 8d nails into the floor. Cut a pair of diagonal braces to the floor at this point and nail them off. Add more diagonal braces to the keel at about 4-foot intervals between the shaft log and stem. After the bracing is

completed, recheck your plumb line at the stern to see if it has shifted while the keel was being braced. If the keel has an edge set in it, sometimes the forefoot will kick over and throw the stem out of plumb slightly, so it is necessary to recheck the stem also.

Next, you have to mount the transom onto the horn timber. With two husky fellows, lift the transom and set the sill into the recess at the horn timber. With your helpers holding the transom in place, drive four 2-inch #12 screws up through the horn timber into the sill. This will hold the transom snugly in the recess. Tack a temporary brace from the floor to each side of the transom. Tack a straightedge under the transom header so a spirit level can be used against it to level the transom. Now, set the transom rake using a level and declevity board.

Once this is done and the braces are nailed down, the transom must be set square to the fore and aft centerline. Hook the ring on the end of a 50-foot tape over a 5d box nail tacked at the centerline on the forward end of the shaft log. Cut a pair of braces, and tack the end of one brace well outboard onto the transom sill and let the other end lay across the horn timber near the stern post. Draw your 50-foot tape taut and note the distance from the center of the forward end of the shaft log to the inner edge of the stop joint at the end of the transom sill. Pass the tape over to your helper on the other side and have him check the same measurement on that side. Adjust the transom until the two measurements are equal, then nail the forward end of one brace to the horn timber. Recheck for movement and nail the other brace to the horn timber. This type of measuring is called hounding or squaring and it is very accurate.

With the transom level athwartships and properly raked, and its sill square to the keel, nail heavy braces vertically to the overhead from each corner of the transom but leave the floor braces in place until the ribbands are all on. Attach the tape to the back of the stem centerline at the *cross spall waterline*, and hound off the top corners of the transom. Adjust the transom and nail temporary braces from the outboard top corners of the transom to the back wall of the shop.

Now bolt in the transom knee with ½-inch bolts—two bolts up through the horn timber and one in through the lower part of the transom itself. Drive two 3-inch #16 flathead screws through the top of the knee into the transom center timber. This completes the set-up of the keel assembly and transom. We will now move on to the mold set-up.

At this point mill up a strongback of 1⅛-inch by 4-inch spruce. Mill enough pieces to extend the length of the boat, plus some 2- or 3-foot pieces for the butt straps to be used for joining the strongback together. Also, you will need six pieces of 1-inch by 1-inch spruce or pine as long as possible for squaring strips. At the same time, mill your overhead braces for the molds, as well as temporary braces to be used from the floor up to the molds.

With your helper, set the first mold into place. (Remember that from amidships forward, the molds should be set up with the cross spalls facing aft. Going aft from amidships, they should be facing forward.) Holding your level vertically against the cross spall and saddle, plumb the mold and tack your temporary diagonal brace from the keel to the cross spall. Next, with your level athwartships on top of the cross spall, level the mold and tack a brace from the floor to the gusset on the mold on both the port and starboard sides. Follow this procedure and set all the molds into place and brace them *temporarily*.

Now take a piece of strongback and lay it along the cross spalls on one side of their centerlines and nail its forward end to the stem with an 8d nail. Recheck the first mold for fore and aft plumbness and hammer 8d nails through the strongback into its cross spall. Do this at every mold and nail the strongback to the transom. All molds should then be plumb, both fore and aft and athwartships. In cases where boats are built on declevity, that is with their waterlines not level, a declevity level must be used in setting the molds square with the waterlines.

Rig your 50-foot tape to the center of the stem (back side) about 6 inches above the strongback. Lay the 1-inch by 1-inch strips on top of the cross spalls, with one on the port and one on the starboard side, and nail their ends to the back of the stem. Using your tape, hound off the first mold as with the transom hounding described earlier, and drive 8d nails through the strips into the cross spalls. Now the mold is squared. Give each mold the same treatment as you work toward the stern. Brace off the molds overhead as you did with the transom and remove the temporary braces to the floor. We now face the next task, which is placing the ribbands.

For ribbands, I prefer western fir, as it is very strong and bends around the molds in a good, fair line. I usually make these ribbands about 1¾ inches square and scarf them together with a 16-inch scarf fastened with both glue and screws. This provides a ribband that goes the full length of the boat. It is uninterrupted by butt straps and is much easier to sight along. When fastening these ribbands on, *keep the splices top to bottom, not inside to outside.* Spruce ribbands are used a lot here in Maine, but they have to be at least 2 inches square and as clear as possible. Spruce has hard and soft spots, which cause unfair bends. For this reason, I prefer western fir. The only exception is on the top ribband, which should be 1¼-inch by 2-inch clear oak, green or unseasoned, for the bend of this ribband is usually extreme compared to those in the rest of the boat.

In fastening on the ribbands, use ¼-inch by 3½-inch hex-head lag screws. You can cut the end off a short ½-inch drive extension and put it in your ½-inch reversible drill, snap on a socket to fit the lags, and you are in business. We used to use 3½-inch #16 flat-head screws and a bit brace, but if you damaged the screw slots, you had a devil of a time getting the screws out. Use flat steel washers on the lag screws. This will give a greater holding power on the ribbands.

The top ribband should be lagged on first, after that, the ribband at the designed water-line.* Lag these on both sides of the boat. Put one pair on at a time, not three or four on a side and then three or four on the other side, as this may pull the boat out of line.

_____

*Many, if not most builders run their ribbands more or less parallel with the plank lines, but in boats of my design, where the shape of the forefoot is critical, I like a lot of ribbands from the waterline on down; hence the DWL ribband.

The sheer or top ribband should be kept about 4 inches above the actual sheer line, to assure fairness in the upper ends of the frames. This will be the last ribband taken off the boat. It's a good practice to use ten ribbands to a side. This will keep them close enough to ensure a fair boat.

With the ribbands all lagged on, check for any hard spots. Let the ribbands into the molds or shim them out until they are fair. After fairing the ribbands, bend in an oak batten at the molds, i.e., against the ribbands as a timber will lay. If this batten bends in fair, you are all set. If not, let in or shim out your ribbands that are unfair to this batten. Be sure to trim both sides of the molds the same amount. This batten can also be used to mark the desired location of each timber on the ribbands.

To prepare for timbering, fit braces from the floor up to the second ribband from the keel, and nail them along between the molds on both sides (one between each mold). Finally, nail braces from the bilge to the floor at each mold between Station 4 and the transom. This is to prevent wracking of the hull when pounding the hot timbers into the timber boxes with your top maul or sledge hammer.

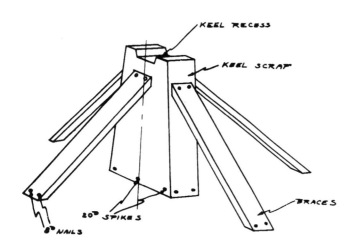
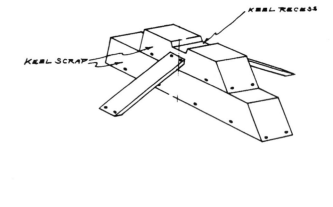

3-1 Keel blocking (forward block to the left, after block to the right).

34

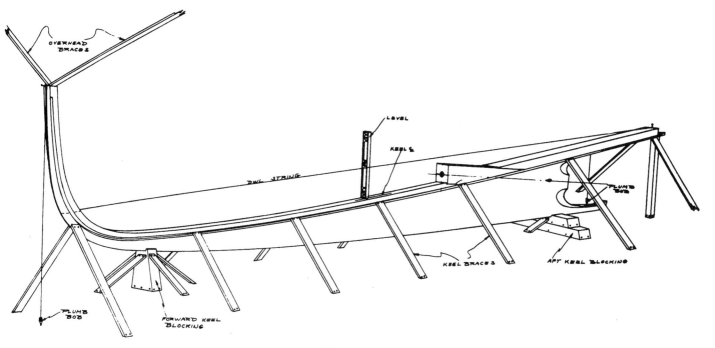

3-2 Setting up and bracing the keel assembly.

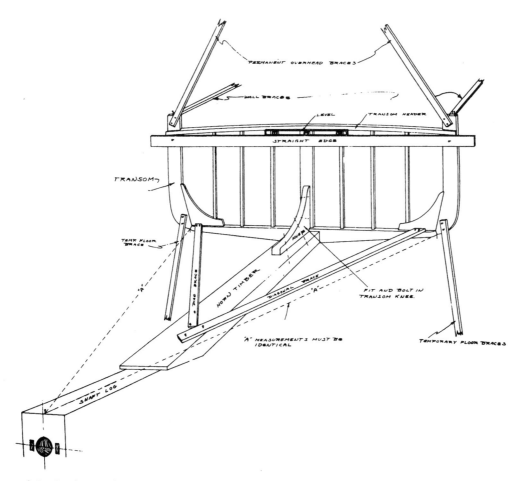

3-3 Setting up the transom.

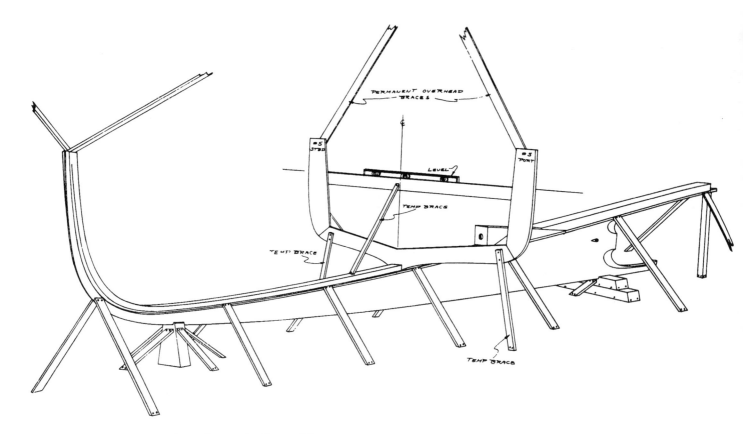

3-4 *Temporarily setting up the first mold.*

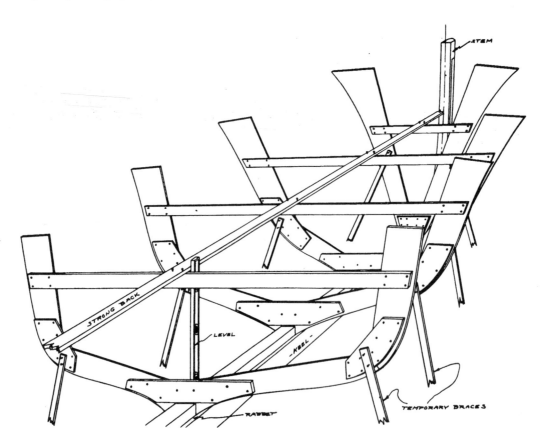

3-5 *Plumbing the molds permanently fore and aft.*

(Left) The molds are all set up and braced, ready to accept the ribbands. The timber heel boxes, keel blocking, and the fairing of the sternpost and skeg show up well in this photograph.

(Right) The transom is framed up and ready for planking. In this case, the frame was set up in place on the horn timber before it was planked.

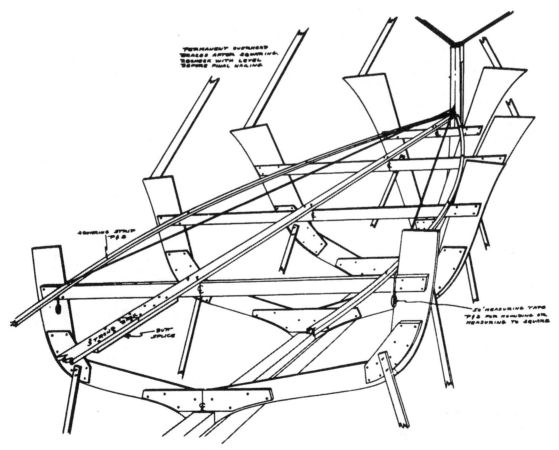

3-6 Hounding and squaring the molds.

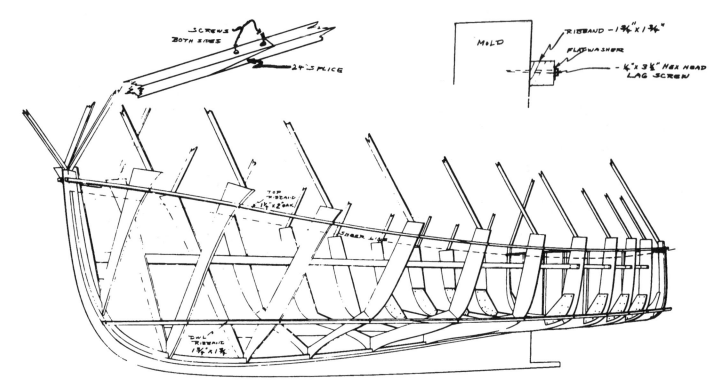

3-7   *The DWL and top ribbands are lagged on first.*

The transom after it has been planked. The ribbands have been lagged on and the timbers have been bent in. In this boat, the cockpit scuppers drain out through the transom rather than through the side of the boat.

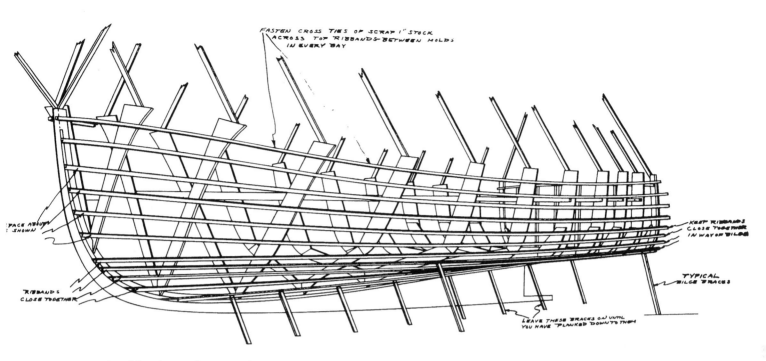

FASTEN CROSS TIES OF SCRAP 1" STOCK
ACROSS TOP RIBBANDS BETWEEN MOLDS
IN EVERY BAY

'FACE ABOUT
' SHOWN

KEEP RIBBANDS
CLOSE TOGETHER
IN WAY OF BILGE

RIBBANDS
CLOSE TOGETHER

TYPICAL
BILGE BRACES

LEAVE THESE BRACES ON UNTIL
YOU HAVE PLANKED DOWN TO THEM

3-8   *The ribbands are all on and the set-up is ready for timbering.*

Chapter 4

Framing

The best bending oak for timbers (frames) comes from butt logs of young growth trees—old growth will not bend worth a darn. These butts should average between 12 inches and 16 inches in diameter and have a smooth, gray bark. Have them sawn live edge about 2¼ inches thick and 8 feet long. Then have the saw mill plane the planks to 2 inches, unless you have your own planer. It is wise to order enough of these planks for the floor timbers as well as the frame timbers, and by so doing you can pick the best pieces for the bending stock. Those planks with a few knots or slight blemishes can be used in the floor timbers, as they are not bent and a few imperfections will not affect their strength. By this, I don't mean that you can use pieces with excessively large knots or checks, but anything within reason is certainly acceptable.

The best timbers are sawn with the grain. Some saw mills will cut the timbers for you, but they straighten one edge of the plank and then saw them out parallel to this edge, so if there is a sweep in the plank, which there usually is, they cut the grain off. It is much better to saw the timbers yourself, following the natural grain of the wood. If you are going to bandsaw them, line off the

planks with a batten, allowing ³⁄₁₆ inch extra for planing. In cutting them with a portable saw, run the saw shoe against a batten tacked to the plank, or cut free-hand along the edge. Timbers for the entire boat can normally be gotten out in a day with a couple of sharp combination blades.

In planing rough-sawn timbers, run each one through the planer on a smooth board the first pass through. The board will give uniform support and the frame will have a better surface than if run through by itself. A board isn't necessary for the second side. I normally use timbers 1¼ inches to 1⁵⁄₁₆ inches by 2 inches for a boat 30 to 36 feet long. This allows you to use a screw with a decent length for fastening the planking. After milling, the timbers should be spread out and painted with a mixture of one-third linseed oil and two-thirds Cuprinol to help keep them from turning dark during steaming. Be sure that the timbers are squared off at both ends. The lower end has to be square to fit into the timber heel box, and, unless you want to take a chance on someone getting some lumps on his head when the maul glances off a rough-cut upper end, you must square off this end also.

You probably have heard of jigs or other

such paraphernalia for pre-bending timbers before actually forcing them into place, but I don't go along with this at all. I have found that taking the timber directly from the steam box and bending it right into place is the best method. *Do it quickly* while the wood is hot and limber. The longer you fool around, the more the timber cools and the harder it is to bend.

I have tried both the steaming and boiling methods. While boiling is good, I still prefer good old steaming. With the right wood and proper steam, it can't be beaten.

You may have a steam box, but if not, you can make do with a section of 12- or 14-inch culvert with a bottom welded on one end or a series of 15-gallon oil or grease drums welded together, after cutting out the bottoms of all but the lower one. The steambox, regardless of its construction, should be about 10 feet long.

Make up a saw horse rig to hold the steam box at about a 30-degree angle, with the bottom resting on a layer of fire brick or sand. Build a brick fire box around the lower end and set up a regular furnace oil burner gun so that it will shoot the flame along the lower end of the steam box into the fire box. You may have to move the burner after you test fire it so the flame points just where you want it. Now fill the steam box about one-third full of water, dump in a gallon of permanent anti-freeze if you desire, and the steaming rig is all ready to go. (Anti-freeze raises the boiling point and seems to make the timbers more flexible.)

In timbering it is ideal to have four men: (1) One man inside the boat to bend in the timber and drive each one into its box in the keel after clamping it off. (2) One man on the floor to guide and pound the timber into the keel box. He should have an electric drill fitted with a bit for ¼-inch lag screws (used to fasten the timbers temporarily to

the ribbands), as well as a ½-inch reversible drill with a makeshift lag driver. The drill and lag driver can be passed up and down as needed. (3) One man at the side of the boat to clamp and fasten the timbers to the ribbands. (4) One man to pass the timbers from the steam box and to tend the water in the box, as well as to keep the box full of timbers. It is not unusual to timber a boat of this size with a four man crew and good bending stock in one day. As a matter of fact, we used to do this most of the time. If the job was not quite done at quitting time, we stayed on until it was.

The day goes like this: Starting early in the morning, fire up your steam rig and fill it with timbers, plugging the open end with burlap bags. While the timbers are steaming, your inside man gets up into the boat and removes the strongback and 1-inch by 1-inch strips from the cross spalls. Have him nail some 2x4's across the top ribband, one between each mold along the entire boat. This will keep the timbers from spreading the boat between the molds. He will have to place these so they are not on frame lines.

One man tends the steam rig so that the others can put washers on ¼-inch by 2½-inch lag screws and place them in open boxes so that they are easily grabbed when needed. Space these boxes of lag screws along each side of the boat at intervals, so that you don't have to look far to find them. You develop a rhythm in timbering. Everyone seems to be gawky and clumsy at the start, but as you go along, every move counts more and more, and things soon go smoothly and quickly. Oh yes, don't forget to have the C clamps all oiled and limbered up. You will need about three dozen clamps to hold a number of timbers in place prior to lagging them to the ribbands. Hang the clamps on the ribbands about amidships, as this is where timbering starts.

After the timbers have been steaming

about an hour or so, get everyone into position and try one. The first timber should go in just aft of the midship mold and line up with it. If the timber bends into place easily, you are all set, but if it is quite stiff, let the others steam another 15 minutes. A word here on bending timbers: The inside man should hold the top of the timber in one hand, with the bottom entered into the box in the keel. He should place his foot quite high on the timber and slide his foot down to the hard turn in the bilge, bending the timber in a big loop at first and then pressing it into the bilge with his foot. The outside man at the side of the boat will also pull with his hands to get the timber out against the ribbands. A good many are broken needlessly by jamming them right into the bilge and hauling in on the top, thus forcing them into a quick bend they can't handle. Remember, keep your foot high on the timber and use a looping and sliding action with your foot. The timber is now clamped into place, and driven down with a sledge hammer until it bottoms in the keel box.

Now, removing one clamp at a time, bore off the ribbands and drive the lag screws into the timber. Bend in the timber opposite this one and fasten it into place. Work toward the transom, bending in a pair of timbers on either side of each mold, with the last pair next to the transom, fastening the timbers to the ribbands as you go. This greatly stiffens up your mold frame and keeps the rest of the timbers from pulling the ribbands out of line. Now you can finish timbering aft of amidships, staggering your work from side to side.

With the aft half of the boat timbered, use the same method going forward—bend and fasten a pair of timbers on either side of the molds and then work back and forth until you reach Station 2. From this point forward, you will have to use your eye and fan or cant your timbers out at the tops, because the distance around the top ribband is greater than the distance from Station 2 to the stem at the keel. The last three timbers forward on either side will have to be bevelled at the heel and screwed directly to the stem, since there are no boxes cut for them.

If the boat has a fairly heavy flare in the bows, you should nail tie straps (1-inch by 4-inch pine or spruce) athwartships to every other pair of timbers along the cross spall line, the area with the most bend in the timbers. Do this in the forward third of the boat. Also, 1⅛-inch spruce braces should be fitted and fastened between the tops of the first five pairs of timbers above the top ribband, then between every other pair for the forward one-third of the boat. These ties and braces are needed to hold the designed flair forward and should not be removed until the hull is planked and the deck frame is completed. Now go home and get a good night's rest.

The next morning the timbers will be all cooled and ready for boring and fastening off their heels. Drive two 2-inch #12 flat-head bronze screws through each heel and into the keel, port and starboard. Counterbore these screws a little deeper than normal in case you have to trim the timber heels for the garboard plank.

You have come a long way and are about ready for planking. Remove the #2 ribbands from the boat to make room for the sheer strake, and the planking crew can take over.

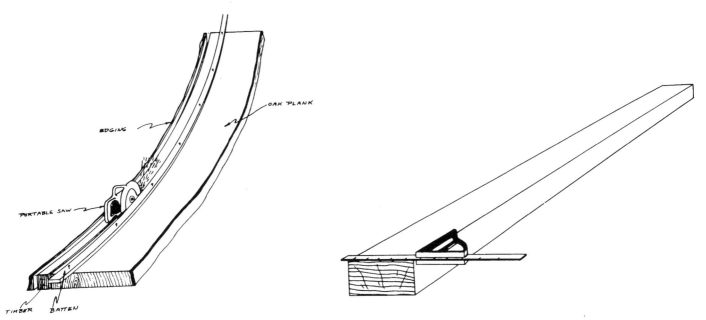

OAK PLANK

EDGING

PORTABLE SAW

TIMBER   BATTEN

4-1 (left)   Sawing out timbers.

4-2 (right)   Be sure to cut both ends of the timbers square before they are steamed.

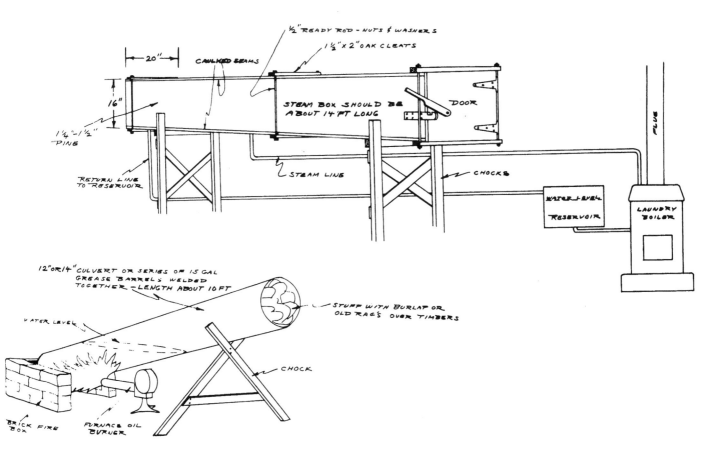

½" READY ROD - NUTS & WASHERS

1½" X 2" OAK CLEATS

20"

CAULKED SEAMS

STEAM BOX SHOULD BE
ABOUT 14 FT LONG

DOOR

16"

1¼"-1½"
PINE

RETURN LINE
TO RESERVOIR

STEAM LINE

CHOCKS

WATER LEVEL

RESERVOIR

LAUNDRY
BOILER

FLUE

12"OR 14" CULVERT OR SERIES OF 15 GAL
GREASE BARRELS WELDED
TOGETHER - LENGTH ABOUT 10 FT

STUFF WITH BURLAP OR
OLD RAGS OVER TIMBERS

WATER LEVEL

CHOCK

BRICK FIRE
BOX

FURNACE OIL
BURNER

4-3   Optional steaming rigs.

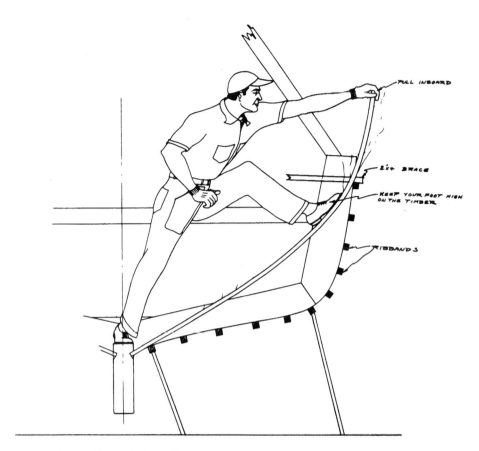

4-4 *Bending a timber—first step.*

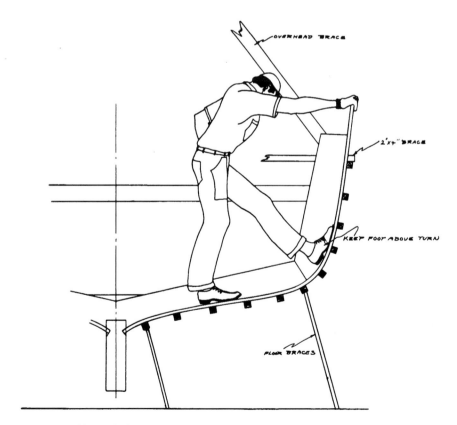

4-5 *Bending a timber—second step.*

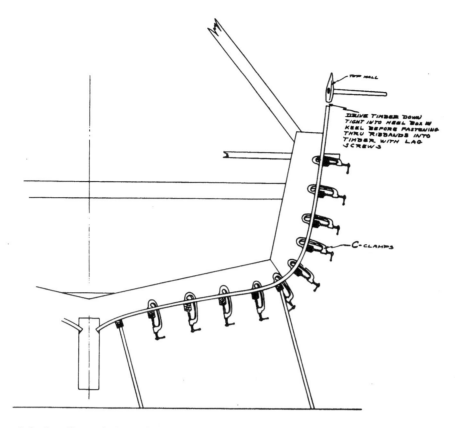

4-6   *Bending a timber—third step.*

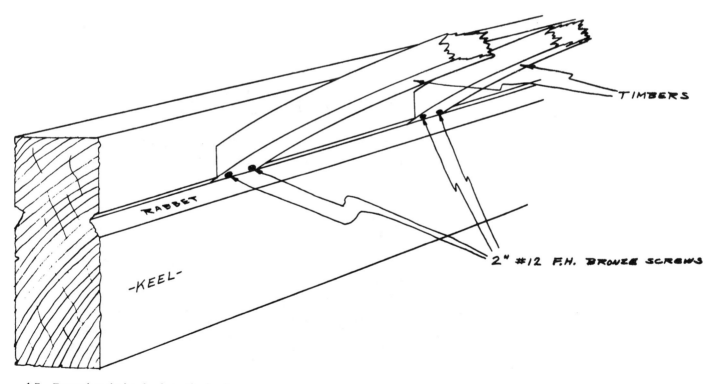

TIMBERS

RABBET

-KEEL-

2" #12 F.H. BRONZE SCREWS

4-7   *Fastening timber heels to the keel.*

(Above) The hull all set up and ready for timbering out. (Right) The temporary bracing shows up well here. This boat has hollow garboards, so the ribband nearest the keel has been shored up to take the strain when the timbers were bent in. The spacing of the ribbands is not always even—they are close together at the garboard and at the bilge where the bend in the timbers is the greatest.

(Above) A closeup of the timbers as they lie against the ribbands, held there temporarily by staging nails. The construction of the molds shows up well here.   (Left) Timbers in place forward, with staging nails rather than lags used to hold them in place against the ribbands. Note how the ribbands are close-spaced below the waterline, a means of holding the designed hull shape in the forefoot area, which the designer considers critical to the boat's performance.

Chapter 5

Planking

Planking is undoubtedly the most satisfying phase in boatbuilding. Its success depends upon the builder's eye, some simple measurements, and a good deal of experience. I will try to put this experience into words and drawings so that any person, with patience, can do a beautiful planking job.

White cedar is used extensively by Maine boatbuilders for planking. Native cedar "boat boards" are ordered from the mill and are live edge, that is, with the bark still on as with the oak mentioned earlier. A good sawyer will get out boat boards with as much sweep or curve to them as possible, which is a great help to the builder, as much of his planking is curved and can be gotten out with less waste than from square-edge stock.

Cedar is a long-lasting wood and comes in lengths to 26 feet. Unless it is very dry it bends easily; in fact it need only be dried for two or three weeks before being used. As with oak, the white, spongy sapwood should be avoided if possible. The knots, which are numerous in cedar boards, sometimes are frightening if you are not used to dealing with them. Only the loose, black ones need to be bored out and plugged; the others only make the wood tougher and less apt to split. Naturally, you will need to work each piece of stock to advantage so there are no knots on seams, butts, or hood ends of the finished plank. Occasionally you will find small rotten areas in an otherwise good board. They can be fixed up by fitting and gluing in dutchmen.

For all its trouble, cedar is well worth it. But be sure to order half again more than you think you will need, select the best for planking, and use the rest for less critical areas of the boat. A few builders use mahogany, either Philippine or African, for planking, but I prefer cedar.

No matter what the planking material, specify about two-thirds of it planed to 1⅛ inches (or whatever the finished planking thickness is to be) and the other one-third left rough-sawn to 1½ inches. The extra thickness will be needed to plank up around the bilge where the planks will need to be backed (hollowed) out and tapered.

Before starting to plank, you will need to make up a sheer lining batten, used to line off the sheer line. The batten should be of western fir about 1½ to 2 inches wide by ⅜ to ½ inch thick and long enough to run a bit more than the length of the hull when bent around the sheer. Joints in the batten should be backed up by butt straps fastened with 5d box nails clinched over on the back side of the batten. Painting the lining batten dark brown or black helps in using it by making it more visible against a light background.

Before any planking is lined out, you should check and make adjustments in the sheer line to get it fair. Do this by nailing the batten along the sheer marks on the molds and on every other timberhead with 5d box nails (galvanized nails are best as they are rough and hold well). Keep the batten standing vertical—not flat against the molds or timberheads—so its outer top corner will be the same height as the sheer. Take great care in adjusting this batten so it is fair, then mark the sheer line along the top edge of the batten onto the molds and timberheads.

Note: In the bows, where the flare is greatest and the deck line full, I generally keep the sheer line a little high (about ⅛ inch), fairing into the designed sheer line about one-third the length of the boat from the stem. This is because sighting around the bows is difficult unless you can stand off far enough to see the entire sheer line at once. Most shops are too narrow for a good standoff view. I find it is better to leave the sheer a little high forward, and afterwards, when the planking is completed, to set up a batten again for sighting and trim the final sheer line in this area. It is much easier to plane a little off than to shim up the covering board.

At this point, you should make up a few lining battens of western fir, about 5⁄16 inch by 1⅛ inch and at least 16 feet long for lining off the edges of the remaining planks.

Now find out the approximate plank widths at several points along the hull by measuring the girth from the sheer to the rabbet at each station and dividing by the number of planks to be used—about 16 or 18 planks for a lobsterboat, which gives about 3¾- to 4-inch planks. The hood ends of the stem should be figured from the top of the garboard, which means dividing by one less plank in calculating the widths. These general widths will need to be altered somewhat to get pleasing lines in the flaring topsides forward. Starting with the sheer strake and continuing halfway down the topsides in this area, each plank should be battened off a little wider than the general measurements indicate in order to take out the apparent hump which would otherwise exist in the plank lines in way of the flare. Your lining batten will tell you the story on this. When you have it where it belongs, it will look good to your eye.

The general plank widths are also altered at the turn of the bilge, where planks are narrowed up, and for the sheer strake, which is made wider for its entire length—but more on this later. Let's now begin to plank, starting with the sheer strake.

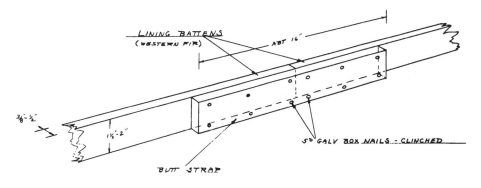

5-1 *Detail of the joint in a lining batten.*

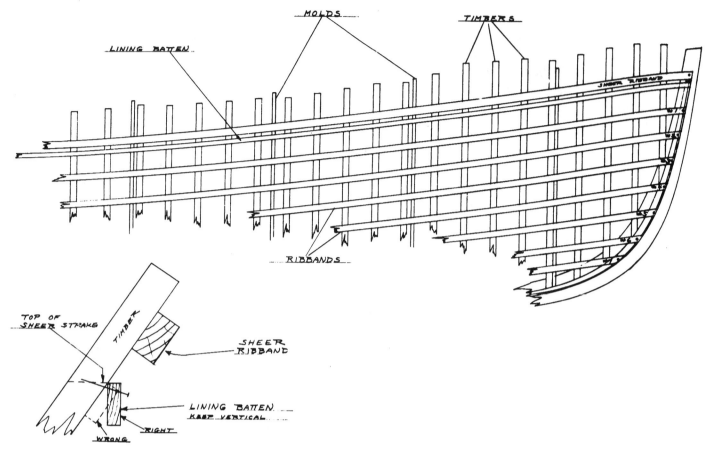

5-2 Placement of the lining batten.

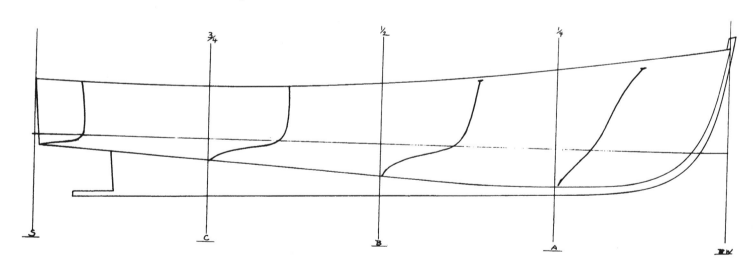

5-3 Girth measurements are taken at these points on the hull.

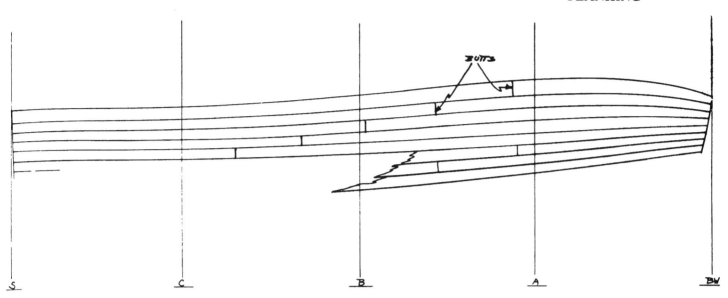

5-4 *The planking layout in way of the flare. Note the width of the planks at* A.

THE SHEER STRAKE

Spiling is the method by which the desired plank line, in this case the top of the forward part of the sheer strake, is transferred from the three-dimensional framework of the hull to one side of the flat board from which the plank will be cut. A spiling batten and dividers are used more or less as described in other boatbuilding books. I use a ½-inch or ⅝-inch pine or cedar batten, or a ⅜-inch plywood batten, 2 or more inches wide and cut roughly to the shape of the line to be spiled. You will take all spiles from one side of the boat, called the pattern side. The side to use is your choice. Tack the batten in place to fit below the sheer line so it is lying naturally. *Don't* try to spring it into shape. Take your dividers and, using a constant setting and starting at the stem, put one point on the sheer line and the other on the batten. Work aft, taking readings at every other timber. Circle all prick marks with a pencil. Use a location

marking system by numbering your prick marks *1, 2, 3,* etc., as you go aft. This helps no end, as you can look back at the boat from the workbench and see where you are. For your numbers, use a felt-tip pen or a dark crayon. These marks are also very useful when taking planking bevels.

Once you have made your marks, remove the spiling batten and lay it on the board from which you will cut the plank. Transfer the spile marks to the board by reversing your procedure—be sure the dividers have not changed setting. Circle the prick points with a pencil and number them, using the same system as used previously. Allow about 1 inch of board above the spile line on this plank (sheer strake) only. The reason for this is that your spile line is taken on the timbers and defines the edge of the inside of the planking—the outside of the sheer plank must be higher because of the flare.

You have to find out how much to allow to get the actual outside point on the plank. Take a block of wood, the thickness of your planking, and lay it at the sheer line on each

51

timber you used for spiling. Using your bevel gauge, set it on the timber and open the blade until it is about level. At the outside edge of the block, measure up to the bevel blade. This will give you the measurement to add to your spile points to obtain the actual top outside edge of the plank. Do this at every other timber and you will get a perfect top edge to your sheer strake. Transfer the initial spile points to the inside of the plank after sawing the top edge and bevel to this line. As you will see, the bevel will decrease as you work aft.

The lower edge of the sheer strake should be lined out using the general widths already established, but adjusted so it is somewhat wider than the other planks. Thus, when the sheer guards are fastened on, it will look generally like the other planking in width.

As mentioned earlier, extra width must also be put in where the flare is in order to get a sweet line. Spot your plank widths on the designated timbers, and adjust and fair with the lining batten. Transfer the final widths to the plank board, measuring down from the spile line, then tack on the lining batten and run your pencil or ball point pen along it. Now you have your forward sheer strake all marked out. (After sheer planks may be sawn from the initial spile line, as their top edges will not need extra wood, since there is no extreme flare aft in lobsterboats.)

In sawing the sheer strake, you can nail two boards together and saw both port and starboard sides at once, or you can saw the one marked board separately, jointing its edges with your jack or jointer plane, and using it as your pattern to make the opposite side. As already mentioned, do all of your spiling from one side of the boat unless you develop a slight hog or bunch in the opposite side, in which case you will have to spile a plank or two on that side to take out this unfairness. However, if the planks are clamped or wedged uniformly along their

full length and brought into place with even pressure, no unfairness should develop.

A word about jointing the plank edges: a 21- or 22-inch hand jointer is the best tool for jointing planks and can be used on all the planking, except for the upper planks in the bows. Here, a 14-inch jack plane will work out better in certain places, such as the bottom edges and even the tops in full, flaring bows. On the bottom edges, you will have to angle the plane in the hollows to get it to cut.

The forward planks should be made as long as you can possibly get them. However, in flaring bows, they are apt to be shorter than desired, because their extreme curve prevents long ones from being sawn out of normal width stock.

We are now ready to hang the sheer strakes. Cut out a couple dozen or more clamp pads from ⅜- or ½-inch plywood; make them about 1¼ inches by 3 inches. Use these between the plank and the clamp foot so as not to bruise the plank. I've seen boats where this practice was not adhered to; when the boats were overboard a couple of weeks, these marks swelled out like a bunch of knots.

Take the bevel at the stem rabbet, using a bevel gauge against a temporary batten tacked along the sheer line, transfer this to the forward end (hood end) of the sheer strake, mark and saw. Then, with a helper holding the plank, check the fit, and, if needed, trim with a block plane until it fits well. Then plane a bevel on the outside edge of the hood end to form about a ¹⁄₁₆-inch caulking seam. Next, starting with the hood end in place and clamped to the stem, bend on the forward part of the plank and clamp it to the timbers, using clamp pads between the plank and clamp foot. Now fasten the hood end in place with three 2-inch #12 bronze screws. Great care must be taken here so as not to split the plank. Your helper can position the rest of the plank as you clamp it on. On hulls with full bows, it may be necessary to steam the plank. The top row of fastenings (2-inch #12 bronze screws will be used throughout for hull planking) should be placed about ¾-inch down from the edge of the plank and near the forward edge of the timber. Put these screws in level—not square with the plank—so you can later cut off the timbers without hitting them. The lower edge fastenings are to be up from the bottom edge of the plank about ½ inch and near the aft side of the timber. A counterbore should be used, so that bungs can be glued in over the heads of the screws.

Another note on sheer strakes which would be helpful is that the fastenings into the last three timbers before the butt should be left out until the after section of the plank is lined up with the forward section and fastened to the butt block. You can then position the after plank and fasten along until you reach the stern. This avoids a quick place in your planking line, which otherwise might

occur where the sheer strakes butt. The oak butt blocks should overlap the adjoining plank edges by ½ inch and should have their outboard corners cut away at 45-degree angles as shown in Figure 5-10 to allow them to drain. Be sure to bevel the butts between all planks for caulking.

Ah yes! the sheer strake is an adventure in itself. Done with care and patience, it will be a most satisfying experience but it is unfortunate that the first plank to be described and to be hung on the boat is the forward sheer strake. Certainly it is not a "typical" plank and at this point it might be helpful to review its differences. It is wider than the other planks because of the sheer guard allowance, it must be specially shaped to eliminate the hump in the flare area, its upper edge needs bevelling wood added, its top row of fastenings must be driven horizontally, and its crooked shape demands a shaped spiling batten. Other planks have some of these features, but in general they are more easily understood, gotten out, and hung than this one.

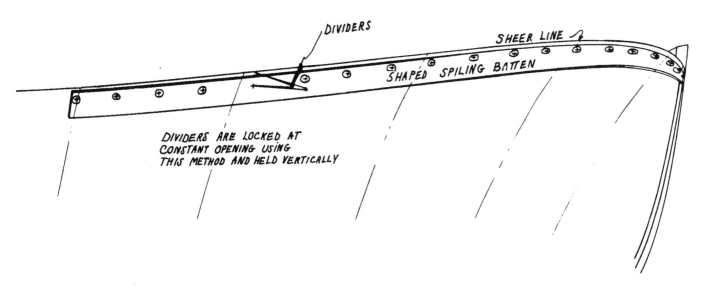

5-5 Using the spiling batten.

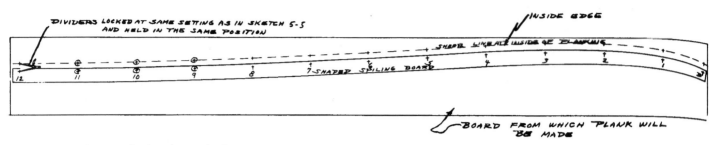

5-6 *Transferring the marks from the spiling batten to the plank board.*

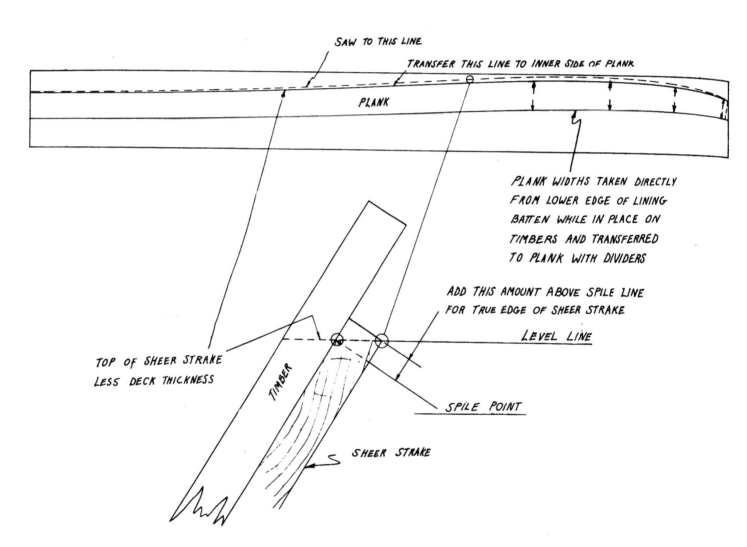

5-7 *Reason for allowing extra wood on the top edge of the sheer strake.*

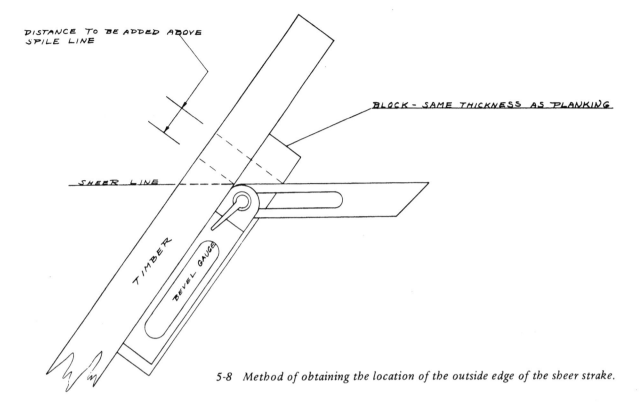

5-8 *Method of obtaining the location of the outside edge of the sheer strake.*

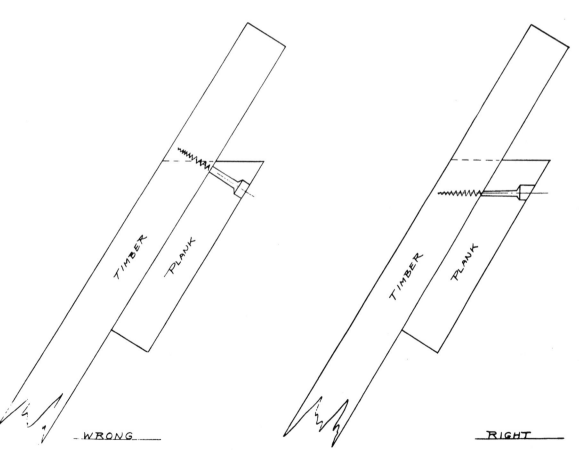

5-9 *Fastening the top edge of the sheer strake.*

THE REMAINING STRAKES

Planking proceeds with the next strake down. Take your smooth plane and plane off the marks on the spiling batten so that it is ready to take the spile of strake #2. If you find that the spiling batten is a little too crooked for strake #2, trim it on the table saw to fit roughly. Take off the next ribband if it is in the way. Using the same procedure that you used on the sheer strake, tack the batten to the timbers and set the dividers. Use your lining batten to determine the lower edge of strake #2, after marking the general widths on the timbers again. As with the sheer strake, this plank will have to be widened out in the way of the flare in order to look good. Be sure to wedge it tightly against the sheer strake by blocking and wedging it from the ribband below. Blocks can be made from excess cut from planks; wedges can be made from 2-inch oak about 12 to 14 inches long.

In a boat of this shape, the planking butts work out well if each one is located about three timber bays aft of the butt above it. Then, after you have hung five or six strakes and are having trouble getting stock long enough, go back more or less under the sheer strake butt and repeat the pattern. The whole idea is to separate the butts by several planks and frames. Also, keep in mind that planks with a lot of shape have to be shorter than straighter ones unless you have unusually long and sweeping planking stock.

The joining edge of each new plank will have to be bevelled to fit well and at the same time leave a caulking seam.* The procedure for doing this is as follows: Since you will be lifting off the shape of the *inside* surface of the plank with your spiling batten, yet marking from it to the *outside* surface of your planking stock, you will first have to get out this plank with square edges, planed and true to the line, so that its inside surface is the same shape as its outside. Once this is done, you can mark one edge to fit the adjoining plank by use of a planking bevel whose tapered blade automatically gives a caulking seam.** Bevels are taken at every other timber and cut into the edge of the plank with a sharp jackknife. This is called *spotting the plank bevels.* After you have spotted the bevels onto the plank, take the plank over to the bench and clamp it in a vise. Using your jack plane with a heavy set, if the bevel is great, rough off the excess wood. Then finish planing down to the spots with your jointer, being careful not to take any off the inside plank edge. In taking plank bevels, set the body of the bevel gauge on the timber and press its blade against the edge of the last plank hung.

As you plank down and approach and round the bilge, you will have to hollow the planks to fit the timbers. Where the hollow is extreme, use thicker planks to compensate or you will have a thin skin. By grinding a curve in your smooth plane blade, you can plane or "back out" up to a $\frac{1}{16}$-inch hollow in your planks. It is a good idea to have such extra blades for this plane. You will see more about planes in Chapter 8 on outboard jointing. You should also have a wooden backing-out plane, which has a curved bottom and blade with which you can plane

---

*Where the hull is quite convex, as it is at the bilge, bevelling wood must be added to the outside width of the plank as was done for the top edge of the sheer strake earlier. How fussy you get in allowing for bevelling wood depends on how extreme the curve of the hull is and how important you feel it is to have the lower edge of your plank come to its marks. In most cases the amount and location of extra bevelling width can be estimated without elaborate measuring.

**This planking bevel was developed to produce a thin caulking seam for a thread of cotton to be rolled in using a caulking wheel. For planking to be caulked using irons, make a seam that has a square shoulder for approximately one-third the plank thickness and a steeper, thus wider, caulking seam for the remaining two-thirds.

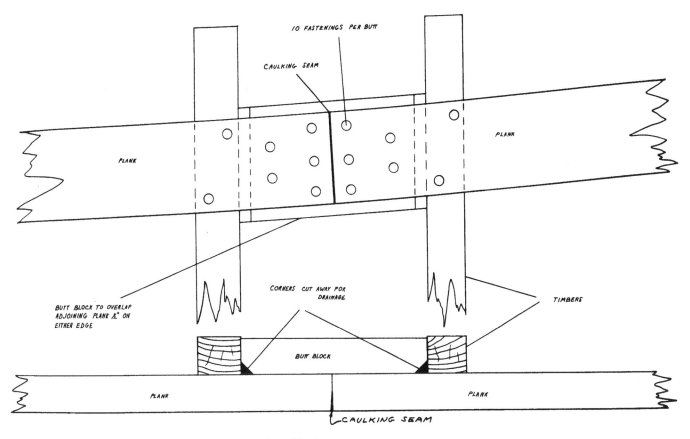

5-10 *The proper shape and location of a butt block.*

a greater hollow. If you are lucky, you may find one in a used-tool store. For the last five or six years, I have been using an electric plane for this. Here again, you should get extra blades so that you can grind them to various curves. On a lobsterboat with hard bilges, some of the planks will require ³⁄₁₆ inch or ¼ inch of hollowing or backing out. I try to narrow these planks in way of the bilge from the normal width. Narrow planks lay up better with less hollowing and less edge bevel—the job is easier all around. These narrow planks can usually be parallel sided (i.e., of constant width).

You can compensate for narrowing the planks in way of the bilge, usually four or five strakes, by widening out the bottom planks that lay on the flat surfaces just below the round of the bilge. Here you can

also compensate for not tapering or shaping them.

In general, you have three areas of planking. The first area would be the top six or seven strakes, which should be made as I have described so far, taking care to keep the lines sweet and fair. Your second area of planking would be as you approach the bilge; in here you have taken out a lot of the curve so your planks have only a slight overhand sweep. As mentioned earlier, this will allow you to use a few parallel strakes unless the boat has an unusually wide beam. Getting out these parallel strakes is relatively simple compared to what you went through to get out the upper strakes. But there is extra work in tapering your plank from normal thickness at the bow to whatever extra thickness you need at the most hollow point, as well as in hollowing or backing out. Use a pattern block to get the right amount of hollowing.

After rounding the bilge, you are in the third planking area—from the bilge to the keel. Before starting to plank here, take another set of girth measurements and deduct 6½ inches for the garboard. Divide the remaining space into strakes, trying not to exceed 5½ to 6 inches at the planks' widest point. Removing ribbands as you go, plank down to within three strakes of the garboard. This last plank down (i.e., the fourth from the keel, counting the garboard) shall have its lower edge beveled off ⅛ inch. The reason for this is that the top edge of the shutter plank (the last one to go on) will go against this edge; the shutter is a drive fit. You will hear more on this later.

Next, you will have to make a pattern of ½-inch or so pine, cedar, or mahogany for the forward piece of the garboard plank. Rough-cut this to fit the rabbet, then scribe it down for an exact fit by holding the dividers so they are vertical and at a constant setting. *Remember this*: since the garboard is *fitted straight down, do not* go at right angles to the curve of the rabbet line—to do so is one of the most common mistakes made in scribing with dividers. After you have marked, lined off, and cut out the pattern, tack some scrap blocks or shims onto the timbers so that when the pattern is clamped on, it is flush with the outside of the rabbet (i.e., shim thickness plus pattern thickness equals garboard thickness). Trim the pattern if necessary for an exact fit and you are ready to trace the lower edge of the garboard directly from the pattern onto your planking stock. From this line lay off widths, and with a batten draw in the upper edge of the garboard, being sure to give it a good upward sweep on the forward end (hood end). Garboards look terrible if they droop at this point. Also, from just aft of amidships, the garboard may

narrow going toward the transom, so that all the transom wood ends are of about the same width. With garboards all milled, the lower edge has to be beveled to leave a caulking seam. This is done with a planking bevel in the same way as described earlier for other planking.

To locate the garboard in its exact position on the hull, it is good practice to mark it at the forefoot joint on the keel. This mark is put onto the pattern and transferred to the garboard. Now, after checking the fit, especially at the hood end, we are ready to steam the forward piece of the garboard, which twists a good deal in the run aft from the hood end. Steam boxes and steaming are described in Chapter 3 on timbering. Before putting the garboard in the steam box, mark and pre-bore the hood end, as it is hard to bore a clean hole in wet wood. When the plank has steamed for an hour or so, take it over to the boat, and, with your helper sitting on the floor to hold the aft end of it, set the forward end in place, being sure that it is in position fore and aft, i.e., that the forefoot joint lines up with your mark. Clamp it into place, wedge it down with blocks and wedges, and bore (through your holes in the hood ends) for the screws in the rabbet and fasten off the hood end. Leave the clamps on until you have fastened off the entire piece of plank with two screws in the rabbet between each timber at its lower edge and one per timber at its upper. By this time, it will have cooled off and taken its shape. Fit and fasten the butt block, then spile, get out, hang, and fasten the after piece of the garboard plank. (A pattern won't be needed for it.)

Now get out and hang the garboard on the other side of the boat, first checking your pattern and trimming it if necessary for a good fit.

The next plank up is the broad strake. This is an easy plank to make, as the top edge of the garboard can be used to mark the lower edge of the broad strake. Remember the *beveled edge on the last plank down from the top* as it will come into play soon. The broad strake will be half the width of the remaining space plus ⅛ inch to allow for its beveled upper edge. Once it's shaped and beveled, wedge and block it to the garboard. Don't forget to spot the bevels on the lower edge of the broad strake and plane on the planking seam. Fasten off the broad strake and you are ready to make the "shutter plank." For this plank, you hang a bottle over the boat—when the shutter is fastened on, you celebrate!

You now have a single plank opening in the bottom. Tack the spiling batten in the opening, shimming it out as you did with the garboard, and, with your dividers, go through your procedure of spiling every other timber. It is my practice to take this spile on the lower edge. Now, transfer this spile onto the planking stock and line off, numbering the spile points. Take this board under the boat, and, with your dividers, take widths at the spile point and transfer them to the plank. Be sure your dividers are as nearly square across the opening as you can judge. After marking off this line with the lining batten, saw the plank carefully. I should mention here that you should leave the line when sawing planks and try not to plane it out completely when jointing.

This is very important: When you take the shutter plank back to the bench to spot the bevel edges (you have to bevel both edges of this plank), be very careful not to spot the bevel on the wrong side. It is easy to do one edge, but both edges can be a little confusing. So, take your time and think!

After you have made your bevels, and have jointed caulking seams on the plank, fit the hood end. With your helper holding the aft end, go along and test the fit. If the plank goes in halfway, it will drive the rest of the way. If it doesn't go in halfway, you will have to take a couple of shavings off until it does. Take a pounding block, made from a piece of oak, about 24 inches by 1 inch or 1¼ inches by 2 inches (an end of a timber will do just fine), kill the edges with a plane and round off the ends to prevent damage to the plank when pounding. Using a two-pound hammer, *never a sledge hammer*, pound the forward end all the way home and set the hood end fastenings carefully with a bit brace. Nurse these screws in; don't use a power screwdriver. Now clamp an oak twister, about 36 inches by 1½ inches by 2 inches, on the aft end of the plank after cutting the butt. With it your helper can twist the plank while another man, whom you will need at this time, tends a prop and pry rig, using a piece of board for a prop and a piece of 2-inch by 4-inch oak about 8 feet long for a pry. He should set this about three feet aft of where you are pounding, with the lower end of the pry near the bottom edge of the plank. Insert a wide chisel at the top edge to keep the top from popping in too fast. Have your man apply pressure on the pry rig to start the bottom edge into the opening. Remove your chisel, take your pounding block, and hammer the plank in as far as you can. Now bore off and drive the screws with a power driver until they fetch up, but *do not force them.* Again using your pounding block, set the plank home and tighten the screws with your bit brace. The plank may not be all of the way in at the prop, but don't let this bother you. Move the pry rig back about 3 or 4 feet and go through the same routine until you reach the last 3 or 4 feet, then take the twister away from your helper, who at this time will be darned glad to give it to you. Place it across the opening at the butt on the inside of the planking and, using a clamp pad, clamp the end of the shutter plank to the twister, and hammer in the last three feet, tightening the clamp as you go. Then fasten off the rest of the plank. Fit the butt block and fasten it in and away you go to spile off and fit the next section of the shutter. Unlike the rest of the planking, separate spilings should be taken on each side of the boat for the shutter planks.

Once the shutter is all in, you may be too tired to reach for the bottle. So, sit back in a pile of shavings and look with pride at a fine planking job!

You now have to plug the screw holes with bungs, which may be purchased or cut from your plank scraps with a bung cutter. Bungs should be set in a good glue, taking care to keep their grain running with that of the planking. When the bungs are all in place, they should be chiseled off, again taking care to cut in the direction of the grain and not to chip them out of the hole. It is a good practice to chip off a piece from the top of the bung to see which direction to attack it from.

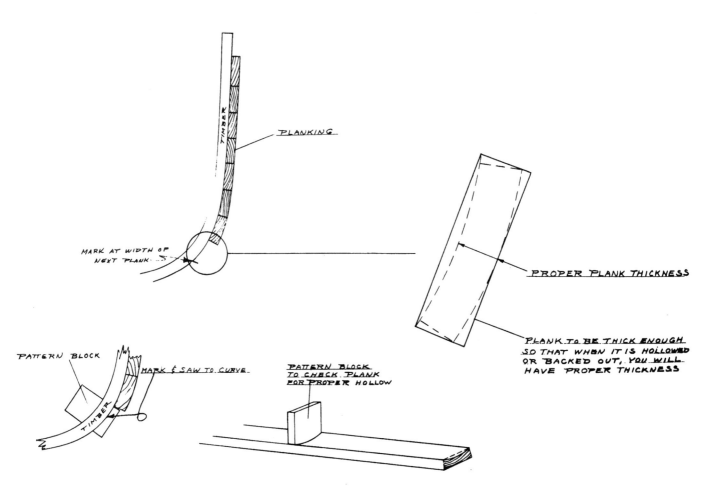

5-11 *"Backing out" planking in way of the bilge.*

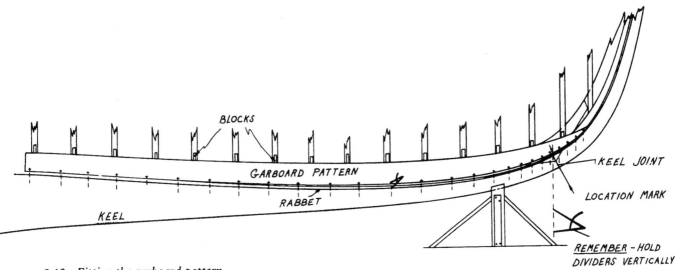

BLOCKS

GARBOARD PATTERN

KEEL JOINT

LOCATION MARK

RABBET

KEEL

REMEMBER – HOLD
DIVIDERS VERTICALLY

5-12   Fitting the garboard pattern.

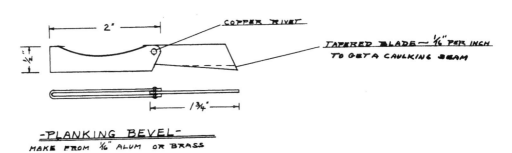

2"

¼"

COPPER RIVET

TAPERED BLADE – 1/16" PER INCH
TO GET A CAULKING SEAM

1¾"

-PLANKING BEVEL-
MAKE FROM 1/16" ALUM OR BRASS

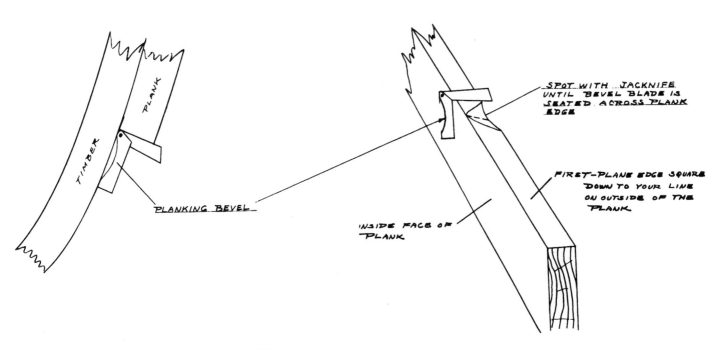

TIMBER

PLANK

PLANKING BEVEL

SPOT WITH JACKNIFE
UNTIL BEVEL BLADE IS
SEATED ACROSS PLANK
EDGE

FIRST-PLANE EDGE SQUARE
DOWN TO YOUR LINE
ON OUTSIDE OF THE
PLANK

INSIDE FACE OF
PLANK

5-13   Taking off and spotting plank bevels.

61

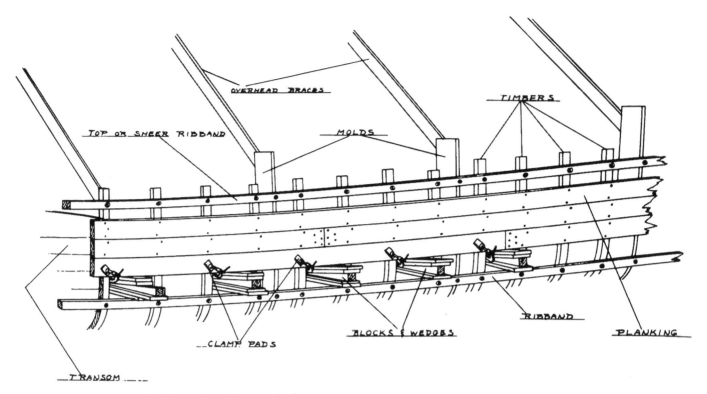

OVERHEAD BRACES

TIMBERS

TOP OR SHEER RIBBAND

MOLDS

RIBBAND

PLANKING

CLAMP PADS

BLOCKS & WEDGES

TRANSOM

5-14 *Blocking and wedging up plank.*

A view of the starboard bow with the boat partly planked up. She is being planked from both the sheer strake and the garboard. You can see where ribbands have been taken off to make room for the planks as they are put on. It is sometimes a good idea to leave one end of a ribband in place to wedge against, as has been done here with the lower one. Notice the shape in the sheer strake and the nice rise of the garboard as it runs forward.

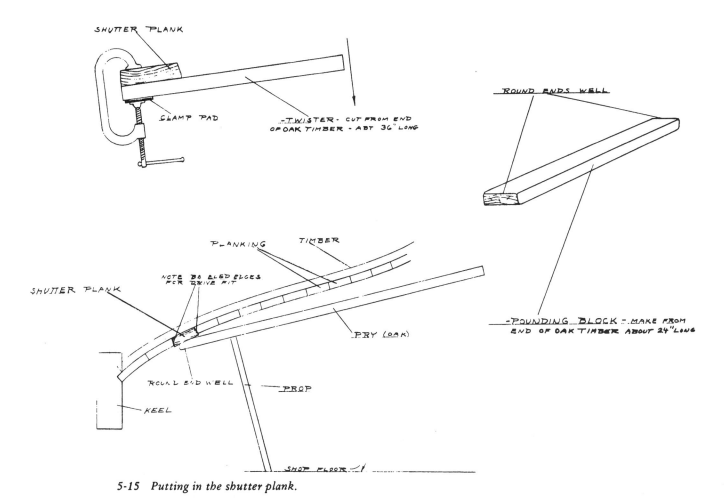

SHUTTER PLANK

CLAMP PAD

-TWISTER- CUT FROM END
OF OAK TIMBER - ABT 36" LONG

ROUND ENDS WELL

-POUNDING BLOCK - MAKE FROM
END OF OAK TIMBER ABOUT 24" LONG

PLANKING   TIMBER

NOTE BEVELED EDGES
FOR DRIVE FIT

SHUTTER PLANK

PRY (OAK)

ROUND END WELL

PROP

KEEL

SHOP FLOOR

5-15   *Putting in the shutter plank.*

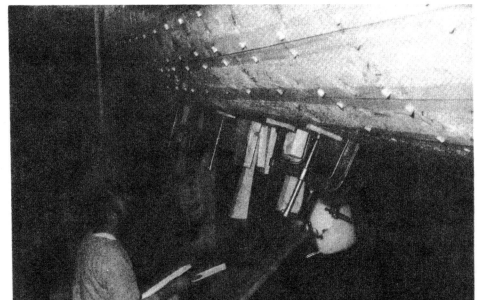

Planking must be wedged together to close up the seams as well as be clamped securely to the timbers before fastening can commence. Here, the planking is being bunged as soon as it is hung, which means that the seams have to be jackplaned off earlier than described in the text.

Chapter 6

Deck Frame

In preparing for the deck frame work, the molds have to be removed, some poppets or props fitted under the hull, and the top ribband taken off.

First, props have to be fitted just under the bilge on either side of the hull at about stations 3 and 6 and at the transom. After fitting the props, cut cedar or pine pads roughly 4 inches by 8 inches and reduce the length of the props by the thickness of these pads. Nail the pads to the props and set the nail heads well into the pads so they won't dig the hull. Position the props and tap their lower ends with your hammer as you go along to set them up tightly, after which they should be toenailed to the floor. Before removing the molds, fit tie braces across the hull about 8 inches below the sheer and nail them to the timbers. With the props and tie braces holding the hull in shape, the molds can be safely removed.

Now rig a staging running all around the boat at the right height for working on the sheer and take off the top ribbands. Assuming that you have made a deck beam mold, you are all set to trim the sheer. This is where a slice or slick would come in handy, but a sharp 1½-inch or 2-inch chisel, along with a drawknife, is the next best

thing. Tack your sheer batten along the sheer, adjust it and mark off with your pencil, and remove the batten.

At this point, you still have your timberheads sticking up out of the hull, and they have to be sawn off. With the beam mold lying across the hull, let's say at the transom, check to see how much you have to trim off the sheer plank to allow the bottom edge of the beam mold to fit neatly onto the sheer plank, and at the same time come down to the marked sheer line. Now trim the plank with drawknife and chisel. Do not take off too much at a time and keep checking with the beam mold for fit. This trim spot should be 5 inches or 6 inches long and next to a timber. Laying your handsaw on this trim spot, saw off the timberhead. Follow this procedure all around the sheer. The only timberheads not cut are those forward that are braced off, as noted in Chapter 4. These stay in until the deck frame is complete. Using the pieces of timber tops that you have sawn, cut and fit them between the timberheads and toenail them to the timbers all around the sheer.

With your electric jointer or jack plane in hand, trim the excess wood between these trim spots and carefully joint the sheer, again being very careful not to cut below your marked line. Check often with the beam mold to ensure the proper angle. Now that the sheer is trimmed and fair, the next operation will be to fit and install the breasthook, and the sheer clamps and shelves.

Before installing the sheer clamps, the breasthook should be fitted and fastened to the stem and sheer strakes. I usually make a ¼-inch plywood pattern of it and get my angles at the stem and outboard edges of the pattern with a bevel gauge, then bandsaw the oak after marking it from the pattern. Clamp the breasthook into place and fasten it with 2-inch #14 flat-head screws through the sheer strakes. A ⅜-inch carriage bolt through the stem and breasthook will secure the breasthook firmly fore and aft.

Now for the sheer clamp: The top edge of the sheer clamp must be lined off in the hull so it can be positioned properly. To do this, make a sample piece of sheer clamp about 18 inches or so long. With your beam mold on the sheer at the first timber in the bow, lay your sample onto the timbers under it. Using your two-foot folding rule or tape measure, adjust the sample until the inboard top corner measures 1⅜ inches below the beam mold, then put a pencil mark on the timber at the outboard edge of the sample. Do this on every other timber for about one-third of the length of the boat from the bow. At midships, where the flare is less, this measurement would drop to 1⅝ inches and carry through to the transom. Take your lining batten and tack it along these marks. If necessary, adjust it to be fair and mark off all the timbers the length of the boat. This completed on both sides, you are now ready to make up and install the sheer clamps.

Because of the length of the sheer clamp, it will have to be spliced. The splice will usually come about amidships, but if you are fortunate enough to get long stock (oak

is usual here), it will be farther aft. This splice should be fitted on saw horses, then all you will have to do, once the forward piece is in the boat, is get the length of the aft piece and cut its aft end to fit the transom frame. This is easy enough to do.

The oak sheer clamps are about 1½ inches by 3¼ inches, and are spiled. They are easy to mill with your portable saw. The forward half of the sheer clamp has quite a bit of overhand sweep. Find an oak plank with about this sweep, spile it off, and saw it to shape. Three or four sliding bar clamps and several 8-inch or 10-inch C clamps are necessary. The C clamps must have deep enough throats to reach down and hold the sheer clamp in place.

After cutting the forward end of the sheer clamp to fit the stem, steam it, clamp it into place, and bore for a ⅜-inch carriage bolt at each timber. I usually counterbore through the planking for the bolt heads, so they bear directly onto the timbers. You will have to be careful not to bore any bolt holes through the plank seams, but instead stagger or angle the bolts from either side of the seam. Work along, bolting off until you come to the splice.

To get the length of the after piece of sheer clamp, have someone hold the forward end of your lining batten at the top of the forward nib in the splice, then mark your batten where it butts against the transom cheek piece. Remember, this will be the back side length. Get the angles with your bevel gauge at the transom, both vertical and horizontal. With the batten laid along the aft sheer clamp, transfer its mark to the sheer clamp, mark the bevels on it, and cut off its end. Clamp the aft sheer clamp in and finish bolting it off. Bolt the splice as shown in Figure 6-6. Bolt down through the breasthook and sheer clamps forward, using two ⅜-inch bolts per side. Be sure to use washers under the nuts.

DECK FRAME

In all probability, you could bend the sheer clamps in cold, but the strain is great and it would have a tendency to pull the sheer strakes inboard, thus creating a hump in the sheer forward. Even with steaming, and with the forward timber tops braced and the tie braces down in the hull, you will still have some pulling, but this can be faired after the deck frame is in.

With the sheer clamps installed, we now have to fit and fasten in the quarter knees. These knees should fit against the transom header and rest on top of the sheer clamp at each side of the boat. Bolt each knee horizontally through both the transom header and timber heads with ⅜-inch carriage bolts, two in each direction.

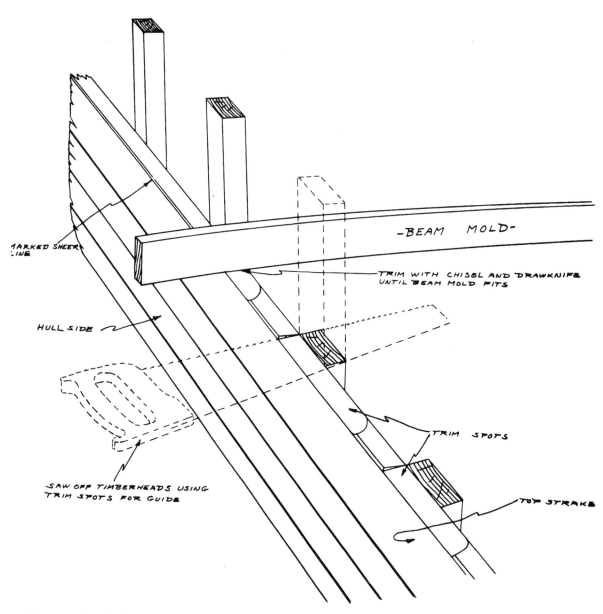

6-1 Spotting the sheer.

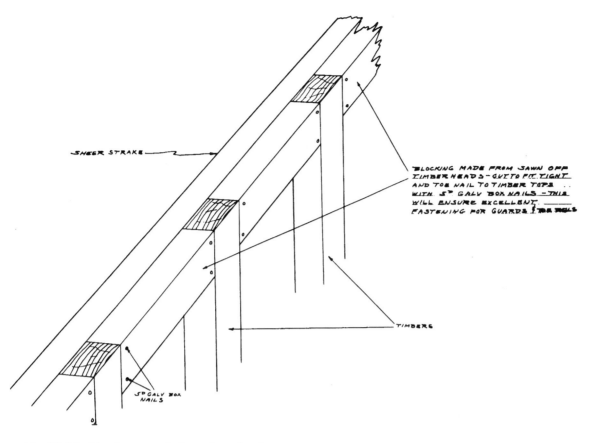

SHEER STRAKE

BLOCKING MADE FROM SAWN OFF
TIMBER HEADS - CUT TO FIT TIGHT
AND TOE NAIL TO TIMBER TOPS
WITH 5" GALV BOX NAILS - THIS
WILL ENSURE EXCELLENT
FASTENING FOR GUARDS & RUB RAILS

TIMBERS

5" GALV BOX
NAILS

6-2   Fit blocking between timbers along the sheer.

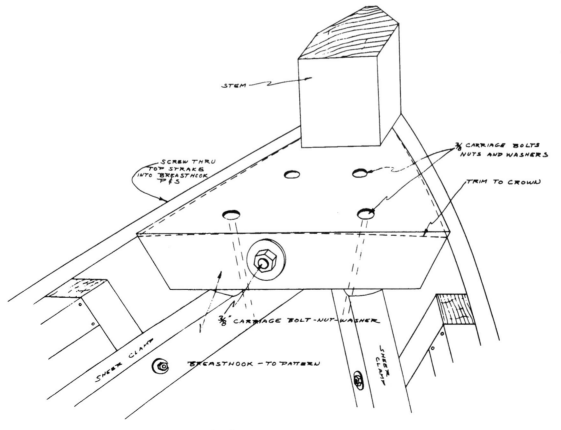

STEM

SCREW THRU
TOP STRAKE
INTO BREASTHOOK
P & S

3/8 CARRIAGE BOLTS
NUTS AND WASHERS

TRIM TO CROWN

3/8" CARRIAGE BOLT - NUT - WASHER

SHEER CLAMP

SHEER CLAMP

BREASTHOOK - TO PATTERN

6-3   Fitting and fastening in the breasthook.

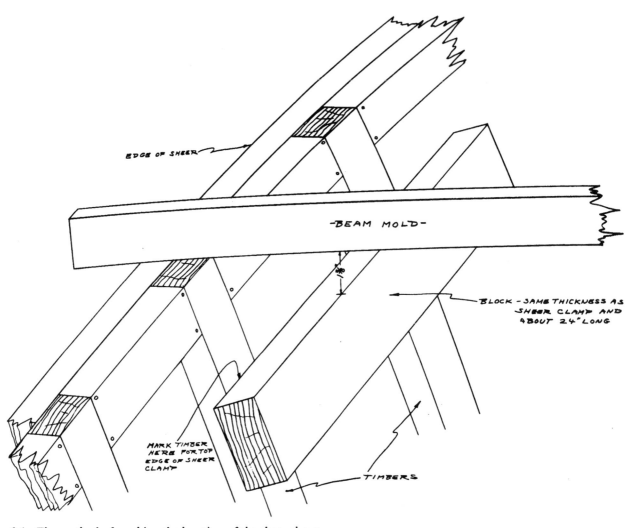

EDGE OF SHEER

-BEAM MOLD-

BLOCK - SAME THICKNESS AS
SHEER CLAMP AND
ABOUT 24" LONG

MARK TIMBER
HERE FOR TOP
EDGE OF SHEER
CLAMP

TIMBERS

6-4   *The method of marking the location of the sheer clamp.*

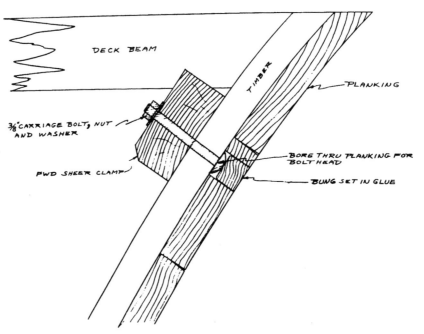

DECK BEAM

TIMBER

PLANKING

3/8"CARRIAGE BOLT, NUT
AND WASHER

BORE THRU PLANKING FOR
BOLT HEAD

FWD SHEER CLAMP

BUNG SET IN GLUE

6-5   *Bolting the sheer clamp up forward.*

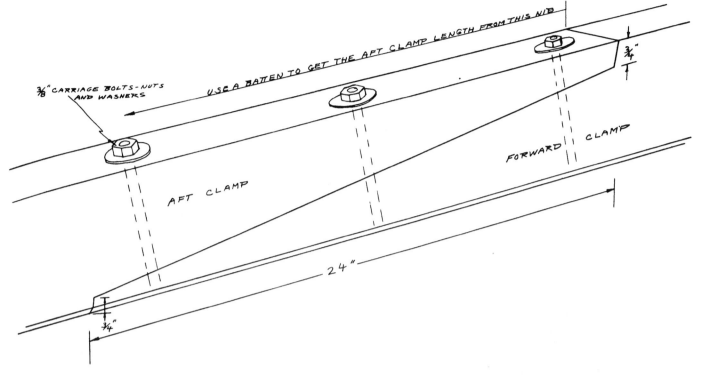

In the diagram:

⅜" CARRIAGE BOLTS-NUTS AND WASHERS

USE A BATTEN TO GET THE AFT CLAMP LENGTH FROM THIS NIB

¾"

FORWARD CLAMP

AFT CLAMP

24"

¾"

6-6   Sheer clamp splice detail.

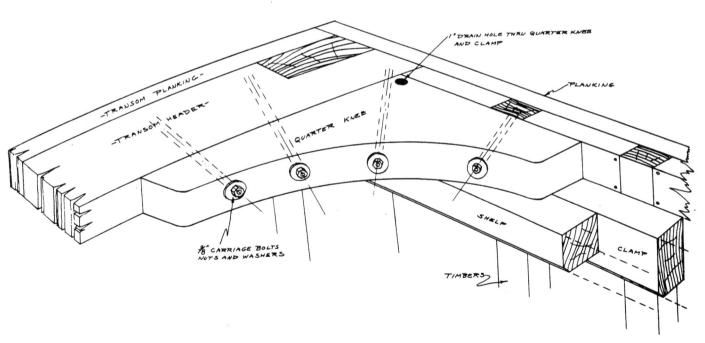

1" DRAIN HOLE THRU QUARTER KNEE AND CLAMP

PLANKING

TRANSOM PLANKING

TRANSOM HEADER

QUARTER KNEE

⅜" CARRIAGE BOLTS NUTS AND WASHERS

SHELF

CLAMP

TIMBERS

6-7   Quarter knee detail.

DECK FRAME

DECK BEAMS AND CARLINS

In milling the deck beams, it is good practice to rough saw each beam, leaving about ⅜ inch of extra wood on each side. This is to allow for springing in the stock, and, believe me, you will see some springing. When the beams have all been rough sawn, lay the beam mold on them again and mark off for the second or final cut. Saw out the beams, just leaving the pencil line and joint the tops with your electric hand plane. To smooth up the lower edges of the beams, you can run them through a thickness planer. It is a good idea to use your jack or smooth plane to take a shaving off the bottom corners. This will prevent fraying of these edges when handling or sliding the other beams or lumber over them.

At this time, I should mention the varying crowns in the first five beams forward. As each one of these beams will have a different crown, the beam mold cannot be used for laying them out. On the lofting, mark the deck centerline above the sheer line and measure between these two lines at each beam location to determine its crown. If you don't want to utilize the lofting, you can use the following rule of thumb for this type of lobsterboat: Spring ⅛ inch extra crown for beam 5, double this measurement for beam 4, then double that for beam 3, etc., except beam 1 (#4–¼", #3–½", #2–1"), which should be about 1½". If you use this method, you will have to fair the top edges of beams 1 and 2. *A word of caution here:* If you should cut these five forward beams, using the regular beam mold, you would end up with a sag in the deck from just behind the stem back to beam 6, the greatest sag being just behind the stem. This would look terrible, so do a good job and make the first five beams individually.

To fit the beams, lay off the last foredeck beam by using a straightedge and your 50-foot tape. Tack the tape eye in the center of the back edge of the stem. Then tack a scrap piece of wood or batten the length of the forward deck with one end against the back of the stem and the other end extending to the aft edge of the straightedge (and fastened at its center), which is laid across the boat. Adjust the straightedge to look about square across the boat, then hound off diagonally from the stem to the aft edge of the straightedge at one side of the boat with your tape. Measure the opposite side and adjust the straightedge back and forth until these measurements coincide. Then mark at the deck edge. The last foredeck beam will now be perfectly square across the boat and the correct distance aft of the stem. You can measure square ahead of this beam, once it has been installed, to position all the beams forward of it.

We will now fit the last foredeck beam. To cut it to length, lay the beam on its aft side at the marks made at the deck edge and spot the top of the beam with your pencil on each end. Stand the beam up with the aft bottom edge on the marks. Your helper should be holding the beam in position across the boat and also helping slide it back and forth while you mark the angles. Lay a small stick, about 6 inches by ⅜ inch by 1 inch, on the timber or block against which the beam will fit, with the stick extending just above the beam. Have your helper slide the beam one way or the other until your spot mark at the top of the beam lines up with the stick. Mark this angle with your pencil. Then lay the stick on top of the beam and sight down to get the angle of the side of the boat. Adjust it to suit your eye and mark the beam. Use this same procedure on the opposite side and cut each end of the beam off with your hand saw.

When you lay the beam in place, after its ends have been sawn off, you will notice that you can move the beam back and forth. You have not made a mistake, as the bottom of the beam hasn't yet been relieved to drop down over the sheer clamp. To do this, slide the beam to one side and measure from the top of the sheer to the top of the beam. This is the amount that will have to be cut from the underside of the beam. Mark the underside of the beam against the top edge of the clamp and use a marking stick against the inner face of the clamp to give you the angle at this point.

Slide the beam to the opposite side and follow the same procedure. After cutting, the beam will fit right into place, but before you fasten it, bevel the middle part of its after side to fit the front of the trunk cabin, which will be installed later on. Afterwards it can be bolted down through the sheer clamp, using a 5/16-inch carriage bolt on each side. Cut in the rest of the forward beams the same way. Fit the mooring bitt blocking from the bitt location forward to the breasthook, using 2-inch by 10-inch oak. Fit and toenail these blocks between the beams with 16d galvanized nails. If strip decking is to be used, you will have to make an oak or mahogany king plank to run down the center of the deck. This should be the thickness of the decking and 6 inches or so wide. It should be screwed to the beams and the bitt blocking with 2-inch #12 flat-head screws.

The aft deck beams can be squared by measuring ahead from the corners of the transom as your transom was hounded off when it was set up. Cut these beams in as you did with the forward beams.

The stud or half beams are cut in with this same method, except that you have to clamp them to your beam mold in order to hold them while marking.

Now that the beams are all in, you have to install the deck carlin. This is the longitudinal member that runs along at the

inboard ends of the stud beams. Make a T-square out of scrap wood—nothing fancy. The length of the blade should equal the distance from the outside of the boat to the outboard side of the carlin. While holding the heel of the T-square against the outside of the boat, slide it along the stud beams, marking the tops of them as you move along. Using a declivity board (milled to whatever tumblehome the cabin side and coaming are to have) and a spirit level, plumb and mark the vertical angle on one stud beam. Set your bevel gauge to this angle and mark off the rest of the stud beams all around the boat. Saw the excess ends off the stud beams and the carlins are ready to fit.

Cut one end of the carlin to fit the notch in the beam and fasten it by nailing through the beam into the carlin with two 16d galvanized nails. Nail the carlin to the stud beams with the same size nails, two to a beam. Unless the carlin can run in one piece, you will have to use a backing block, with the same section as the carlin, at the butt joint. Cut this block to fit between two stud beams and screw through the carlin into the block with 2¼-inch #14 flat-head screws.

With your electric plane, and also your sharp jack plane, trim the deck beam ends at the sheer and the top of the carlin.

To give added support to the deck beams, a shelf will be made up and fastened to the inboard face of the sheer clamp as shown in Figure 6-17. Take bevels for the outboard face of the shelf, which is usually of oak and about 2 inches by 3 inches in cross-section. Chamfer the lower inboard corner and bolt the shelf in place under the beams as shown in the sketch. We now move along to the tie rods.

The tie rods are usually made from ⅜-inch rod, cut to length and threaded for nuts on either end. Starting alongside the second stud beam from the last full beam forward, counterbore through the planking to the timber closest to the stud beam. Now, with a long ⅜-inch auger, bore through the timber and run the bit through and bore the carlin. Plug the hole on the inboard side of the carlin for a spur center and counterbore back for the nut and washer. Drive the tie rod in and tighten the nut over the washer at the inboard side of the carlin. The tie rods should be installed at every other stud beam from this one to the stern deck frame.

A fashion piece should be fastened to the transom header across the top edge of the transom. This piece should be the thickness of the decking, about 3 inches wide, and milled to the transom radius. Mill and fasten on the aft king plank. The outboard top edge of the sheer strakes should now be chamfered for the sheer guard, using a marking gauge. The deck frame is ready for decking.

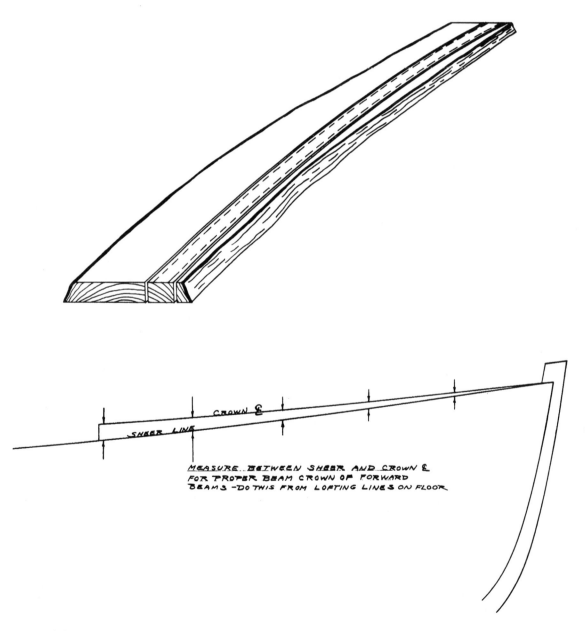

6-9 *Picking the crown of the forward deck beams from the lines.*

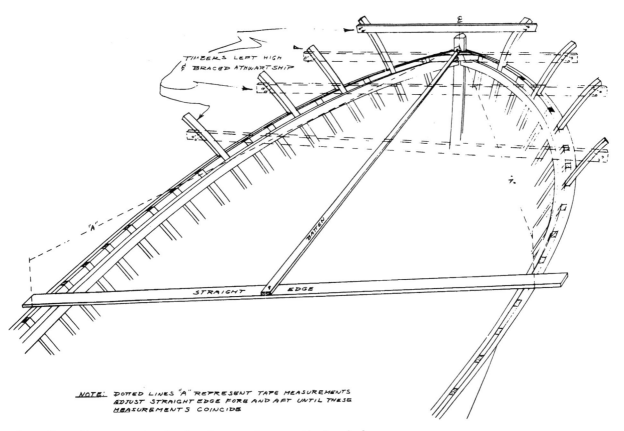

NOTE: DOTTED LINES "A" REPRESENT TAPE MEASUREMENTS
ADJUST STRAIGHT EDGE FORE AND AFT UNTIL THESE
MEASUREMENTS COINCIDE

6-10   Hounding or squaring for the aftermost beam on the foredeck.

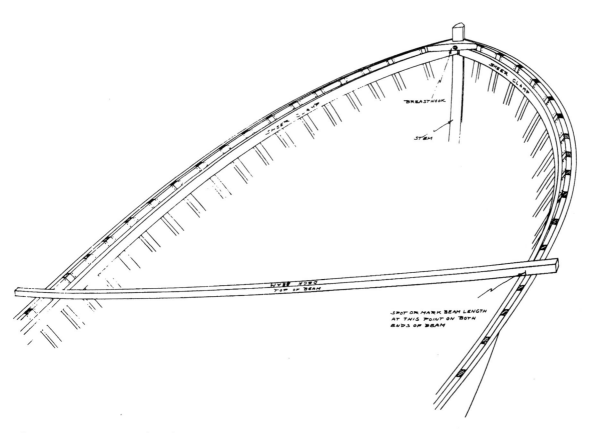

6-11   Getting the beam length.

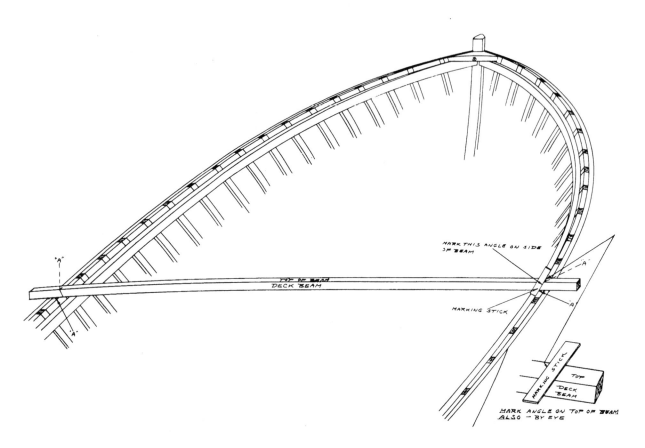

MARK THIS ANGLE ON SIDE OF BEAM

TOP OF BEAM
DECK BEAM

MARKING STICK

MARKING STICK

TOP

DECK BEAM

MARK ANGLE ON TOP OF BEAM
ALSO - BY EYE

6-12 Marking the cutting angles on the beams.

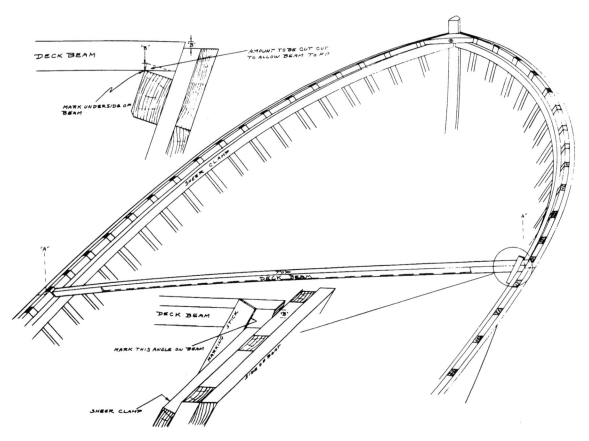

DECK BEAM

AMOUNT TO BE CUT OUT
TO ALLOW BEAM TO FIT

MARK UNDERSIDE OF
BEAM

SHEER CLAMP

TOP OF
DECK BEAM

DECK BEAM

MARK THIS ANGLE ON BEAM

MARKING STICK

TOP OF BEAM

SHEER CLAMP

6-13 Fitting a deck beam.

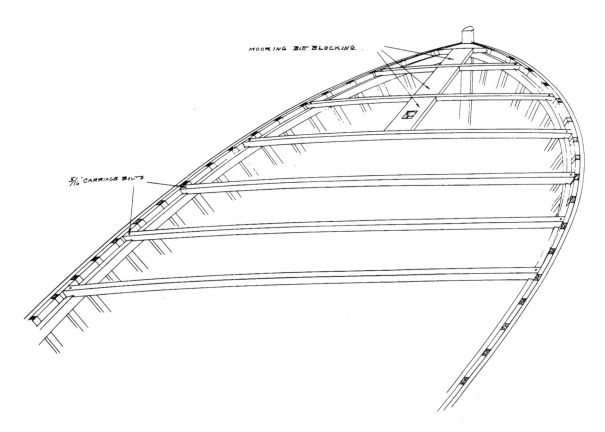

MOORING BITT BLOCKING

5/16" CARRIAGE BOLTS

6-14   *The completed forward deck frame.*

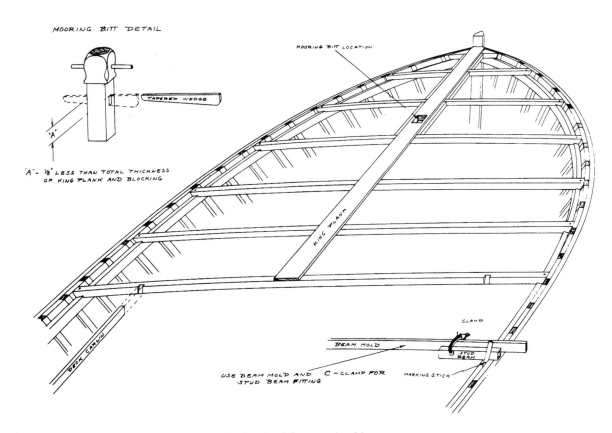

MOORING BITT DETAIL

MOORING BITT LOCATION

"A" - 1/8" LESS THAN TOTAL THICKNESS
OF KING PLANK AND BLOCKING

TAPERED WEDGE

"A"

KING PLANK

DECK CARLIN

CLAMP

BEAM MOLD

STUD BEAM

USE BEAM MOLD AND C-CLAMP FOR
STUD BEAM FITTING

MARKING STICK

6-15   *Fitting the stud beams. Note also the detail of the mooring bitt.*

A partly framed-out deck, looking forward. The stud beams are being put in, their crown being set by the beam mold that is lying across the boat. The cockpit was put in this boat before the deck was framed and provides a good working platform. Note the filler blocks between the tops of the timbers, and the sheer clamp and shelf upon which the deck beams rest.

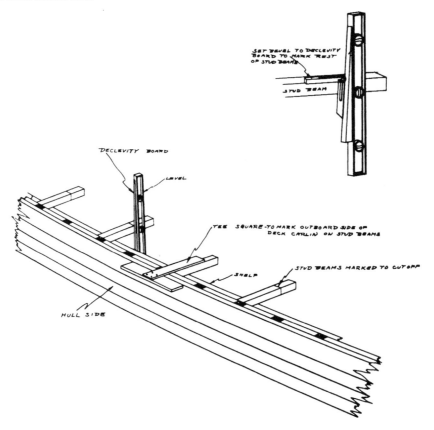

6-16 Marking and cutting the stud beams.

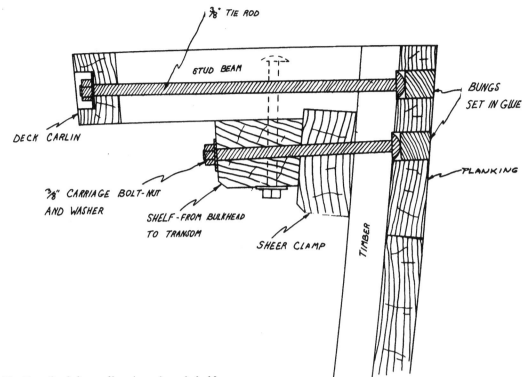

6-17 *Detail of the carlin, tie rod, and shelf.*

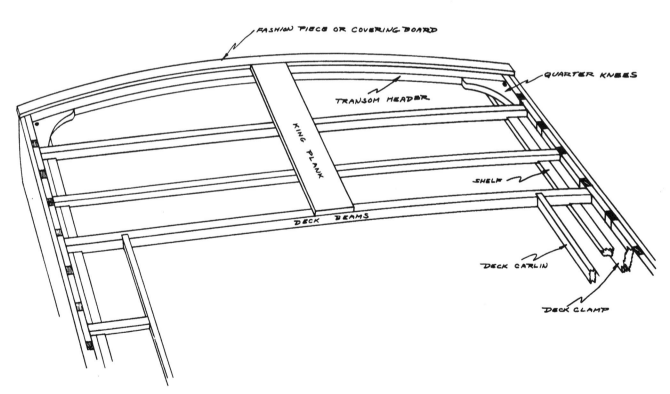

6-18 *After deck frame ready for decking.*

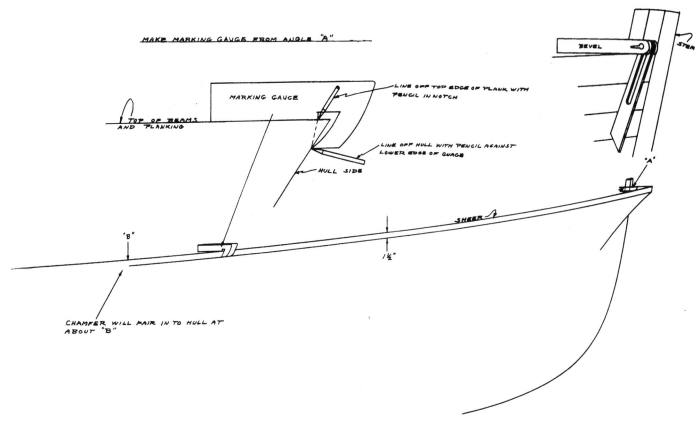

6-19 *Chamfering the sheer edge for the sheer guard.*

Chapter 7

Interior Framing

FLOOR TIMBERS

The first task of interior framing will be installing the floor timbers. These members are undoubtedly one of the most important items of structure in the entire boat, as they hold the bottom in shape. Floors, being sawn members, provide the stiffening to absorb the tremendous beating often encountered during winter fishing.

The main thing to ensure a strong bottom is that there are enough well-fitted floor timbers. There are various ways to place these floor timbers. Each builder has his own idea, and most methods are satisfactory. Some builders prefer to set them against the hull timbers, while others like to set them directly on top of the timbers. The method I prefer is to place the floors halfway between the timbers. My reasoning is that with the floor timbers in this position, the bottom is much less susceptible to puncture from logs or debris. For example, we'll say that the timber spacing is 10 inches on centers. This leaves 8 inches between the 2-inch hull timbers, and, with the floor timbers taking up about 2 inches of this, there are only 3 inches of unreinforced

planking on either side of a floor timber. This, to my way of thinking, is very strong and spreads stress and strain more evenly along the bottom.

In the forefoot area, say for the first four timbers, it is advisable to have the floor timbers in every bay. From this point aft to about three feet ahead of the engine, they may be in every other timber bay. But from three feet forward of the engine to three feet aft of it, floor timbers should again be in every timber bay. In the remainder of the boat aft of the engine, every other bay is satisfactory.

In preparing to mill out the floor timbers from 2-inch oak, you will need patterns. Half-inch pine pattern stock is good to use, as it is easy to work in the boat. It is not necessary that these patterns fit perfectly— their top edges must be nearly level, however, since the floor timbers themselves will be scribed down later. Take your level, dividers, and saber saw into the boat with you, as this will save you countless steps in running back and forth to the bandsaw to cut out patterns. If you have the time, you can get these patterns from the loft floor, but the quickest way really is to make the patterns right in the boat with the saber saw.

Once the patterns are completed and the oak for the floor timbers is in the shop, the floors have to be marked and bandsawed out. It is a good plan here to saw the floor timbers about ⅜ inch larger than the pattern to allow for springing up as with the deck beams described in Chapter 6.

After the initial cutting with the bandsaw, run the top edges of the floor timbers over the jointer or joint them with an electric hand plane. Go back to the bandsaw and saw each floor to the pattern line, but first be sure to check to see if the floor timber did spring, and re-mark it if necessary before sawing.

Get back into the hull with the floor timbers and set them all in place for scribing down, starting in the forefoot. Place your spirit level on top of each floor timber in turn and adjust each one with small wedges until it is level. Shove these wedges in from either end of the floor timber, so they won't interfere with scribing. In scribing, be sure to keep your dividers vertical. Don't scribe at right angles to the hull or your floor timber will not fit. Scribe both sides of the floor timber, moving along and repeating this process until all of the floor timbers have been so scribed.

Back at the bench, trim the floor timbers to the scribe lines and set them back in the boat. They all should fit the hull perfectly, their tops should be level, and, if your work so far has been fairly accurate, their tops should also be fairly near the finished height. There remains only the final trimming to the proper height so the cabin sole will be level when fastened to the tops of the floor timbers.

Moving back to the forward area, run a chalkline just above the floor timbers back to the forward engine floor timber and level it fore and aft. Measure down to a point that would represent the underside of the cabin sole on every floor timber, and make a tick mark.

The tops of the floor timbers in way of the engine beds should be level also to facilitate making the engine beds, but they will be higher than those forward. Don't forget to cut out reliefs for the engine base in the center of these floor timbers.

In the aft area, you will have to go through the same procedure, which I feel is good practice, as you will have level floors to build on instead of having to make shims to level the floor timbers here and there afterward.

Now, back to the bandsaw for the final sawing. Using your combination square set at the tick marks, line off the actual height of the floor timbers and saw and joint their top edges. And be sure to cut good-sized limber holes in the floor timbers.

If you have a drill press, bore ½-inch holes down through the center of the floor timbers for drift pins. The drill press will give you good, straight holes, but this can also be done by eye with a ½-inch reversible drill.

Apply a generous coat of Cuprinol to the floor timbers and lay them back in place in the hull. Mark the position of each side of the floor timbers on the hull, move them out of the way, and bore ⅛-inch pilot holes out through the hull. With the floor timbers back in place, and with your helper standing on them, you can bore from the outside for 2-inch #12 screws and fasten them in.

The holes into the keel for the drift pins are 1/16 inch smaller than the holes through the floor timbers and should go into the keel 6 or 7 inches. Bore these, using a stop or mark on the drill (a piece of tape will suffice), about ¼ inch deeper than the drift pin, to be sure the pin will tighten on the floor timber and not bottom out. The heads of the drift pins should be peened well so that the ½-inch washer used under them cannot come off when driving the drifts home. Also, the points of the drift pins should be rounded off or ground to a slight taper. After the drifts are all driven, one in each floor timber, you can move along to the engine beds.

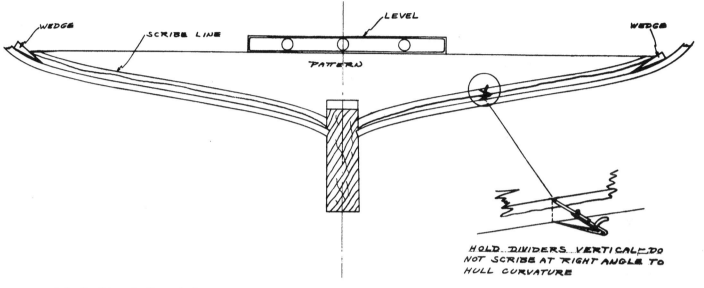

7-1 *Scribing the floor timber pattern.*

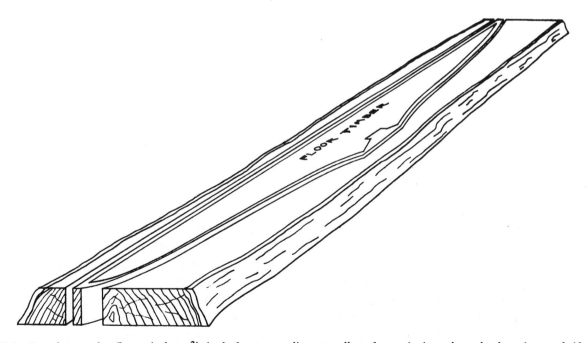

7-2 *Rough saw the floor timbers ⅜ inch from neat lines to allow for springing, then check and remark if necessary for final sawing.*

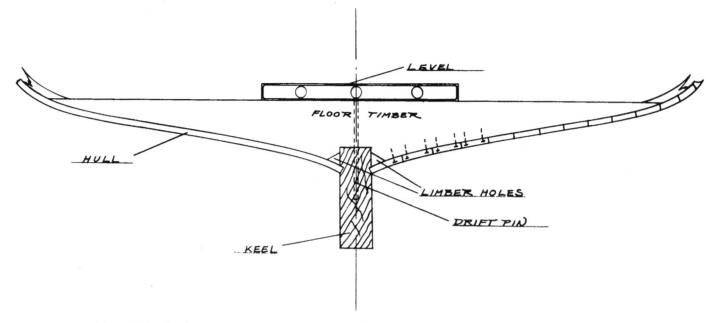

7-3   *Floor timber in place and fastened.*

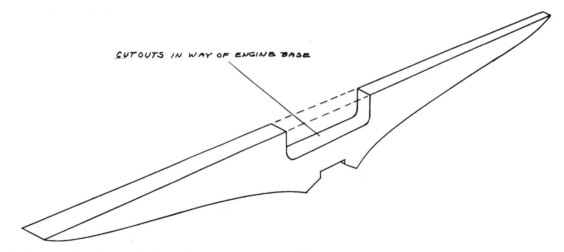

7-4   *Floor timber in way of the engine.*

ENGINE BEDS

Most, if not all, marine engines in the size range for this boat, be they diesel or gas, will be equipped with engine mounts bored for 22½-inch bolt centers athwartships. I side my engine beds 4 inches thick and set them so that they are 20 inches apart. This means that the holddown bolts are 1¼ inches outboard from the inside edge of the beds. The beds should not be less than 10 feet long, particularly if you are using diesel power. This will spread your loading over a minimum of 10 floor timbers, which is a must with the high power being used nowadays in lobsterboats. The floor timbers should be notched out 1 inch in way of the engine beds and by the same token, the engine beds should be notched out 1 inch on their bottom edges, to fit over the floors.

This notching should be executed *very carefully*, taking care to get neat fits, so the beds have to be driven in place. There is no point in notching them otherwise. The notches lock the beds fore and aft as well as athwartships.

In order to get your pattern for the engine beds, you will have to run a chalk line up through the shaft log. This is done in the following manner: First, bandsaw a round plug of 1-inch cedar or pine to fit the shaft hole aft. Then bore a fine hole in the center of the plug to run the chalk line through. Feed the string through the hole and knot the end, so it won't pull out when drawing the string taut from inside the boat. Using a batten or edging, push the forward end of the string up through the shaft log. Have your helper pull the rest of the string inside, and you can drive the plug in the shaft hole at the sternpost.

Now, climb back into the boat and nail a straightedge about 3 feet long, vertically with its lower corner on the centerline of the keel at the forward engine floor timber. Be sure that the straightedge is plumbed with a spirit level and braced off to prevent movement. Have your helper draw the string taut, and, with you at the forward end of the shaft log, have him raise or lower the string along the edge of the straightedge until the string is vertically centered in the shaft hole at the forward end of the shaft log. Tack a 5d box nail in the straightedge against the string and secure the string tightly to it.

Place a piece of pattern stock on the notched floor timbers long enough to span all of them, and, with your level just touching the string, have your helper put a tick mark on the pattern near the forward end, and also one aft about where the shaft coupling will be. Now, with the pattern lying on its side, take your straightedge and line off the shaft centerline.

From the engine plan determine the height and the fore-and-aft location of the mounts, and mark this on the pattern. (Normally, the forward engine mounts are below and the aft ones above the shaft line.) Now mark out the top edge of the pattern, taking off ¼ inch for the shims under the mounts. You can always raise the engine this way, but it's a hell of a job to keep lifting the engine up with falls or a "come-along" and cutting the beds away to suit. Mark the bottom edge of the pattern for the notches over the floor timbers.

Take your pattern down to the bandsaw and saw it out. Then mark around the pattern on two pieces of 4-inch oak bed stock, and mill, apply Cuprinol, and drive them into place. Bore and drift pin the engine beds to the floor timbers just as you did in pinning the floor timbers to the keel. This operation is finished, except for removing the string and the plug.

Probably at this stage it would be a good idea to bore the shaft log for the inside stuffing box and the sternpost for the stern bearing. This is accomplished with a boring bar or shaft. If you aren't able to borrow one, it is not very expensive to make one. The boring bar should be a couple of feet longer than the shaft log and made of 1-inch cold-rolled steel shafting. Each end should be turned down to accommodate the chuck on your ½-inch reversible electric drill. At about 6 inches from the shoulder on the bar at each end a square hole is cut through to take a ⁵⁄₁₆-inch square, tool-steel bit. An Allen set screw should be fitted to hold the bit in place. Now pick up an oak block about a foot long and 1¼ inches thick, set your dividers, and mark out two plugs the diameter of the shaft log hole. Before sawing the plugs out, bore 1-inch holes on the same centers for the boring bar. Now saw out these plugs, leaving the line so that they will fit snugly in the shaft log and sternpost.

83

Grease the plugs in the boring bar holes, using water pump grease or something similar, and drive them into place in the shaft log and the sternpost. These will be your boring bar bearings.

Insert the boring bar, with the bit set for the diameter of the stern bearing shank, and start boring the sternpost, checking for depth as you go. If a full cut is too much for the machine, bore the hole in two or three settings of the bit. Use the same procedure in boring for the inside stuffing box, and you can then remove the plugs and the boring bar. The stuffing box and bearing will be fastened with ½-inch hanger bolts.

The rudder stuffing box should be bored for, seated, and installed at this point, as it would be uncomfortable to do the job after the cockpit is framed up. One-eighth-inch firm rubber gaskets, usually red in color, should be used under the flanges of both the shaft and rudder stuffing boxes.

BILGE STRINGERS

I don't believe in bolting the bilge stringers through the timbers in boats of this size, as I feel that bolts are a weakening factor. Instead, I fasten in two layers of 1-inch by 4-inch oak, using 2-inch #14 flat-head screws, two to each timber. Another advantage of double stringers is that you can stagger your butts. The stringers are to run on both sides of the boat along the turn of the bilge under the cockpit from the transom to about amidships, where they will rise in a natural sweep to the stem. Be sure to apply Cuprinol to the stringers and every other piece of wood that you put into the hull.

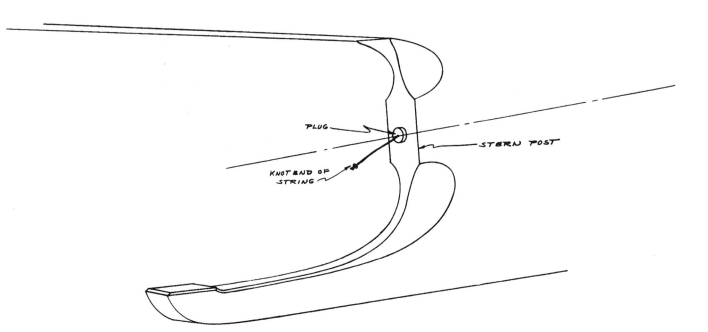

7-5 Determining the shaft line for locating the engine bed. Run the string through the shaft hole and the plug, then drive home the plug.

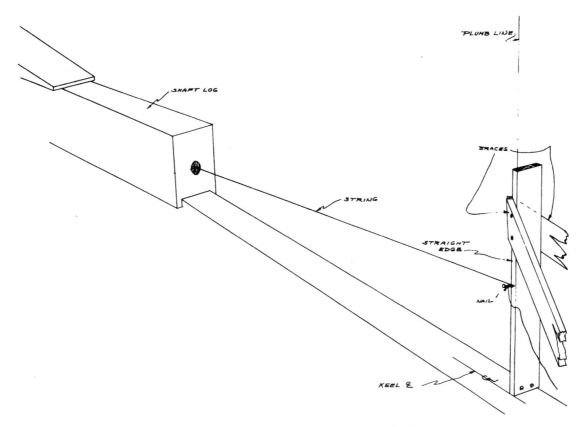

7-6 *Locating the engine bed. Inboard setup of the string that represents the shaft.*

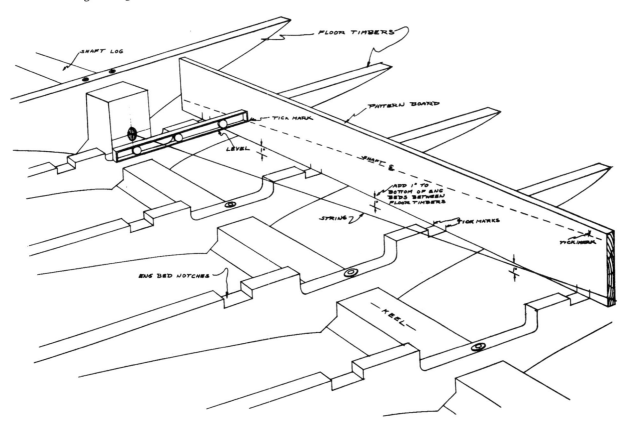

7-7 *Making the pattern for the engine bed.*

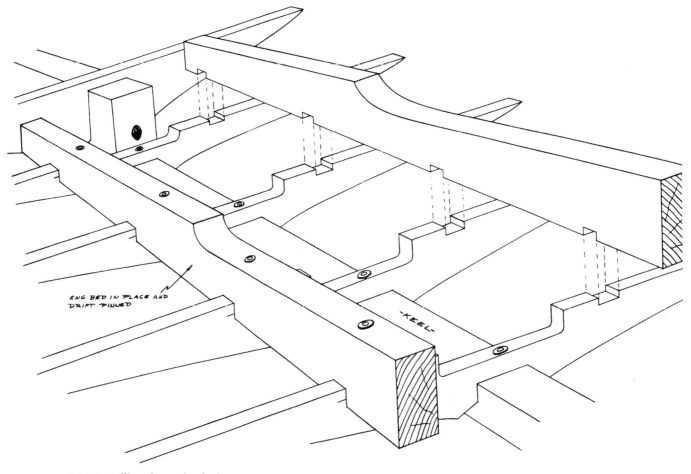

ENG BED IN PLACE AND
DRIFT PINNED

-KEEL-

7-8   *Installing the engine bed.*

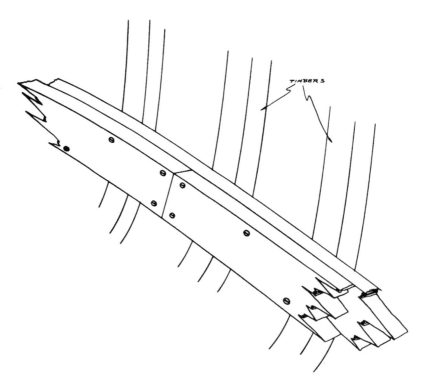

TIMBERS

7-9   *Laminated bilge stringer—two layers, screw fastened.*

COCKPIT FRAME

The cockpit stringer should be about 1½ inches by 2 inches and screwed to the timbers with 2½-inch #14 flat-head screws, two to each timber. To locate this stringer, measure down the proper distance, as shown on the plans, from the carlin at the bulkhead and measure down likewise at the transom, put tick marks on the timbers at these measurements, and run a string between them. Draw the string good and taut and tie it off. Bring your level down until it just touches the string, with the lower corner of the level touching the timber. Mark the timber at this point. Repeat this operation on every other timber until you finish one side. I set a string up on both sides, so that this marking or spotting can all be done at the same time. Spile these stringers to shape if they need it, mill them out, and fasten them in. You are now ready for the cockpit beams.

Saw the cockpit beams, which are about 2 inches by 2 inches, just as you did the deck beams, the one exception being that these beams have only 1 inch or so of crown. The cockpit is to be watertight and self-bailing, so the reason for crowning the beams is so that the water will run to the sides of the boat and out through the scuppers. If the beams were straight and the deck flat, the water would collect in the center at the transom as the cockpit deck is also sloped aft.

A slip stick is used to get the length of the cockpit beams. Use two pieces about 1-inch square with the ends cut on a 45-degree bevel. You can adjust these sticks to the bottom length of the beam and hold them together with a small clamp. While the slip stick is in place and resting on the stringers, get the angle for the beam end, using your bevel gauge. Now place the slip stick on the beam itself and make tick marks to indicate its lower edge length, then mark the angle on both ends of the beam, using your bevel gauge. Lay the beam into position after cutting the ends, and notch the underside of each end to fit the stringer, the same as you did with the deck beams. Cut about ⅜ inch out as this will allow the beam to fit down well. Screw the ends of the beam to the stringer with 2½-inch #16 flat-head screws. Repeat this procedure on each beam until you have done them all.

You will have to screw 1-inch oak pieces to the transom frame to receive the cockpit deck planking. The framing for the hatch is as per Figure 7-15. There will be two strongbacks running under the beams, one on each side of the hatch openings. They should run from the engine hatch all the way to the stern. Props are to be fitted from every other floor timber up to the strongbacks. Strongbacks should be of oak about 2 inches by 4 inches, laid flat. Use temporary props to brace them up so you can check that the tops of the beams are in line with a straightedge laid fore and aft. Knock out the temporary props as you fit and fasten in the permanent ones. Now, with the straightedge laid crossways, flat against the side of a beam, toenail the beam into the strongback. Hatch partners should also be 2 inches by 2 inches and have their ends notched and fastened into the cockpit beams in the same way as the deck carlins were to the deck beams. Do this to all of the beams and, by golly, the interior framing is complete!

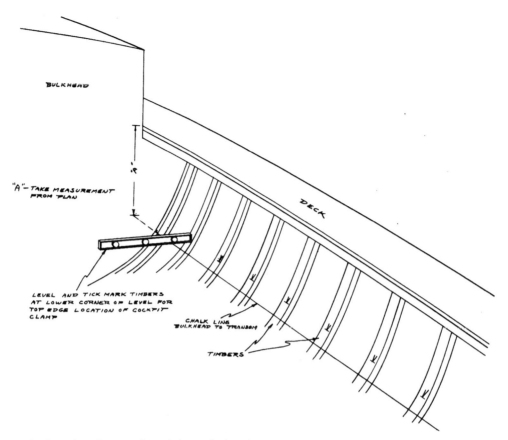

BULKHEAD

"A"-TAKE MEASUREMENT FROM PLAN

DECK

LEVEL AND TICK MARK TIMBERS AT LOWER CORNER OF LEVEL FOR TOP EDGE LOCATION OF COCKPIT CLAMP

CHALK LINE BULKHEAD TO TRANSOM

TIMBERS

7-10 *Spotting the top edge of the cockpit stringer on the timbers.*

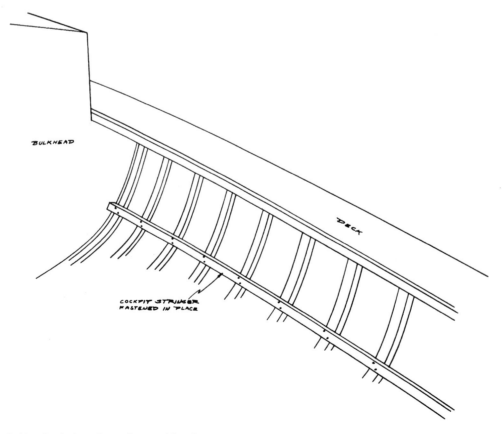

BULKHEAD

DECK

COCKPIT STRINGER FASTENED IN PLACE

7-11 *Cockpit stringer fastened in place.*

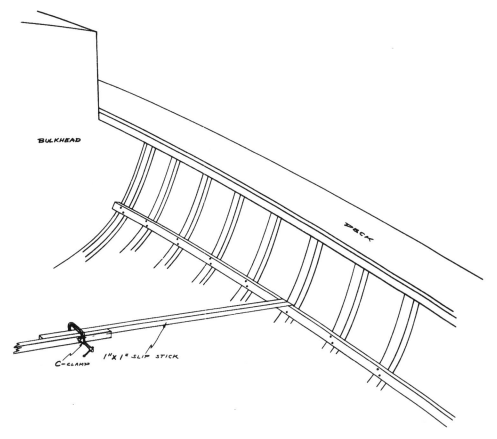

BULKHEAD

DECK

C-CLAMP   1" x 1" SLIP STICK

7-12   Using a slipstick to get the bottom length of the beams.

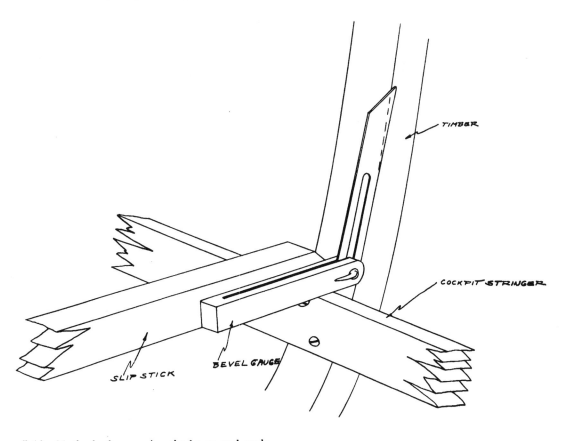

TIMBER

COCKPIT STRINGER

SLIP STICK   BEVEL GAUGE

7-13   Method of measuring the beam end angle.

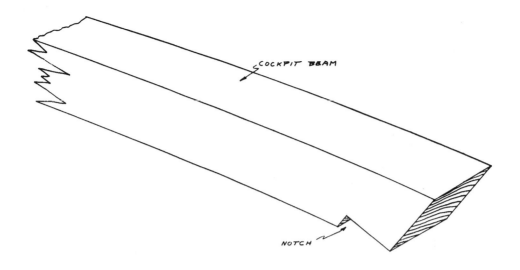

7-14   Notch the beams to fit the cockpit stringer.

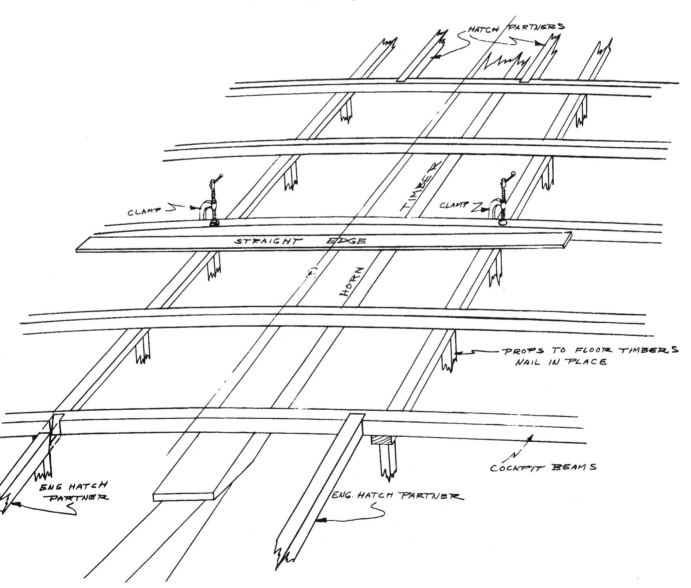

7-15   Installing the framework for the cockpit sole.

The sheer clamp, bilge clamp, engine bed, floor timbers, and cockpit deck framing all show up well here. The cross bracing forward helps hold the shape of the flaring bow until the deck is on.

Chapter 8

Finishing the Hull

CAULKING

It has been my experience that boats of this type, properly planked, need very little caulking. I say this knowing that boats I helped to build 20 years ago are still tight The caulking cotton itself sometimes lasts only about 8 to 10 years, so you can see that a careful planking job pays off.

Some builders feel that the planks have to be married, in their term, by caulking the whole boat with a caulking iron. I don't go along with this, as I feel there is plenty of time when the boat is older to do this. If she is caulked hard to begin with, you will always be caulking her. (This does not apply to larger boats 45 feet and up, as they have heavier planking, larger seams, and are subject to much worse sea conditions. These larger vessels are caulked with oakum in addition to cotton caulking.)

Cotton caulking comes in both the soft type for use with a caulking iron and the twisted type, often called wicking, for rolling in the seams with a caulking wheel. I use the soft in the garboard, planking butts, hood ends, and plank ends around the transom, and the twisted cotton in the plank seams. About a pound of each will do a boat of this size.

The cotton in plank seams is to be rolled in first. In preparing for this, you will note that the cotton comes in a skein. The twisted cotton looks like a cotton rope with six strands. Cut the skein up into lengths about 20 feet long. With your helper standing about 10 feet away from you to unwind the cotton, you separate the cotton by taking two strands in one hand and the other four strands in your opposite hand, and walk toward your helper, winding the cotton into balls around your hands. Your helper will be unwinding the twist as you work toward him. Repeat this procedure to divide the four-strand length of cotton, and you will have three lengths of two-strand cotton from one six-strand length. After doing this to all the six-strand lengths of cotton, you will have a number of two-strand cotton balls. This procedure is similar to your grandmother balling her yarn from yarn skeins. As a matter of fact, my grandmother used to help me do this if she happened to be visiting the boatshop at the time.

A word about caulking wheels. You can purchase a straight-handled caulking wheel from the ship chandleries or marine supply stores. This is a satisfactory tool, but I prefer a pistol grip type. My grandfather used to make his from lignum vitae or ironwood. These were good and would last quite a while. However, I made a pattern for my present one, and had it cast in bronze. This has been ideal, as it has good weight, fits my hand perfectly, and rolls the cotton deeply with less effort, or at least it feels that way to me. The pistol grip type pushes on the wheel with direct pressure from your arm and wrist, as there is no twisting action with your hand and wrist as there is with a straight caulking wheel.

Take a two-strand ball of twisted cotton in your left hand, and, twisting the ends of the cotton together, hold the ends on the seam, say at the side of the boat at the transom. With the caulking wheel in your right hand (if you are right-handed), roll in the ends of the cotton strands. Leave an inch or two of cotton beyond the plank ends at the transom, which you will later tuck in with your caulking iron. Unroll the cotton ball about 6 feet and twist the two strands into a rope. With your caulking wheel, roll in about 6 inches of cotton at this point. Move along doing this at about 6-foot intervals until you come to the end of your length of cotton. With another ball, continue on, being sure to overlap the previous length of cotton by about 2 inches. Then go back and roll all the cotton in. Caulk all the seams except the garboards in this fashion.

Two strands of soft-strand cotton will be used in caulking the garboards as mentioned before. You will want to sit down when driving cotton, so a caulking stool should be made, or perhaps you can locate a milk bottle crate. The crate is handy because you can reach under yourself and grab it about anywhere to move it as you work along.

Find yourself a cardboard box to lay the soft cotton in and separate the bundle into two coils. Then pull the two opposite ends of cotton up over the edge of the box so that you can readily grab them without fishing for them. The caulking iron should be held with your thumb and three fingers. The forefinger is kept free so as to feed the cotton up over the caulking iron blade.

A caulking mallet should be used in driving home the cotton, but I imagine that these are very scarce and finding one could be quite a task. However, you can do the job with the side of your 20-ounce hammer. It's a little rough on the head of your caulking iron, but not as bad as you would think.

In starting to caulk the garboard, drive the ends of the cotton into the seam at one end of the garboard (bow or stern) and go along tucking in the cotton. By this I mean to use your forefinger and iron to make mini-loops with the double strands of cotton and tap with the caulking mallet or hammer to hold them in place. Go along for 5 or 6 feet, tucking these loops into the garboard and then go back over this area with solid blows to set the cotton in tightly. Proceed along in this manner until within a foot or so of the garboard butt. Now, caulk the butt, leaving about 6 inches of cotton sticking out at the top and bottom. This excess cotton will be driven into the respective fore and aft seams. Resume caulking the garboard seam and continue up the stem until you reach a point about 6 inches below the waterline forward. From this point to the top of the stem rabbet, use only a single strand of soft cotton. You also should use a single strand of soft cotton in caulking around the wood ends at the transom.

This is about all that I have to say about caulking, except to remind you to be sure to leave about 2 inches of excess caulking on either end of all the planking butts, and to drive it into the adjacent seams just as you did for the garboard.

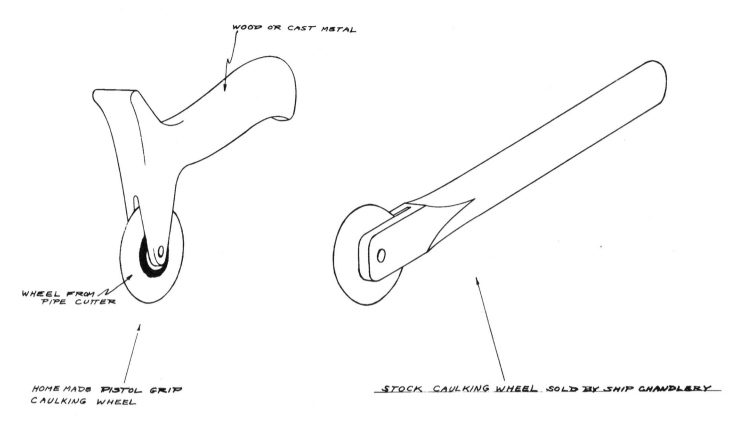

WOOD OR CAST METAL

WHEEL FROM
PIPE CUTTER

HOME MADE PISTOL GRIP
CAULKING WHEEL

STOCK CAULKING WHEEL SOLD BY SHIP CHANDLERY

8-1 *Caulking wheels used to roll in twisted cotton.*

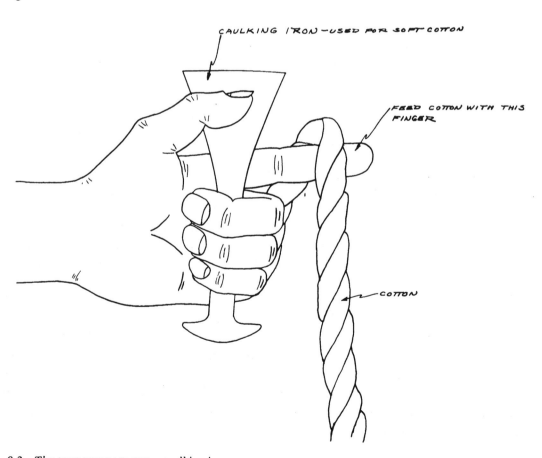

CAULKING IRON —USED FOR SOFT COTTON

FEED COTTON WITH THIS
FINGER

COTTON

8-2 *The proper way to use a caulking iron.*

The hull being caulked. The ends of the stranded cotton, or wicking, will be tucked into the wood end seam at the corner of the transom when it is caulked. At the top of the sheer strake just under the guard can be seen the bungs over the heads of the sheer clamp fastenings.

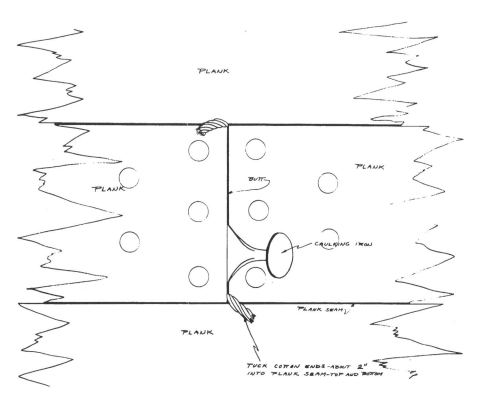

PLANK

PLANK

PLANK

BUTT

PLANK

CAULKING IRON

PLANK SEAM

PLANK

TUCK COTTON ENDS-ABOUT 2" INTO PLANK SEAM-TOP AND BOTTOM

8-3 *Caulking the butts.*

OUTBOARD JOINTING

Outboard jointing requires a combination of bull work and sensitive feel in your hands for shape. There is no job on the entire boat that will make your muscles ache like this one. You will have muscles ache that you thought you didn't have if you do the entire job alone. But if three or four men do it together, it is not so rough.

It has been my experience to work like the devil the first day in jointing the seams. Using your jack plane, joint off the planking butts first, they may be irregular because of differing twists in the planking. Then jack the planking seams the full length of the hull. In the bows, this jacking or planing will be minimal, as the planks are generally flatter in this area. However, along the bilges quite a bit will have to be planed off from the seams. Take off shavings as long as you can reach. When you have jointed off the hard places and slight bumps, you will find that you can walk right along and take off very long shavings. Remember this: It is a *very important practice* to take long shavings all the while you are jointing up the hull. Short strokes will produce dips and lumps all over it.

Assuming that you have completed the seams on the first day, go home and get a good night's rest. Your muscles will let you know when it is morning.

Take your aching body back to work. Rig a staging along the bilge with stage planks and saw horses. When you finished jacking the seams yesterday, you left a somewhat hex shape to the bilge planks. Planing these high points off and developing a generally round shape is called rough rounding of the bilge. Take it easy today by rough rounding the bilges with your jack plane. Feel with your hand by rubbing your hand up and down around the bilge as you plane along. You can do this job sitting down and, by taking

frequent rests, you will probably do one side of the boat today and the other side tomorrow.

The next day you will start to get hardened up. Your muscles will feel much better and you will accomplish a lot more. Finish planing the bilges and then move ahead to the forefoot area and jack plane this area fair.

The worst of the job is over at this stage. The remaining part of the planing will be generally to dress the whole boat with your smooth plane. Keep the blade sharp! The smooth is a lighter plane than the jack, with a finer set to the blade, so this is an enjoyable task.

When you have completed planing the hull, saw off the wood ends flush with the transom, plane them with your smooth plane, and the outboard jointing is finished.

SANDING

In my early years of building boats, we sanded them entirely by hand. This sounds like a terrible job, but for perfection, you still can't beat it. Believe it or not, it is relatively easy, if performed right. Make a block of wood about 3½ inches by 5 inches from planking scraps and tack a piece of inner tube or rubber around the bottom of it. Then wrap your sandpaper around the block (50-grit production paper to start with). Hold the block in your right hand, and use your left hand to exert pressure on the block toward the hull. Move the block back and forth with your right hand, and, again, as in planing, use long strokes.

Sanding should be started by rubbing diagonally up and down on about a 45-degree angle. Go over the entire boat in this manner. Then sand fore and aft all over the boat, using the same grit sandpaper. For a final sanding (fore and aft only) use an

80-grit production paper. It is not necessary to sand the bottom below the waterline with 80-grit sandpaper.

To speed up the sanding job and make it easier, we have in recent years been using a flexible-back sanding disc pad in an electric drill. This disc comes in 7-inch and 9-inch diameters and has a semi-stiff foam pad on its base. Used with care, this does a remarkable job and is used extensively around boatyards now.

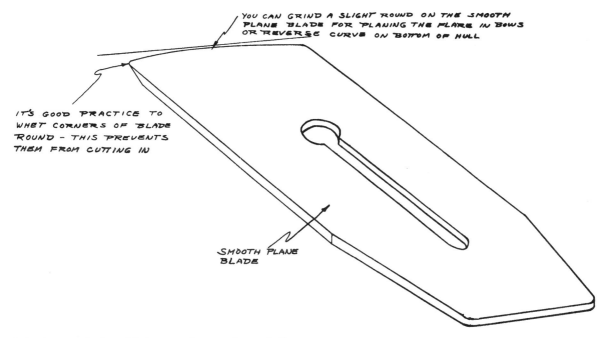

8-4 *A smooth-plane blade ground to produce a hollow.*

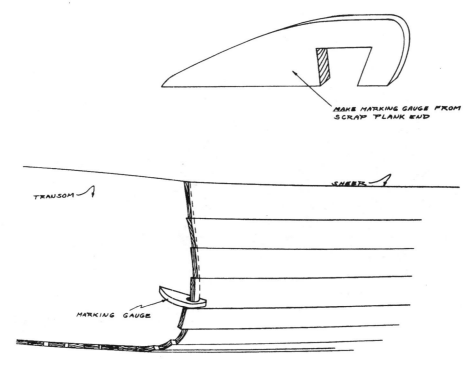

8-5 *Marking the outside of the planking for sawing at the transom.*

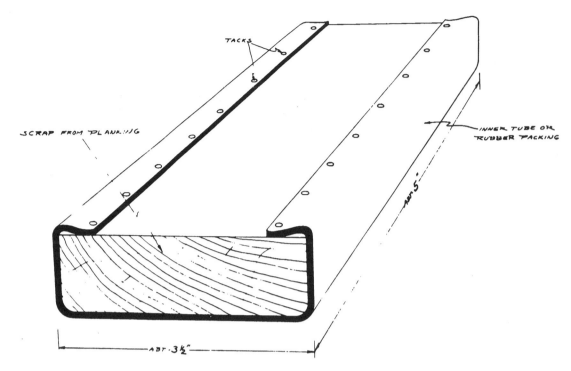

TACKS

SCRAP FROM PLANKING

INNER TUBE OR
RUBBER PACKING

ABT. 5"

ABT. 3½"

8-6 A homemade sanding block.

A properly smoothed-up hull, before painting. This one is planked with mahogany.

SCRIBING THE WATERLINE

The waterline has to be scribed into the hull at this point. The easiest method is to tack straightedges across the bow and transom at the waterline. Level and brace these straightedges to hold them in place. Using a chalk line or string over the straightedges, have one man hold the string at the forward position and another man hold it at the transom. With the forward man holding the string in close to the hull, but not quite touching it, have the man aft move outboard until the string just touches the hull, then draw it taut. Put a tick mark on the hull about 20 inches aft of the stem. Do this about every 20 inches for the length of the hull, with the forward man moving outboard and the aft man moving inboard as you go along, to position the string for the tick marks. Set the straightedges for the opposite side of the boat and tick mark that side of the hull. Now tack on the lining batten, being sure to keep the batten vertical so that the top edge of the batten is tight against the hull. Run your race knife or scribing tool along the top of the batten. This cuts a fine groove in the hull to mark the waterline. A scribing tool can be made by bending over the tang of a file to a right angle and grinding a v hook on it with a bench grinder. This tool does a very satisfactory job.

PRIME COAT OF PAINT

Be sure your seams and the hull itself are free of dust. The prime coat of paint should be a flat coat well thinned to penetrate the surface of the planking. When brushed on, you should be able to see the grain of the wood through it. A 2½-inch oval brush is best for this, but these are getting hard to find and are very expensive. But they hold more paint than a regular flat brush and save time.

In applying the prime coat of paint, brush the paint into the seams by working the brush at an angle (about 30 degrees) across the seams. Use plenty of paint for this, as it seals the cotton and gives the seam compound something to grip to. This is called priming the seams, and, for large boats, you can get a seam brush to do the job. Brush out any excess paint on the planking as you work along the hull, until you have completed painting the topside planking. The bottom of the hull should receive the same treatment, with antifouling bottom paint. First, read the directions on the can, as some bottom paints require red lead under them.

In the past, seams were filled with a compound made up of white lead, whiting, and sometimes varnish. You would dish out a glob of white lead on a board and knead in whiting with a putty knife until you could handle and knead the compound with your hands. This made beautiful-looking seams when new, but the putty cracked with age. Now there are many newer compounds that have superior characteristics.

You will have to fill the seams with a putty knife. Some men prefer a wide knife and others prefer the narrower, 1½-inch width. I prefer the 1½-inch putty knife, as it is easier to force the compound into the seam, and you can go along faster. I don't feel that a wide knife, no matter how hard you press on it, gets the compound into the bottom of the seams.

As you go along, recess the compound by running your forefinger along the seam. This will give you a concave and neat-looking seam.

Filling the garboard seam is difficult with a putty knife, and is simplified by making a couple of tools out of wood. Make a putty board out of thin plywood about the shape of a wide (6 or 7 inches) putty knife, and a spatula with which to push the compound from the putty board into the garboard seam. This spatula should be about 10 inches long and resemble a double-edge knife. While holding the putty board with a load of compound on it up next to the garboard seam on the keel, and with the spatula in your right hand, work the compound into the seam along the garboard.

With the puttying completed, the hull is ready for a fine sanding, using 80-grit pro-duction paper with your sanding block, after which the final coats of paint may be applied. Be sure to sand and wipe between each coat. A really good paint job will require five coats; three thin primes, one full prime, and semi-gloss or gloss for the final coat. Use 100-grit production paper before the final coat.

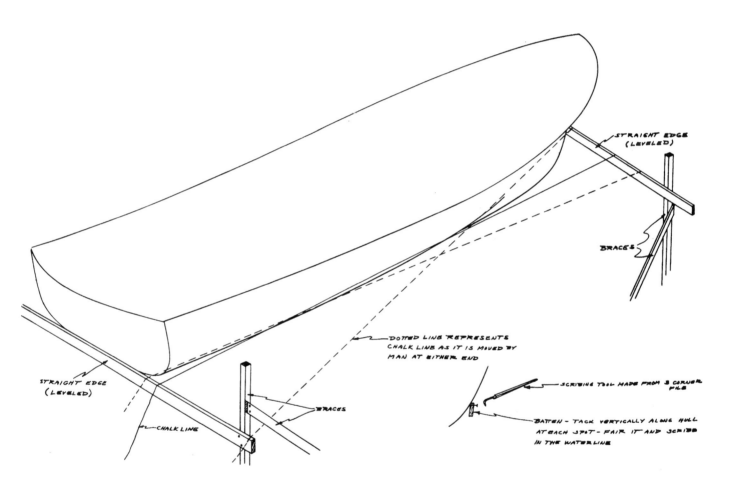

8-7 *Method of spotting and scribing the waterline.*

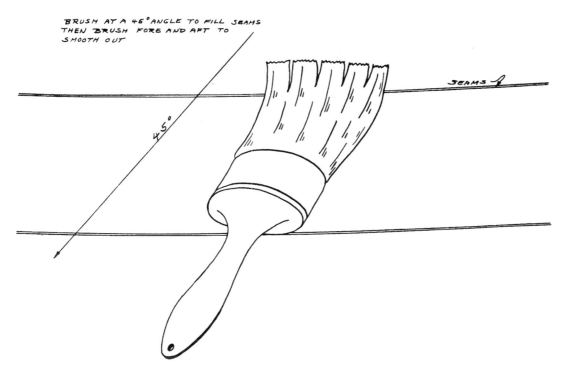

PLANKING

BRUSH AT A 45° ANGLE TO FILL SEAMS
THEN BRUSH FORE AND AFT TO
SMOOTH OUT

45°

SEAMS

8-8   Priming the seams and planking with a regular brush.

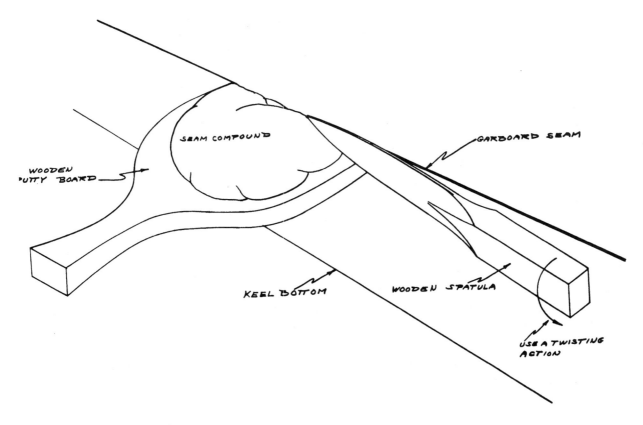

WOODEN
PUTTY BOARD

SEAM COMPOUND

GARBOARD SEAM

KEEL BOTTOM

WOODEN SPATULA

USE A TWISTING
ACTION

8-9   Puttying the garboard seam.

Chapter 9

Decking, Guards, and Rails

PLYWOOD AND FIBERGLASS DECK

I should say something about plywood to be used with fiberglass. If you don't use marine grade plywood, don't use anything less than the best exterior grade under your fiberglass. In inaccessible places, such as the underside of the cockpit deck, it is wise to give the bottom and edges of the plywood a coat of fiberglass resin.

If you should desire fiberglass-covered plywood decks, it is advisable to use two layers of plywood glued together, which in a sense makes a solid one-piece deck panel. Use ½-inch plywood for the bottom layer and ⅜-inch or ½-inch plywood on the top one, keeping the joints between the two layers well staggered. "Anchorfast" nails, 1½-inches long in the bottom layer and 2-inches in the top layer make an excellent fastening job. The outboard edge of the plywood deck should be routed off with a ⅜-inch rounding bit so that the fiberglass can be carried down over the deck edge and covered with the sheer guard.

Trim the inboard edges of the plywood at the carlin and forward and aft deck beams, and nose off the sharp corner of the plywood to allow the fiberglass to be folded down over the inboard edge of the deck.

Fiberglassing the deck should be done in two layers, 2-ounce fiberglass mat underneath, and a top layer of 10-ounce glass cloth. The mat is easy to handle, so I'll not discuss this further, but the cloth should be cut into manageable pieces and rolled up on rods made from 1-inch by 1-inch scrap. Then each piece can be unrolled neatly in place when needed. Nails should be set in the deck with a hammer and nail set, and filled over with plastic auto body filler. This filler does not shrink much and dries quickly enough to be sanded in a few minutes.

An advantage in using two layers when fiberglassing is that the joints can be staggered, just as in the plywood decking. This eliminates tedious sanding and fairing of the laps.

Shop heat is another factor in fiberglassing. The ideal working temperature is 65 to 75 degrees.

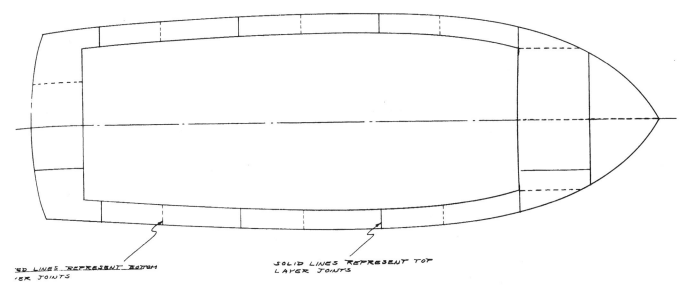

9-1   Layout using 4-foot by 8-foot sheets of plywood for the deck.

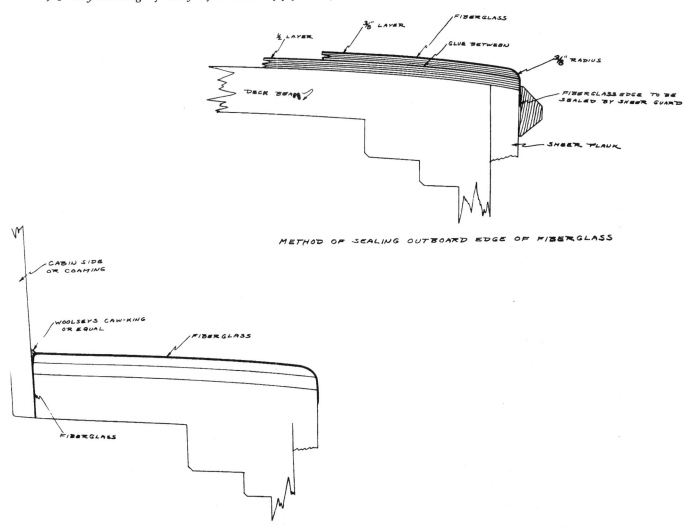

½ LAYER

⅜" LAYER

FIBERGLASS

GLUE BETWEEN

⅜" RADIUS

DECK BEAM

FIBERGLASS EDGE TO BE
SEALED BY SHEER GUARD

SHEER PLANK

METHOD OF SEALING OUTBOARD EDGE OF FIBERGLASS

CABIN SIDE
OR COAMING

WOOLSEYS CAW-KING
OR EQUAL

FIBERGLASS

FIBERGLASS

METHOD OF SEALING INBOARD EDGE OF FIBERGLASS

9-2   Sealing the edges of fiberglass cloth.

STRIP-LAID CAULKED DECK

Laying strip decking is usually started by bending a batten around on top of the inboard edge of the deck carlin, carrying it forward across the forward deck beams to the king plank, and fairing it, using the side deck T square (see Chapter 6) for width measurements. Do this on both sides (port and starboard), and leave the battens tacked in place so as to have something to fit the ends of the center or filler decking (which is put on first, laid fore and aft) against. Use care in shaping these deck planks, as their outboard curve will have to be fair so the first strip will bend nicely against it. Your smooth plane will come in handy for this work. Once the filler deck is in place, forward and aft, get the angle of the forward end of the first strip by setting the heel of the bevel gauge along the edge of filler decking with its blade along the king plank. Transfer this angle to the first strip and mark and saw its end. You should have your smooth plane with you to trim the sawn end to the line if needed. These strips are usually about 1½ to 1⅝ inches wide by 1 inch thick. Edge nail the end of the first strip to the king plank, then face nail it into the beams as you bend it around the deck, using 2-inch "anchorfast" nails. Saw the butts square, using a combination square and handsaw.

Nail the first strip the entire length of the deck, cutting its after end to fit against the fashion piece at the transom. The second and subsequent strips will be fitted to the king plank forward in the same manner, but your nailing sequence will differ here. Edge nail each of these strips to the preceding one along its entire length with a 3-inch "Anchorfast" nail between each deck beam. Be sure to stagger the butts well as you go along, but make sure each one lands on a deck beam. Then face nail the strips to the beams with 2-inch "Anchorfast" nails. If you are going to use covering boards on the edge of the deck, don't forget to allow for this in stripping. If not, lay the strips right out to the edge of the hull.

Should you plan on using a covering board around the edge of the deck, you will fasten on about six courses of strips. Then you will have to make patterns for the inside edge of the covering board. As in previous pattern work, transfer and mark the inside edge of the covering board onto the stock to be used for this piece. Mark the outboard edge of the covering board with a marking gauge and saw it a bit outside the line, as you may have to plane some off the inside edges for a final fit. Clamp the covering board into place with door clamps once it fits well, and mark the outside edge neatly. Now take the covering board and saw the outboard edge to this line. Apply Cuprinol to the bottom side of the covering board and fasten it into place with 2-inch "Anchorfast" nails into the timber heads, filler blocks, and sheer strake, as well as the deck beam ends. The sheer edge should now be trimmed and faired, using your jack plane.

You will notice that I didn't mention planing on any caulking seams in strip decking. This is because it is very difficult to keep a strip deck from leaking, and, in this case, a planed caulking seam wouldn't help any. Once the deck is laid, the seams are forced open with your caulking wheel, which is dipped occasionally into a cup filled with cotton and oil. Then a single strand of twisted cotton is rolled into all the deck seams. Caulk the butts with a stiff, narrow putty knife, opening them first if necessary with a ½-inch chisel by tapping it lightly with a hammer.

When the caulking is all done, sharpen up your jack plane and plane the deck evenly all over and sand it, using a sanding block in a diagonal motion as you did on the hull, or use your flexible-back sander. If you have an orbital vibrating sander, it is also useful for this job. If you should use this machine, be sure it is a dual-action model so the final sanding can be with the grain to get rid of the swirl marks. Then you can fair up the edges of the decking to the carlins and deck beams using planes, a spokeshave, and a chisel.

Now prime paint the deck, using flat paint, as you did on the hull, being sure to prime the seams as you go along as they will not be puttied and in time will fill up with paint. Then apply Cuprinol to the underside of the deck.

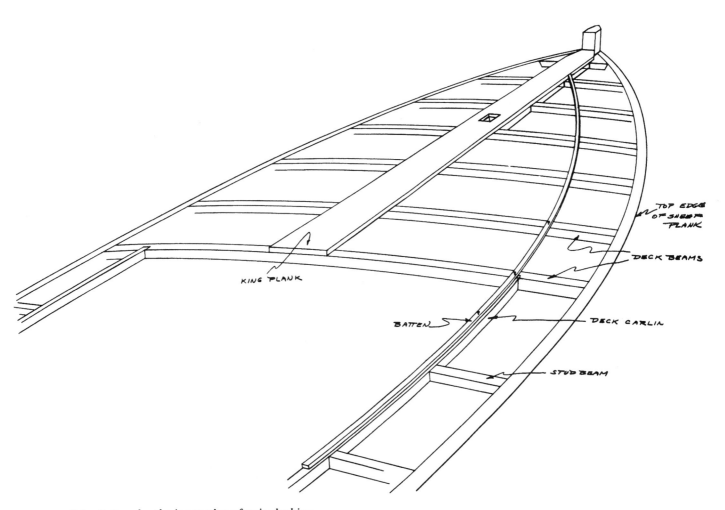

9-3 Batten for the inner edge of strip decking.

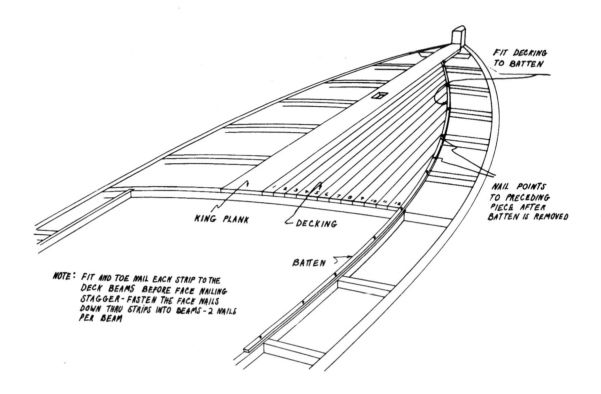

FIT DECKING
TO BATTEN

NAIL POINTS
TO PRECEDING
PIECE AFTER
BATTEN IS REMOVED

KING PLANK

DECKING

BATTEN

NOTE: FIT AND TOE NAIL EACH STRIP TO THE
DECK BEAMS BEFORE FACE NAILING
STAGGER-FASTEN THE FACE NAILS
DOWN THRU STRIPS INTO BEAMS-2 NAILS
PER BEAM

9-4   Center or filler deck installed, forward starboard side.

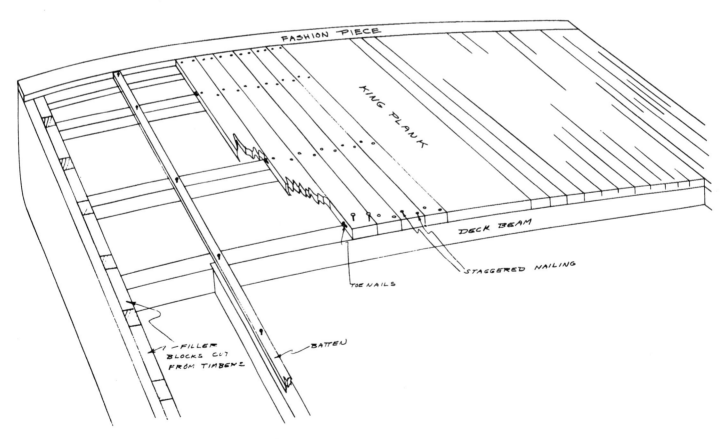

FASHION PIECE

KING PLANK

DECK BEAM

STAGGERED NAILING

TOE NAILS

FILLER
BLOCKS CUT
FROM TIMBERS

BATTEN

9-5   Installing the center or filler decking at the stern.

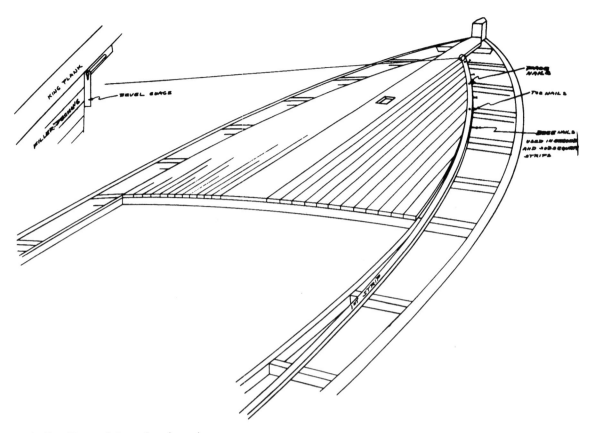

9-6   Bending and fastening the strips.

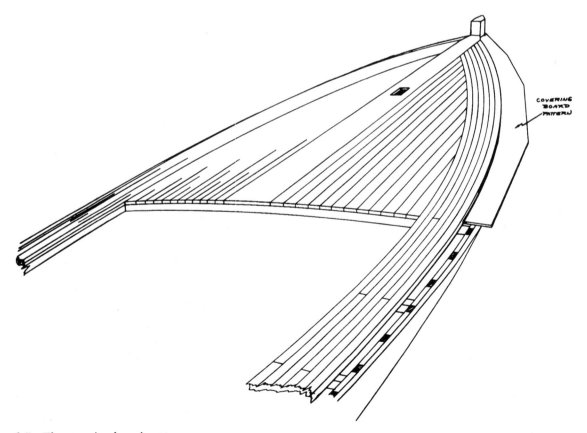

9-7   The covering board pattern.

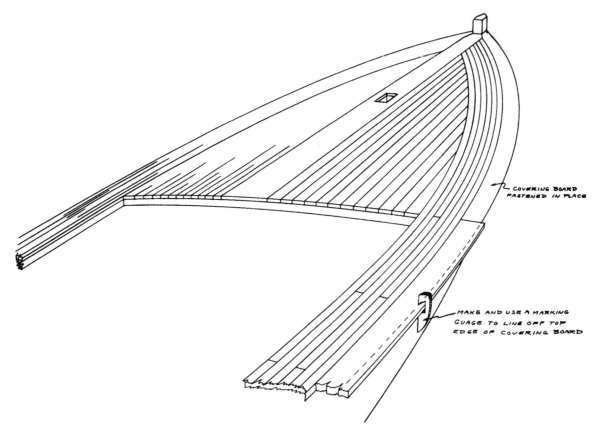

9-8 Marking the top edge of the covering board.

COCKPIT DECK

The cockpit deck can be laid, using the plywood and fiberglass combination, or it can be planked with 1⅛-inch by 4-inch western fir and then caulked. In either case hand holes or hatches should be cut in over the stuffing boxes for access to the shaft and rudder stock.

PLYWOOD AND FIBERGLASS COCKPIT

If you should use the plywood and fiberglass combination, the flat surfaces should be treated in the same manner as the deck, except that the fiberglass will have to be run up and over the top edge of the mopboards, which are of ¾-inch plywood and are spiled to fit around the outer edges of the cockpit and are about 5 inches high. Use 1½-inch #12 screws to fasten the mopboards to the timbers.

After fiberglassing, the ⅜-inch by 2-inch cockpit ceiling or sheathing can be installed, starting about 1 inch under the sheer clamp and working down to the mopboard in parallel strakes. Fasten it with "anchorfast" nails. The lower pieces of ceiling will lay against the top edge of the mopboard and help hold the fiberglass in place. At this time, while you're in the business of milling out ceiling, it would be a good idea to get out enough stock to ceil up the cabin (done later on) as well as the cockpit. Ceiling can be of pine, cedar, or mahogany and should have its exposed corners chamfered to make a V joint. In the cockpit hatch opening, you

108

should carry the fiberglass down over the edges about 2 inches and then fasten in some oak landing strips about 1 inch by 1½ inches for the hatches to rest on. In a wooden boat, the edges of the fiberglass have a tendency to separate from the wood. I suppose the water and dampness work on them, so it is good practice to fasten a retainer of some kind on these edges wherever possible. The hatches can be fitted with brass or stainless steel trim. If you should have an engine box in the cockpit, the rabbeted sill will hold the fiberglass edges down.

The cockpit scuppers can be fiberglassed out if you use the plywood and fiberglass combination. Remember to block in behind the mopboard in the scupper area so that you have solid wood through the scupper hole, as shown in Figure 9-14. The scupper hole is located aft on either side of the cockpit, just forward of the transom frame. For a fiberglassed scupper, the hole should be about 2¼ inches in diameter to allow enough room to fiberglass it. The inner and outer edges of the scupper hole should be well rounded so that the fiberglass will flow smoothly around them.

It is also a good plan to rout a ⅛-inch-deep rabbet in the hull planking around the outer edge. After fiberglassing, tack through the fiberglass while it is still wet into the rabbet with ⅝-inch copper tacks and seal over the tacks with resin.

After the fiberglass has set up, cut out a piece of leather about 2½ inches by 3 inches and place it over the scupper hole on the outside of the boat. Tack the forward edge to the hull with ⅝-inch copper tacks. This will act as a check valve to prevent water from coming in through the scupper, but yet the water will run out of the cockpit.

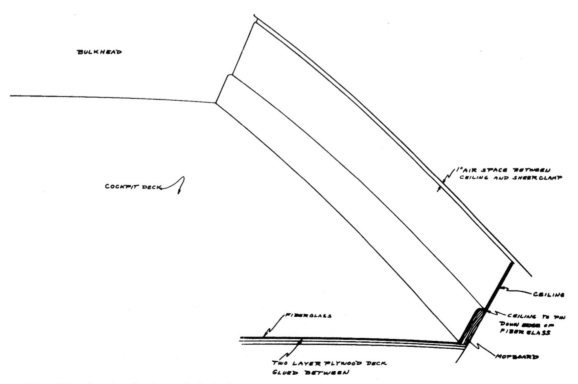

9-9 Fiberglass detail—the cockpit deck.

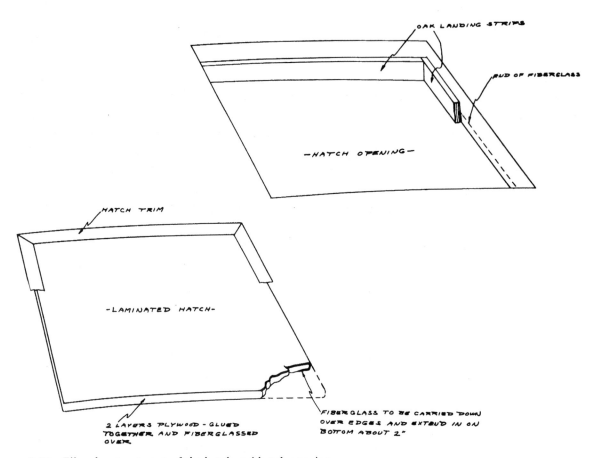

OAK LANDING STRIPS

END OF FIBERGLASS

—HATCH OPENING—

HATCH TRIM

—LAMINATED HATCH—

2 LAYERS PLYWOOD - GLUED TOGETHER AND FIBERGLASSED OVER

FIBERGLASS TO BE CARRIED DOWN OVER EDGES AND EXTEND IN ON BOTTOM ABOUT 2"

9-10 *Fiberglass treatment of the hatch and hatch opening.*

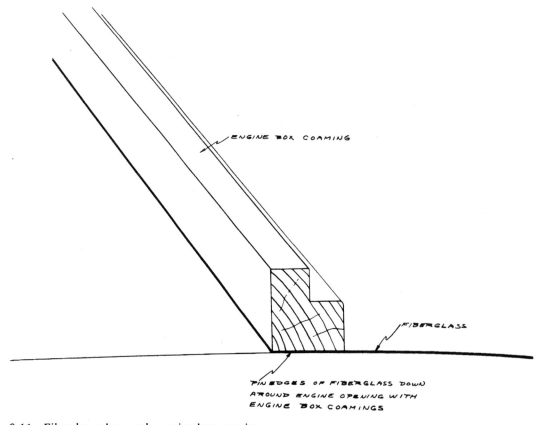

ENGINE BOX COAMING

FIBERGLASS

PIN EDGES OF FIBERGLASS DOWN AROUND ENGINE OPENING WITH ENGINE BOX COAMINGS

9-11 *Fiberglass edges at the engine box opening.*

PLANKED AND CAULKED COCKPIT

Should you desire a planked cockpit deck, you will have to plane about a 1/16-inch caulking seam on one edge of each plank. Then you should fit the hatch strips around the hatches for the decking to fit against. These strips are the same thickness as the decking and are about 1⅛ inches wide, beveled on their inside edges for the hatches to lay tightly against. (The outside edges of the hatches will, of course, have to have matching beveled edges.) Screw these strips to the partners or the beams with 1¾-inch #12 flat-head screws. Keep each strip centered on the beams and partners so that you can land the decking around the outside edges and also have landing inside for the hatches.

The mopboard can be made from planking material and should be about 1 inch thick by 5 inches wide, with its top edge chamfered to match the cockpit ceiling. Also, its bottom edge will have to be under-beveled so that you can caulk the seam easily. Counterbore and screw the mopboards into place against the timbers with 1½-inch #12 flat-head screws, and bung them off. Block behind them for the cockpit deck scuppers.

Deck scuppers can be either of 2-inch lead or made of fiberglass. If you choose the former method, a 1/16-inch rabbet will have to be cut in the mopboard inside and in the hull planking outside, to receive the flared end of the lead. The sharp corners on either end of the scupper hole should be rounded off so as not to cut through the lead when flanging or rolling its edges into the rabbets.

It is sometimes easier to roll the flange on the inner edge of the lead scupper in a mock-up at your workbench vise. After doing this, push the scupper through from the inside, setting the flange into bedding compound. Peen the inside edge into the rabbet with a small ball-peen hammer and nail through the flange into the mopboard with ⅞-inch brass escutcheon pins. Now go outside and, using your handsaw, saw off the lead scupper about 5/16 inch away from the hull. Stick the handle of your ball-peen hammer into the scupper, and, with a rolling motion, start flaring this edge. Smear some bedding compound on the outside rabbet and finish peening until the flange lies flush with the hull. Nail through this lip with escutcheon pins also.

Fit the cockpit decking down and fasten it off, counterboring as you go. The last three or four pieces of decking at the outboard edge of the cockpit on either side should not be fastened until the scuppers have been completed, as the last piece out is under-beveled to fit the mopboard. Once the decking is down and fastened, bung the screw holes. Trim off the bungs, using your 1½-inch chisel, and you are ready to caulk the cockpit deck.

Use a caulking wheel for caulking and roll a double strand of twisted cotton in all of the seams, except the outboard ones. These will have to be caulked with a caulking iron and mallet, or hammer, using soft cotton. The butts and hatch strips will also have to be caulked with an iron.

Make up your hatches and roll cotton in their seams and set them in place.

The cockpit deck is ready to be evened up with your jack plane, and to be sanded and painted. Don't bother to putty the seams, just work paint into them; it will surprise you how they fill up.

Cockpit ceiling or sheathing can be installed as described earlier for the plywood and fiberglass cockpit.

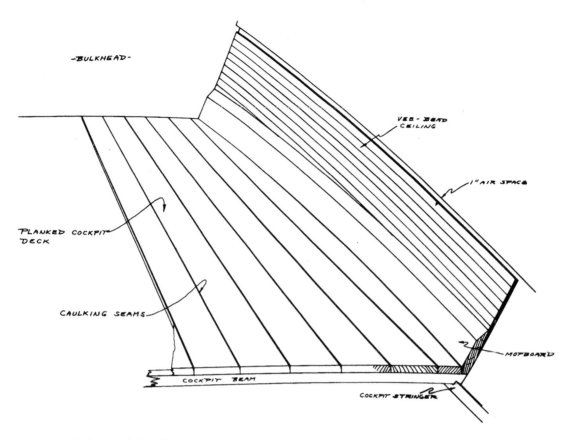

-BULKHEAD-

VEE - BEAD
CEILING

1" AIR SPACE

PLANKED COCKPIT
DECK

CAULKING SEAMS

MOTBOARD

COCKPIT BEAM

COCKPIT STRINGER

9-12   *A planked cockpit sole.*

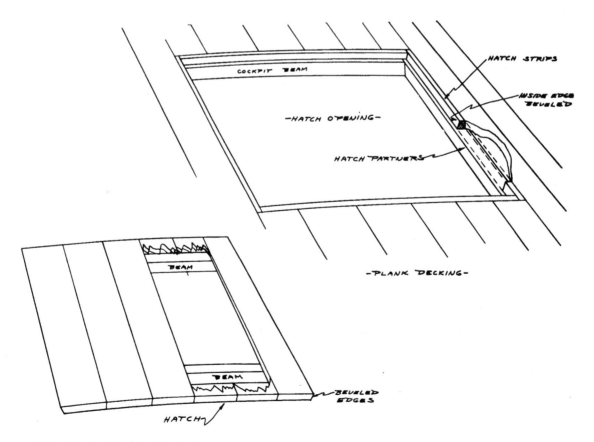

COCKPIT BEAM

HATCH STRIPS

INSIDE EDGE
BEVELED

-HATCH OPENING-

HATCH PARTNERS

-PLANK DECKING-

BEAM

BEAM

BEVELED
EDGES

HATCH

9-13   *Planked deck hatch detail.*

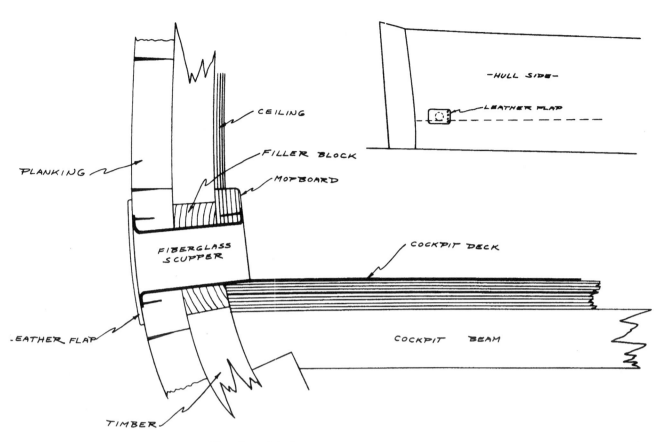

CEILING

PLANKING

FILLER BLOCK

MOT BOARD

HULL SIDE

LEATHER FLAP

FIBERGLASS SCUPPER

COCKPIT DECK

LEATHER FLAP

COCKPIT BEAM

TIMBER

9-14 A fiberglass scupper for a fiberglassed deck.

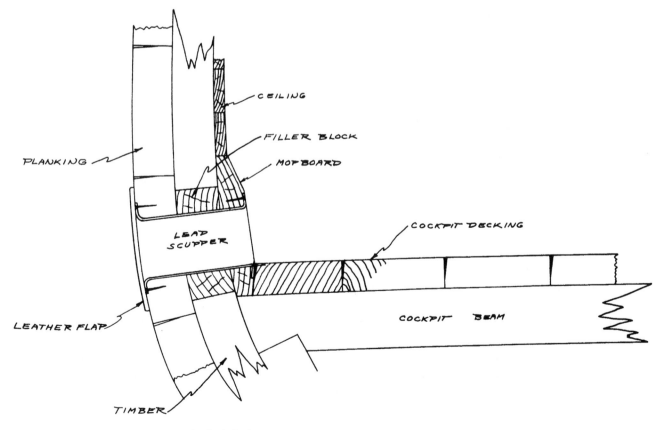

CEILING

PLANKING

FILLER BLOCK

MOT BOARD

LEAD SCUPPER

COCKPIT DECKING

LEATHER FLAP

COCKPIT BEAM

TIMBER

9-15 A lead scupper for a planked deck.

GUARDS AND RAILS

To prepare for the toe rails and sheer guards, the edge of the planked deck has to be beveled, or chamfered, about ⅜ inch in on top and ⅜ inch down on the side of the boat. This will lower your guard so that the fastenings will go into the timber heads and timber blocks that were fitted between them. The top edge of the sheer guard should be kept about ⅛ inch below the edge of this bevel (about ½ inch lower than the deck). The outer edge of the toe rail should be kept out to the edge of this bevel, making a neat and practical arrangement.

The first operation will be the buffalo rails, which go against the stem to support the bow chocks. These are sawn pieces the thickness of the toe rails, and are a fussy fitting job, as they have to be let into the side as well as the back of the stemhead. After recessing the stem, make a pattern for one side and saw out both buffalos to it. Bed and fasten the starboard piece after you get a good fit, then fit the port one to it, leaving the center joint until last for a tight seam. Buffalos should be of oak or mahogany, and about 4 feet long. They should be hollowed on their underside so their edges fit tightly against the deck. Their aft ends taper to the same size as the toe rails, usually 1⅛ inches by 1¼ inches.

With the buffalos all bedded and fastened into place, move on to the toe rails. All of the joints in the toe rails and guards should be sawn joints. In other words, the ends should be held against each other and a handsaw run through the joint. This will give you a perfect fit. Bear this in mind, as you will be doing it a lot. Hollow the bottoms of the toe rails to get a tight fit on the deck, and bed and fasten them, using 2-inch #10 flat-head screws, about 10 inches apart, counterboring for their heads so they can later be bunged. The aft sections of the toe

rails from the bulkhead to the transom should have about four 4-inch-long scuppers on their bottom edges. Lay these off and clamp or temporarily screw the aft toe rails together bottom to bottom. Bore through the rails at the ends of the scupper holes with a 1-inch bit, take the rails apart, and bandsaw between the holes. Clean the edges of the scupper holes out with a spoke shave and jackknife, and sand the corners smooth. Now fasten on the aft sections of the toe rails and trim the joints and ends. Bung and sand them smooth.

The sheer and stern guards should be made about the shape shown in Figure 9-19. Mill them from 1⅛-inch by 2-inch oak and chamfer them on both the top and bottom corners to receive a half oval of brass or stainless steel. The guards are to be hollowed slightly on their back side, so as to fit tightly against the hull. These also should be bedded and screwed on with 2½-inch #14 flat-head screws, counterbored for bungs. Fastenings should be about 10 inches apart. Saw the joints as you did in fitting the toe rails. After fastening, trim the joins and ends, and bung and finish them by sanding.

The final guard job will be the quarter guards. These are usually about 10 to 12 feet long and the same in section as the sheer guard. Both their forward and after ends should be well rounded so as not to catch on anything and fray. The brass or stainless steel half oval should go around the aft end of each quarter guard, with its end fastened to the transom. The forward end of the quarter guards should have a slightly rounding taper about 8 inches long.

Hollow out the backs of the quarter guards, and bed and fasten them on with the same size screws that you used in the sheer guards. Bung over the screw heads and sand them so they are ready for paint.

Finally, the stemhead should be shaped to look about like the design in Figure 9-18.

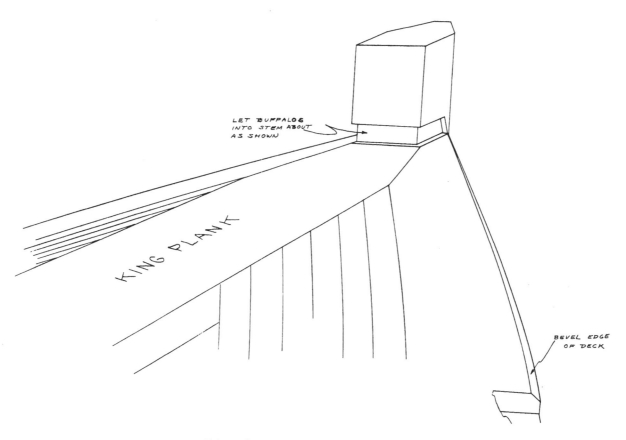

LET BUFFALOS
INTO STEM ABOUT
AS SHOWN

KING PLANK

BEVEL EDGE
OF DECK

9-16   Recess in the stem for the buffalo ends.

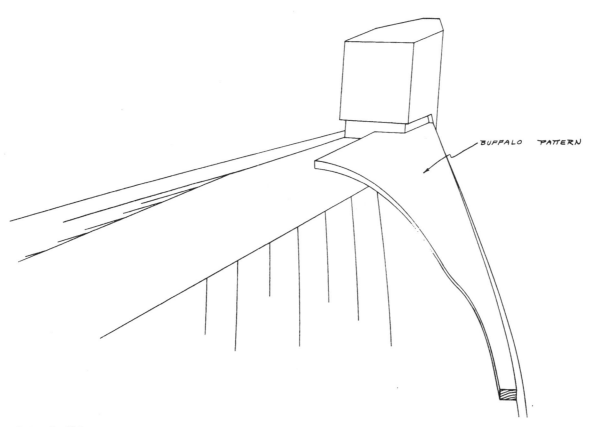

BUFFALO   PATTERN

9-17   Buffalo pattern.

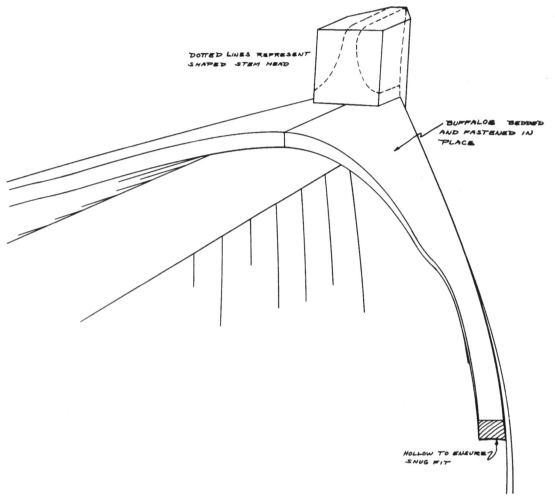

DOTTED LINES REPRESENT
SHAPED STEM HEAD

BUFFALOS BEDDED
AND FASTENED IN
PLACE

HOLLOW TO ENSURE
SNUG FIT

9-18   The buffalos installed.

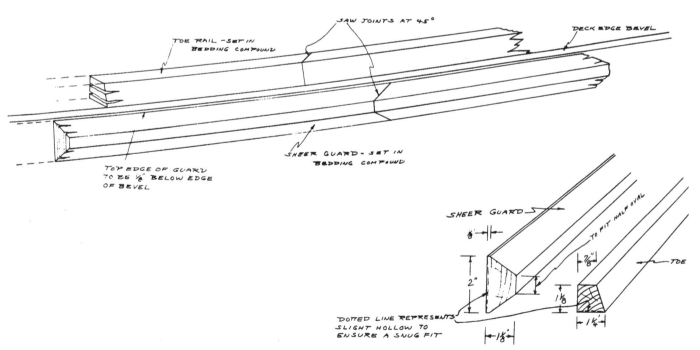

SAW JOINTS AT 45°

DECK EDGE BEVEL

TOE RAIL - SET IN
BEDDING COMPOUND

TOP EDGE OF GUARD
TO BE ½" BELOW EDGE
OF BEVEL

SHEER GUARD - SET IN
BEDDING COMPOUND

SHEER GUARD

TO FIT HALF OVAL

TOE

2"

⅝"

⅞"

1⅛"

1⅛"

1¼"

DOTTED LINE REPRESENTS
SLIGHT HOLLOW TO
ENSURE A SNUG FIT

9-19   Sheer guard and toe rail details.

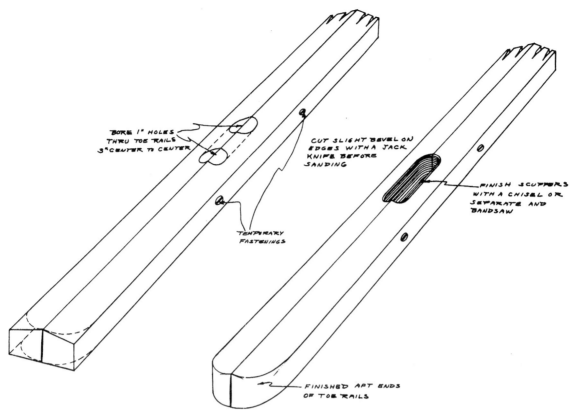

BORE 1" HOLES
THRU TOE RAILS
3" CENTER TO CENTER

CUT SLIGHT BEVEL ON
EDGES WITH A JACK
KNIFE BEFORE
SANDING

TEMPORARY
FASTENINGS

FINISH SCUPPERS
WITH A CHISEL OR
SEPARATE AND
BANDSAW

FINISHED AFT ENDS
OF TOE RAILS

9-20 Toe rail scuppers and aft end details.

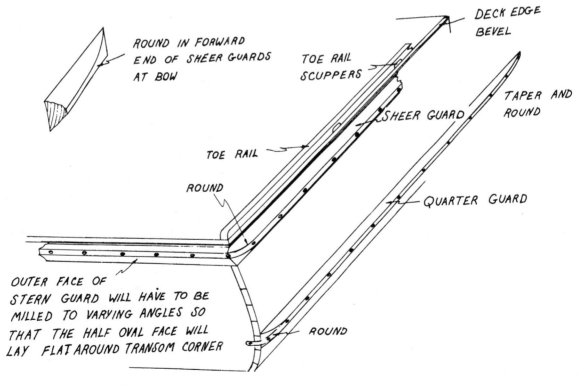

ROUND IN FORWARD
END OF SHEER GUARDS
AT BOW

DECK EDGE
BEVEL

TOE RAIL
SCUPPERS

TAPER AND
ROUND

SHEER GUARD

TOE RAIL

QUARTER GUARD

ROUND

OUTER FACE OF
STERN GUARD WILL HAVE TO BE
MILLED TO VARYING ANGLES SO
THAT THE HALF OVAL FACE WILL
LAY FLAT AROUND TRANSOM CORNER

ROUND

9-21 Guard and toe rail endings.

Chapter 10

Deck and Cabin Joinery

The first stage of cabin construction is to mill out a number of the pieces, such as cabin beams, corner posts, cabin side cleats, pilothouse beams, and aft posts for the pilothouse. In addition, you will need some ½-inch pattern stock with which to make up the cabin side pattern. Make two beam molds if you haven't already done so, one for the trunk cabin beams with 7 inches of crown in 10 feet and one for the pilothouse beams with 4½ inches of crown in 10 feet. Bandsaw the beams out of 1⅛-inch oak plank, roughly ⅜ inch oversize to allow for springing. Then lay your beam mold back onto the beams and mark them again, as you did with the deck beams. You should saw neatly on both edges of the beams this time, as the crown is quite pronounced and truing up the edges with your jack plane is harder to do than with the deck beams.

After bandsawing and truing the edges of the beams, use your smooth plane to take a shaving or two off the bottom corners. Then sand the beams, treat them with Cuprinol, and paint them, with the exception of the last coat. This will save you a lot of overhead painting later. Set the trunk cabin and pilothouse beams to one side after painting,

where they will be all ready to cut in when you need them.

The next task is to make up the corner posts of the trunk cabin and the cabin side cleats. There should be at least one cabin side cleat midway between the corner posts and the bulkhead cleat, and more if the cabin side is long or has several windows, as there should be a cleat between each window. These cleats should be of oak, about 1½ inches by 2 inches in section, with the inboard edges and bottom ends well rounded or chamfered.

The corner posts are more difficult. Get the proper angle for the posts by setting the heel of the bevel gauge against the after edge of the forward deck with the blade against the deck carlin at the side of the boat. You will need a dry oak or mahogany plank planed to 3 inches from which to make these posts. Set the bandsaw to the angle you picked off and saw the posts out. Then plane them clean with your jack plane. Rabbet the posts with your table saw to receive the cabin side and front. Saw the rabbets a little undersize and plane them out the rest of the way with your rabbet plane. You may leave the outer and inner corners of the posts hard, except nose the sharp edges off with sandpaper, or you can round the outside corner from about ½ inch above the deck to the top of the post.

The 3-inch by 3-inch corner posts, left about 6 inches longer than needed, can now be set at the correct angle and diagonally bolted into place at the bottom through the deck beam. Use your spirit level and declivity board to check for the correct tumblehome, and brace the tops of the posts from overhead to hold them in place athwartships Then rig braces from the top of the posts to the overhead to hold them in proper fore and aft alignment. The tops of these braces should be angled aft so as not to interfere with the cabin front installation. Now, standing on the staging, sight across the posts and check that they are in line with each other. Make adjustments until the posts line up to suit your eye, then nail off the braces.

The cabin front and sides should be at least 1-inch thick and are normally made of Philippine mahogany or pine, but some builders use western fir. Unless you are fortunate enough to purchase 24-inch-wide boards, you will have to spline two pieces together and glue them up. Splines made of ⅜-inch plywood about ¾ inch wide are very strong and take glue well. Cut a ⅜-inch-wide by ⁷⁄₁₆-inch-deep groove in the edges of the board with your dado saw so that the spline doesn't bottom out when the edges are fitted together.

Run the glue into the grooves and onto the splines, then clamp the boards together with door clamps. After tightening the clamps, wipe the excess glue off the boards with a paper towel or rags. Be sure to use *waterproof glue*. After the glue dries these boards will have to be planed along the glue joint with your jack plane and sanded with your dual-action vibrating sander.

Before you can cut the cabin sides and

front out of these boards, you need to make patterns for them. Clamp a piece of pattern stock along the inboard edge of the deck carlin and reach underneath to mark the back side with your pencil. Saw the excess wood off below the pencil mark on your table saw and joint the edge with your jointer or jack plane. Now tack the pattern back into place in the boat and tack a straight piece of pattern stock to the pattern at the forward post. Be sure it fits into the rabbet. Move aft to the after face of what will be the bulkhead location (or wherever you want the cabin to end), and, using your level, tack a straight piece of the pattern stock vertically to the lower end of the first piece. Mark the height of the cabin side on the forward upright of the pattern at the corner post and on the aft upright at the bulkhead.

Lay the pattern on the cabin sideboard and mark the forward and aft ends, and the lower edge. Put a tick mark on the board at the height marks on the uprights, and connect them with a straight line. This side of the cabin can be sawn out, jointed, and laid on the board for the other side, which is then sawn out and jointed. The cabin windows can be laid off and cut out with a saber saw, as it is a lot easier to cut them out now than to do it from a staging after the cabin sides are in place.

Now that the cabin sides are ready for installation, you will have to make a pattern for the cabin front. Do this as you did in making the pattern for the sides, except you will be fitting into a rabbet on both ends. Leave the top edge of the cabin front about 1½ inches high because its crown is greater than that of your beam mold, due to its rake. The top can be marked and trimmed off after the cabin beams are in place.

The cabin front will be installed first, and will drop into the rabbets from above the deck and slide down to fit the bottom edge of the deck beam. Bed the front, where it lies against the posts and deck edge and beam, in adhesive sealer or butyl rubber compound. Now tap on the top edge to drive it down into position, using a scrap block to pound on. Fasten the cabin front into the corner post rabbets with 1¾-inch #12 flat-head screws, counterboring for their heads. Go inside the boat and stagger-fasten along the lower edge into the beam, placing the screws about 6 inches apart.

After the front is all fastened in, go through the same motions and install the cabin sides. Also fasten the vertical cabin cleats at the bulkhead and wherever else you have planned to put them. Remove the overhead braces from the corner posts, and, using your declivity board and level against the cabin sides, brace them off at several locations to the correct tumblehome, usually about ⅜ inch per foot. Run these braces from the cabin side tops outboard and be sure to nail them securely.

Next, we have to mill and install the cabin beam clamps or carlins. These are of oak, normally about 1⅛ inches by 4 inches and are fitted to the inside top edge of the cabin sides. The beam ends will box into these pieces so they should be screwed securely into place through the cabin sides.

Notch out the trunk cabin clamp for the bulkhead beam, which goes in first, using a handsaw and 1-inch and ½-inch chisels. These notches will be the same width and depth as your beam, and will be cut ½ inch into the clamp athwartships. After marking the notch out on the beam clamp with your combination square, take your handsaw and saw just inside your lines, being particularly careful not to saw below your bottom line where it would show. On the top edge of the clamp, which will be hidden, you can run the saw right out to the ½-inch-depth line. These saw cuts will save you a lot of chiseling in cutting out the notches. Lay off

the clamp for the other beams, spacing them evenly about 10 inches apart, and cut out all the beam notches.

Fitting the cabin beams will be done in the same manner as you fitted the deck beams. Lay the beam on its side and tick mark the length so it will be fully seated in the notches. Stand the beam upright and adjust it back and forth until the tick mark at the top corner of the beam lines up with your marking stick. Mark both ends in this fashion and saw them off. Now tap them into the notches with your hammer. Fasten into the ends of the beams through the cabin sides and clamps with 8d galvanized nails or 2¼-inch #12 flat-head screws. Set up a strongback on props under the beams to hold them in line until the cabin top is in place just as you did for the cockpit beams.

Now that the cabin beams are all fastened in and aligned, the top edges of the cabin front and sides have to be faired. Keeping your straightedge parallel to the fore and aft centerline, lay it across the beams and have your helper slide it athwartships while you mark across the cabin front with your pencil held up under the straightedge. Use your saw, jack plane, and spokeshave to trim off the tops of the corner posts and plane the front down to the line. Then install the header across the cabin front, crowning and beveling its top edge to fit fairly. Trim the ends of the beams and the top edges of the cabin sides, and the cabin top is ready to be fitted on. If there is to be a companionway hatch or a hatch ahead of the windshield, don't forget to put in the partners for it.

The cabin top should be two layers of ⅜-inch plywood glued together and covered with fiberglass (same practice as in plywood deck). With two layers, you won't have to install butt blocks under the plywood joints. Apply glue to the top edges of the cabin front and header, nail the bottom layer of plywood to the beams and around the edges with 3d galvanized box nails, then cover the surface with glue and nail on the top layer, using 5d box nails. In both layers, keep the nails at the cabin sides and front well back from the edge, as you will have to remove considerable wood when rounding off the corners for fiberglassing. Set the nails and fill the holes, seams, and nicks, if any, with plastic auto body putty, such as "Snowball" or "White Lightning." After the body putty dries, sand the entire roof and round off the corners at the cabin sides and front to about a ⅜-inch or ½-inch radius.

Tack a batten about 1½ inches below the cabin top along the sides and across the front. This is to keep the resin from running down and saves a lot of clean-up work. Apply a coat of resin to the cabin roof and lay on 2-ounce fiberglass mat, saturating it with resin to hold it in place. Butt the joints and fit the mat down to the batten around the cabin and to the aft edge of the cabin top at the bulkhead, where your trim moldings will cover it. Then lay on 10-ounce fiberglass cloth over the mat and saturate it with three or four coats of resin. After the final coat of resin has dried to a tacky stage, remove the battens from the cabin sides and the front, because once the resin hardens you will have to tear the battens off in pieces. If you are careful in measuring the catalyst for the resin, you can control the set-up time, and if you catch it just right, you can put on all coats of resin the same day.

When handling fiberglass, the glass fibers can get into your skin and be very irritating. For protection there are paper throw-away suits that you can buy, which I would recommend, as fiberglassing is rough on clothes. Another word on fiberglass: Colors can be added to the resin to bond in a permanent color.

The front and sides of the cabin will have a half round molding to seal the edge of the fiberglass, as well as hide it from sight. Corner knee molding should be made to fit around the corner posts. These are fun to do, because they are light to handle and intricate. Leave these corner knees a little oversize so that after the other trunk cabin moldings are on, you can fair them in perfectly with a chisel, rabbet plane, and spokeshave. Then sand them, and they will look as if they had grown there.

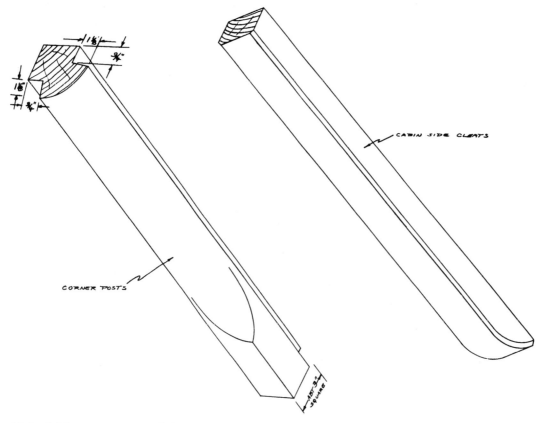

1 1/8"
3/4"
1 1/8"
3/4"

CABIN SIDE CLEATS

CORNER POSTS

1/8' 3 1/2 SQUARE

10-1   Cabin corner posts and cleats.

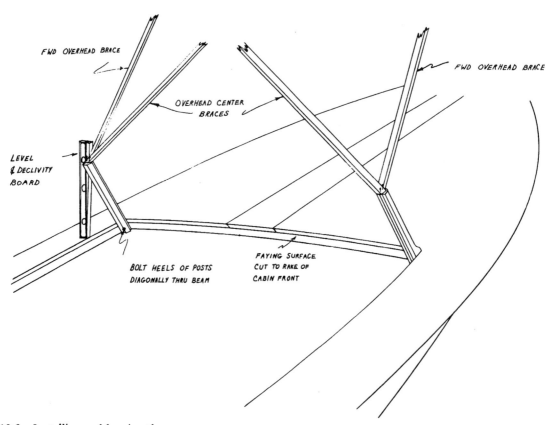

FWD OVERHEAD BRACE

FWD OVERHEAD BRACE

OVERHEAD CENTER
BRACES

LEVEL
& DECLIVITY
BOARD

BOLT HEELS OF POSTS
DIAGONALLY THRU BEAM

FAYING SURFACE
CUT TO RAKE OF
CABIN FRONT

10-2   Installing and bracing the corner posts.

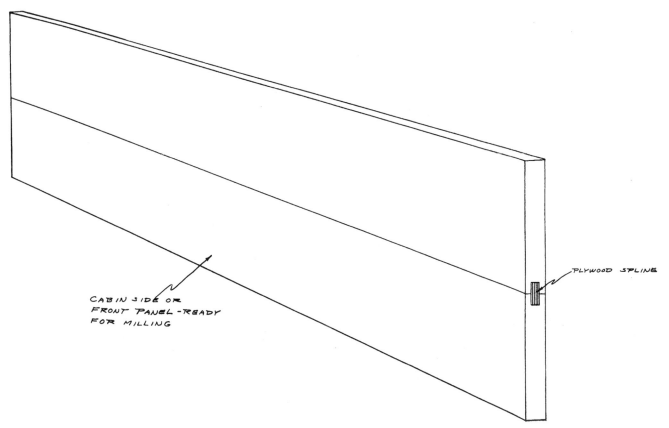

CABIN SIDE OR
FRONT PANEL - READY
FOR MILLING

PLYWOOD SPLINE

10-3   Glued and spliced panel for the cabin side or front.

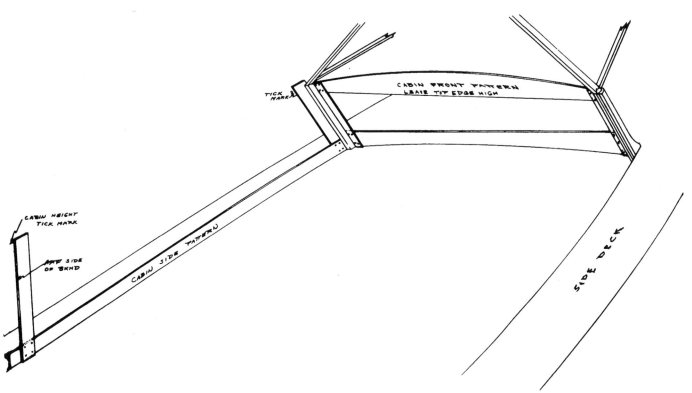

CABIN FRONT PATTERN
LEAVE TOP EDGE HIGH

TICK
MARK

CABIN HEIGHT
TICK MARK

AFT SIDE
OF BKHD

CABIN SIDE PATTERN

SIDE DECK

10-4   Cabin side and front details.

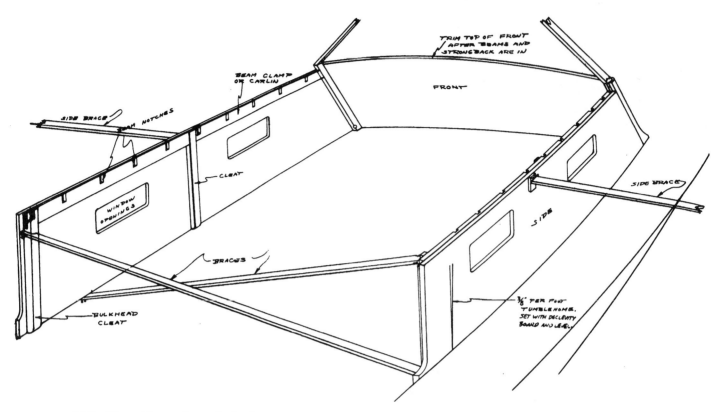

10-5 *The cabin trunk—ready for beams.*

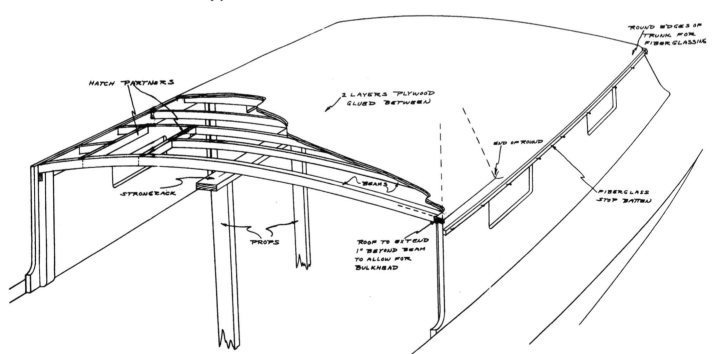

10-6 *The cabin trunk—ready for fiberglass.*

124

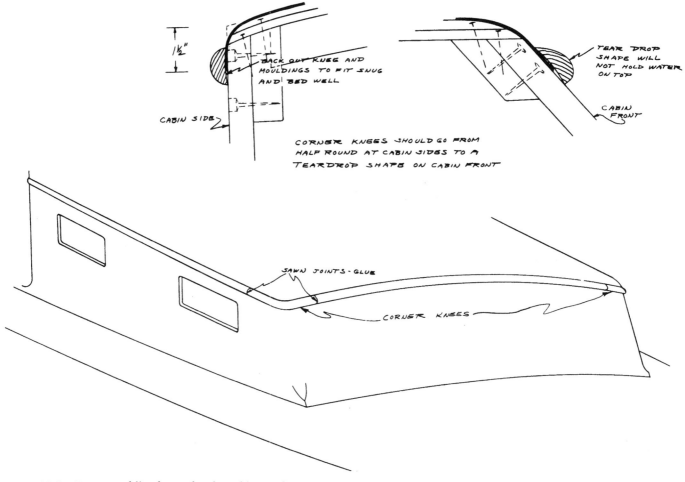

10-7 *Corner molding knees for the cabin trunk.*

COAMINGS AND MOORING BITT

The cockpit coamings, which are the same thickness as the cabin sides, have to go in at this point. These are normally made of oak, and, when in place, their top edges will be about 1¼ inches above the deck. The side coamings will fasten to the deck carlins and butt onto the cabin sides, where they are held in line by oak dowels through the butt. Bed the coamings in adhesive sealer and fasten them with 1¾-inch #12 flat-head wood screws, counterboring for their heads. The screws should be spaced about 6 inches apart and staggered so as to hold firmly.

The aft ends of the side coamings have to be grooved in about ½-inch to receive the ends of the aft coaming. Get the length of the aft coaming from the bottom edge of the deck beam. Saw it to the right tumble-home angle and drive it into the side coaming grooves from the bottom. Don't forget the bedding compound. Fasten this piece to the beam as you did the side coamings to the carlins. Bung the screw holes and trim the bungs off with a chisel. Then sand the coamings for painting.

The mooring bitt should be made up and installed at this point, but first cut a 3¼-inch-square hole for it in the kingplank if you haven't already done so. The head or top of the bitt should be about 4 inches square and 5 inches high. The shank, which goes down through the deck and blocking, should be 3¼ inches square and about a foot long. This will give you a ⅜-inch shoulder around the bitt at the 5-inch mark to set on the deck. Measure the depth through the bitt hole in the deck to the bottom of the blocking. Deduct ⅛ inch from this and tick mark the shank—measuring from the shoulder on the bitt downward. Square this mark around the bitt shank with a combination square and pencil. This will be the top of the mortise through which a tapered tenon or wedge will be driven athwartships.

Make your tenon of ⅞-inch oak about 14 inches long, and 1¼ inches at one end and 1¾ inches at the opposite end. Center the

tenon on the aft side of the bitt shank with the top edge on the mortise mark that you squared around the shank and mark along the lower edge of the tenon. Square to the sides of the shank and lay out for the mortise.

Bore the mortise out with a ¾-inch bit and clean it out with chisels. Test fit the tenon to be sure that it will drive in. Now finish shaping and sanding the head of the bitt and bore athwartships for a ½-inch bronze pin about 10 inches long. Drive in the bronze pin and center it.

The last operation will be to bed the bitt shoulders and drive the bitt down through the deck opening with a top maul and a scrap block of wood. Now drive the tenon home, drawing the shoulders down tightly to the deck. Another chore is finished.

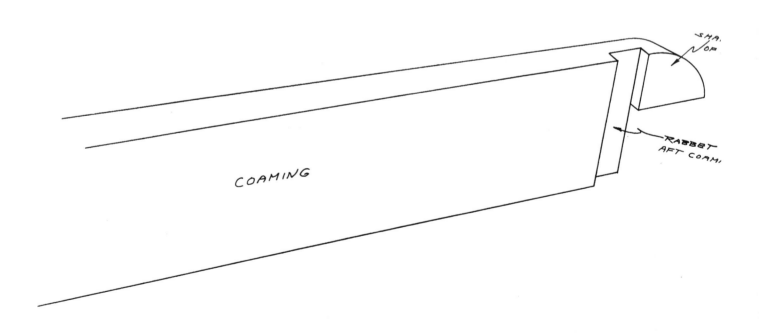

10-8 *Detail of the after end of the coaming.*

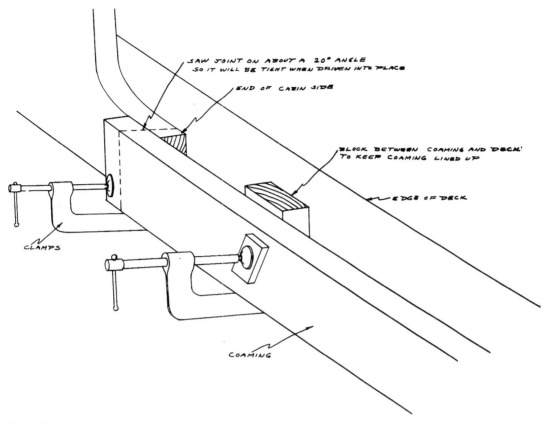

SAW JOINT ON ABOUT A 20° ANGLE
SO IT WILL BE TIGHT WHEN DRIVEN INTO PLACE

END OF CABIN SIDE

BLOCK BETWEEN COAMING AND DECK
TO KEEP COAMING LINED UP

EDGE OF DECK

CLAMPS

COAMING

10-9   *Fitting the forward end of the coaming.*

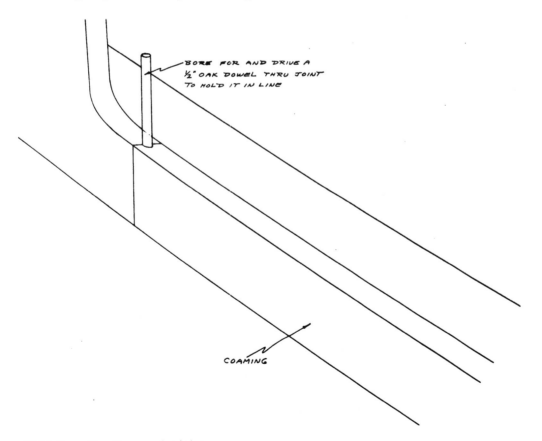

BORE FOR AND DRIVE A
½" OAK DOWEL THRU JOINT
TO HOLD IT IN LINE

COAMING

10-10 *Dowelling the coaming joint.*

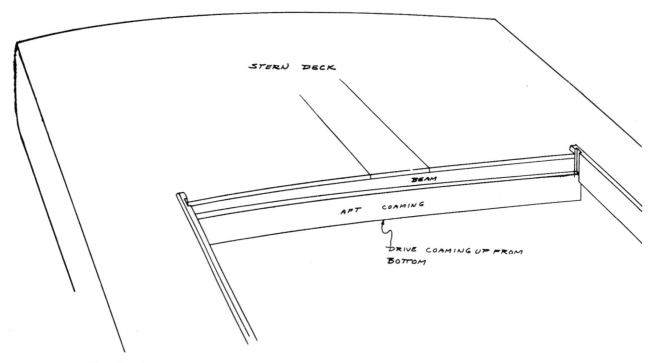

STERN DECK

BEAM

APT COAMING

DRIVE COAMING UP FROM BOTTOM

10-11   Installing the aft coaming.

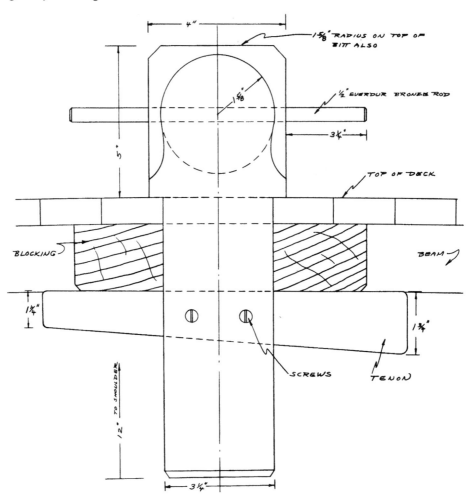

4"

1⅝" RADIUS ON TOP OF BITT ALSO

⅞"

½" EVERDUR BRONZE ROD

3¼"

5"

TOP OF DECK

BLOCKING

BEAM

1¼"

1¾"

12" TO SHOULDER

SCREWS

TENON

3¼"

10-12   Mooring bitt detail.

MAIN BULKHEAD

You will have to have a pattern for the main bulkhead. To begin, make up three pieces of ½-inch pine pattern stock long enough to extend from the cabin top down to the keel. These pieces should have one edge jointed and marked so that you don't have to fool around sighting the pieces to see which edge is the straight one. Then you will need some wide pieces in way of the hull sides and the cabin roof crown and various other pieces as shown in Figure 10-13.

Make the pattern about as shown, and once the boundary pieces have been scribed down to a good fit, nail them together with 3d galvanized nails. Patch blocks at the joints can be made from scrap pattern stock. Tack the straightedges in place, one on either side of the companionway and one on the opposite side of the boat at the side of the trunk cabin.

Remember when scribing vertical pieces to hold the dividers horizontally and not at right angles to the hull. By the same token, horizontal pieces should be scribed with the dividers held vertically.

The bulkhead pattern may have to be in two pieces so it can be removed, in which case you can use the inboard straightedge at the companionway for a separation joint by extending it to the bottom of the hull.

The bulkhead is made of plywood. Remove the patterns and place them on the plywood, which should be lying on sawhorses. Mark and saw out the bulkhead shape with your saber and portable saws. If you have help, you can saw most of the plywood on the bandsaw.

Treat the edges of the bulkhead with Cuprinol or paint and install it in position inside the hull. It should be fastened in well, preferably with screws, as it is an important transverse strength member.

An ideal bulkhead is made of two layers of ½-inch plywood, glued together with staggered joints, which will give you a solid 1-inch bulkhead with no joints to work.

The bulkhead pattern shown is for a full bulkhead. In most fishing boats, the owners will want the engine located just ahead of the bulkhead unless the boat is large enough to have room for all or most of the engine under the cockpit, in which case there will be a flush hatch in the deck, or, depending on the type of engine, a 6- or 8-inch-high engine box.

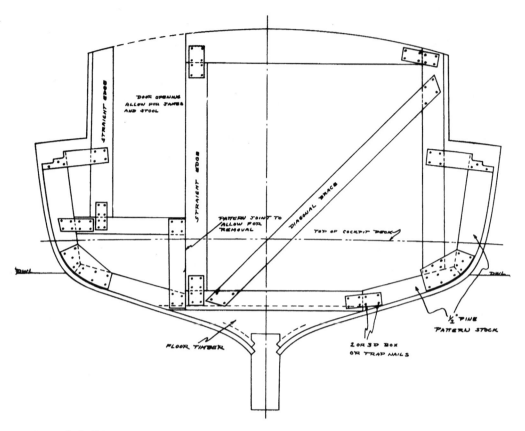

10-13 Main bulkhead patterns.

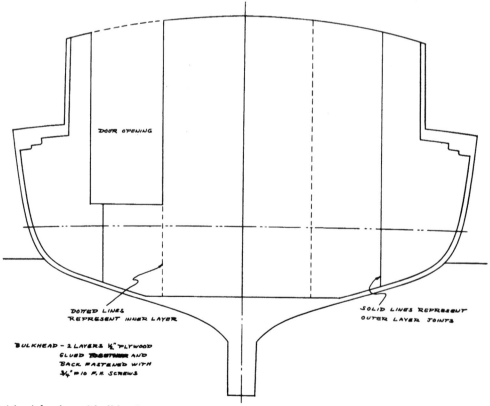

10-14 A laminated bulkhead.

PILOTHOUSE

The pilothouse construction is similar to that of the trunk cabin with a few exceptions. The pilothouse beams, roof, and molding will be done in the same manner.

The windshield makes the difference. Instead of having a solid piece front, as in the trunk cabin, the pilothouse will have a framed front for windows. The front may also vary, depending on which type of windshield that you prefer—flat, vee, or hexagonal. Mill the pieces for it from the same stock that you used for the trunk cabin.

FLAT WINDSHIELD

The flat windshield is the easiest to make, because you only have the two corner posts to contend with, as in the trunk cabin. The vee windshield requires three posts and the hexagonal type, four.

The flat windshield can be made up at the workbench, using mortise and tenon glued joints to connect the uprights and athwartship pieces. Fasten 1¼-inch by 2-inch oak cleats behind the uprights. The windows are set into the windshield rabbets, well bedded, and held in place with retainer strips made of pine, cedar, or mahogany.

The rabbets are usually routed out to a depth of ⅝ inch and are about ⅜ inch wide. The retainer strips should be made about ⅜ inch by ⅝ inch to allow them to protrude ¼ inch (the thickness of the glass) out beyond the windshield. After fitting, nose the sharp corners off with 80-grit production paper. This gives the windows a framed look, so to speak, particularly if the strips are painted a trim color.

On most fishing boats, only the window in front of the helm is hinged to open. Be sure to make its frame big enough when laying out the windshield, so the window

glass will all be the same size and be in line athwartships with the opening window in place. The opening window should be made with its top and bottom edges beveled so that water cannot lie in the landing at the bottom and so that spray will not be driven easily in through the top. The hinge at the top of the window is fitted with a neoprene gasket, which should extend at least 1 inch beyond the ends of the window.

The window frame is of half-lapped joint construction and should be clamped and the joints glued while it is in place in the windshield. After sanding the joints, plane the edges of the window so that it doesn't bind anywhere. It is a good idea to have a ¹⁄₁₆-inch clearance around the frame. Also, round off the top back corner of the window to allow it to open without binding. Now rabbet out the frame, bed the glass, and fasten in the retainer strips, using 1-inch escutcheon pins.

The final piece of woodwork will be to fit and fasten in the landing pieces for the opening window. They should be about ¾ inch by 1½ inches with about ⅜ inch extending into the window opening all around, so that the window has something to land against. These pieces should be well bedded, preferably with adhesive sealer, and fastened to the windshield with 1½-inch #10 oval-head chrome-plated screws.

After painting the window, the hinge and neoprene hinge gasket can be put on. Then fasten on the window quadrants, which are used to adjust the opening of the window.

Another item I should mention here is the 1-inch-thick oak backing cleat to which the bottom edge of the windshield is fastened. This should be marked out on the 1¼-inch board that you will mill from. Set the board in position on the trunk cabin at the proper rake and scribe it down to fit against the cabin top. Mark a line parallel to the scribe line to give the finished piece an inch of thickness. Then set your bandsaw to the rake angle of the windshield, and saw out and fit the piece between the posts. Fasten it down by screwing up through the cabin roof. To do this, set the cleat in place between the posts and mark along both its edges onto the cabin roof. Remove and then bore ⅛-inch pilot holes down through the roof. With your helper holding the cleat back in place, bore up through the cabin roof into it with a counterbore and drill for screws (1½-inch #12 flat-head). Remove the cleat once more and apply bedding compound. Finally, with your helper holding the cleat back in place, drive the screws home.

The side wings of the pilothouse, which are from the same material as the windshield, can also be made up on the workbench, rabbeted for windows, and have their top pieces notched out for the roof beams. The corner posts can be made up and attached to the side wings at this point.

You should have made up and installed backing cleats on the trunk cabin roof, similar to the cleat for the windshield, to screw the bottoms of the side wings to. With these cleats in place and the side wings trimmed to a good fit, you can set the wings in place, brace them from overhead using your declivity board and spirit level (⅜ inch per foot), and fasten both them and the windshield into place. The inboard aft edge of each side wing should have a 1¼-inch by 1¼-inch vertical cleat screw fastened through the side wing.

Now install the aft corner posts. They should be bolted through the deck carlins with ⅜-inch carriage bolts. It is good practice to cut out a ⅜-inch-deep box in the cockpit deck in which to set the heels of the aft posts. Make sure you bed the post heels well in the boxes. Securing the posts in this way really stiffens up the pilothouse aft. On the hauling side of a lobsterboat, the aft post will be set inboard about in line with

the edge of the engine hatch or box to keep that side of the boat clear for working.

Install your aft roof beam and another one about halfway forward. If there is some fore-and-aft curve in the cockpit deck coaming when viewed from above, you will have to take this into account when getting the actual length of the latter beam. You will normally find that this beam will have to be longer in order to bow out the roof line so that the curve at the roof lines up with the curve at the coaming. Now cut in the rest of your roof beams and fasten them into place through their ends. Then nail a strongback under them along the centerline and prop it up from the cockpit deck so the beams all come fair. Straighten them up athwartships with your straightedge and temporarily nail them to the strongback to hold them in line until the plywood roof is on and fastened.

The pilothouse roof is of fiberglass-covered plywood with moldings at its edges and is put together and finished just as the trunk cabin roof was.

V OR HEX WINDSHIELD

The side wings with corner posts attached should be in place before work is commenced on the windshield itself. Unlike the flat windshield, the v or hex one is best built right in place on the boat. Either one or two center posts are needed and are made similar to the corner posts described earlier. Great care should be taken in setting and aligning them. To do this, lay off and mark their locations on the trunk cabin roof and bore down through with a ⅛-inch drill for pilot holes. With the posts fitted, bedded, and braced in position, fasten them by driving screws up through the trunk cabin roof, taking into consideration the angle of the posts when back boring and driving screws.

For the hex windshield, you can make a simple jig out of plywood and scraps to hold the two center posts at the proper angle. Fasten the jig to the trunk cabin roof. Once this is done, it is an easy matter to position the posts athwartships, trim their heels and fasten them up through the cabin roof.

The centerposts of a hex windshield must be specially treated to get their alignment just right. Here's how it is done. With a short piece of batten, get the length between the rabbets along the bottom of the windshield from the corner post to the nearest center post. Tick mark the batten at this length and adjust the top of the center post to match the tick mark. Set the top of the other center post from the other corner post in the same manner. Mark these positions of the center posts on the jig and then sight from the corner post to the nearest center post from the staging at the side of the boat and adjust the top of the center post if needed to make it line up. When the align-

ment looks good to your eye, fasten the tops of the center posts to the jig and brace them off to the overhead.

Once the centerposts are in and braced you can saw out and fit the top and bottom pieces of the windshield. Again, keep in mind that the opening window must have a larger opening both ways to accommodate the window frame so that the window glass will all be in line when the window frame is in place. After fitting, bed the bottom edges of the bottom pieces, and fasten them in place. Apply glue in the rabbets at the tops of the posts and fasten in the top pieces. The upright end pieces, which are fitted next, are to be half lapped onto the top and bottom pieces and glued as well as screwed to the posts. Using clamp pads and waxed paper, clamp the half-lapped joints with C clamps and allow them to set overnight. Now that the basic windshield is completed, it may be finished off as described earlier for a flat windshield.

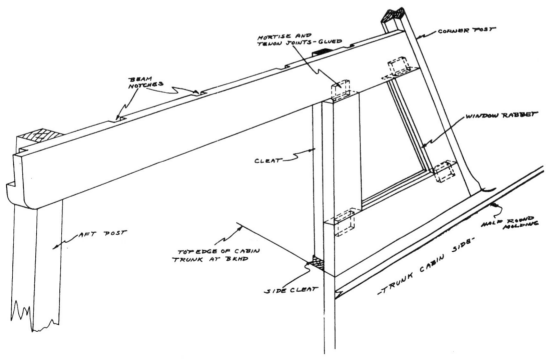

10-15 The pilothouse side wing.

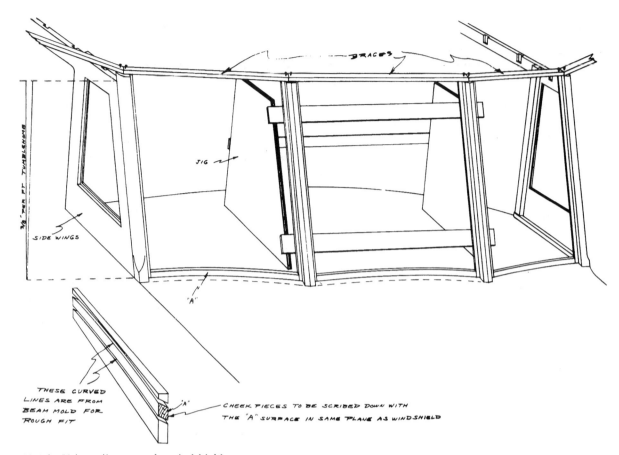

BRACES

JIG

SIDE WINGS

⅜" TPER FT TUMBLEHOME

"A"

THESE CURVED
LINES ARE FROM
BEAM MOLD FOR
ROUGH FIT

"A"

CHEEK PIECES TO BE SCRIBED DOWN WITH
THE "A" SURFACE IN SAME PLANE AS WINDSHIELD

10-16   Using a jig to set the windshield center posts.

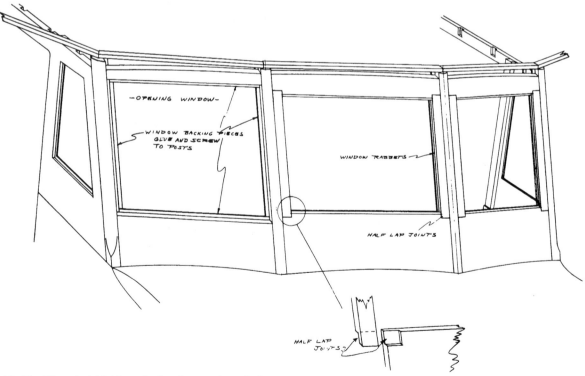

—OPENING WINDOW—

WINDOW BACKING PIECES
GLUE AND SCREW
TO POSTS

WINDOW RABBETS

HALF LAP JOINTS

HALF LAP
JOINTS

10-17   The windshield ready for the opening window.

*Looking forward from the cockpit.
The main bulkhead, pilothouse, and
windshield have been completed.*

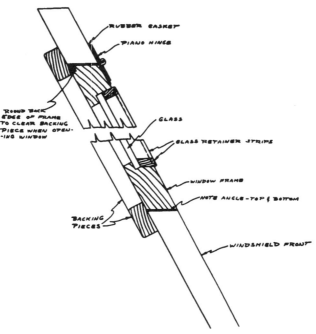

RUBBER GASKET

PIANO HINGE

ROUND BACK
EDGE OF FRAME
TO CLEAR BACKING
PIECE WHEN OPEN-
-ING WINDOW

GLASS

GLASS RETAINER STRIPS

WINDOW FRAME

NOTE ANGLE - TOP & BOTTOM

BACKING
PIECES

WINDSHIELD FRONT

10-18   *Detail of the opening window.*

GRAB RAILS

Grab rails are required on both the trunk cabin and pilothouse roofs. These can be through-bolted or screwed down into the beams. Since the type of roof construction we are using is very strong, you can bolt the grab rails between the beams using large washers under the nuts on the underside.

I prefer the shaped or grooved type of grab rail myself, as you can easily slide your fingers along it as you walk forward or aft. However, some prefer the looped hand grip type. I guess it is just a matter of preference, as they are both satisfactory.

The grab rails should be made of oak about 1⅛ inches wide by 2¼ inches high so as to be substantial. The sliding or grooved type can be made with your table saw and router. You can round the ends with a band-saw and spoke shave. The openings in the looped or grab type can be made by clamping their bottom edges together and using a drill press with a Forstner or similar bit to bore the holes through the grab rails which form the ends of the loops. Take the clamps off and finish sawing with the band-saw. Round the corners with a router and sand them. The grab rails are now ready to be fastened to the roof tops.

The next job will be to construct the trunk cabin windows. Some customers want fixed windows, in which case you should follow the same procedure that you used in the fixed windows of the pilothouse.

If opening windows are wanted, there are bronze marine windows or portlights that you may use. These are easy to install, and they have finishing rings for the outside, if you should desire them. There are also aluminum marine windows; these should be installed adhering to the instructions furnished with them. They usually have to be primed with chromate paint before applying regular paint.

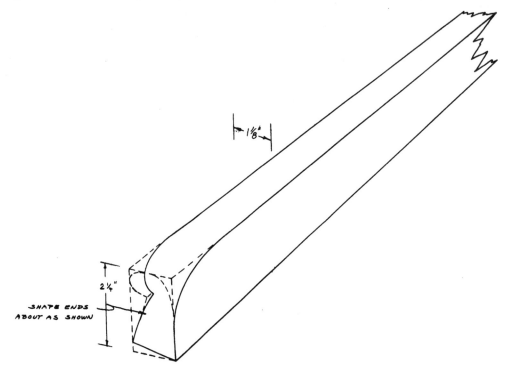

10-19 Detail of a groove-type grab rail.

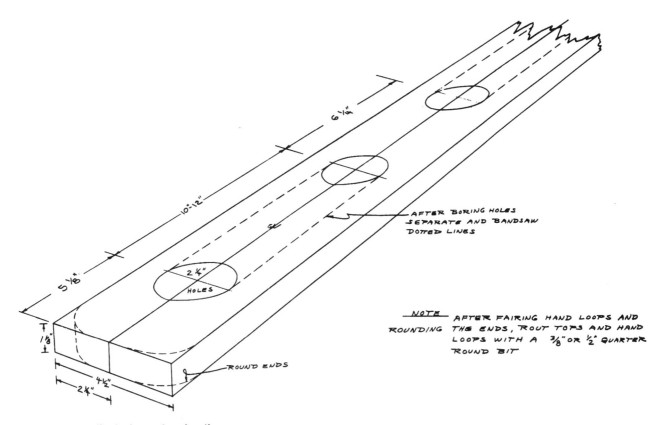

Figure labels (as drawn):
6 ¼"
10"-12"
6"
5 ¼"
2 ¼" HOLES
1 ¾"
4 ½"
2 ¼"
AFTER BORING HOLES SEPARATE AND BANDSAW DOTTED LINES
ROUND ENDS
NOTE AFTER FAIRING HAND LOOPS AND ROUNDING THE ENDS, ROUT TOPS AND HAND LOOPS WITH A ⅜" OR ½" QUARTER ROUND BIT

10-20 Detail of a looped grab rail.

FORWARD HATCH

If the boat is to have a forward hatch in the trunk cabin, I would recommend one fitted with a plexiglass top as shown in Figure 10-21, as it lets in a good deal of light. The plexiglass should be at least ¼ inch thick; ⅜ inch is better. Both thicknesses can be screwed directly to the frame after bedding with adhesive sealer. Don't peel the protective paper off either side of the plexiglass, except in way of the bedding, until installation is complete. Boring should be done in a drill press with the bit turning quite slowly. On ¼-inch plexiglass, #10 flat-head screws about 1½ inches apart should be used. On ⅜-inch plexiglass, #10 screws should be used about 2 inches apart. After planing and sanding the edge of the plexiglass flush with the hatch cover edge, sand off all the sharp corners. On the top of the plexiglass, mark a line with your combination square about 2 inches in on all four sides. Cut and peel the protective paper from this 2-inch-wide area and paint to this line. Then the rest of the protective paper can be peeled off.

Make the hatch coaming and hatch cover frame out of 2-inch mahogany. Mahogany is very good for this job as it is a stable wood when glued and fastened. The coaming should be well bedded and fastened down with 3-inch #16 flat-head screws, after which the inside finish band can be fitted and fastened with 1-inch escutcheon pins, using glue under the top edges and on the ends. The best corner joint that I have ever seen is the one I have shown in Figure 10-23.

Now add the hinge and fasten on the quadrants, and the hatch is complete.

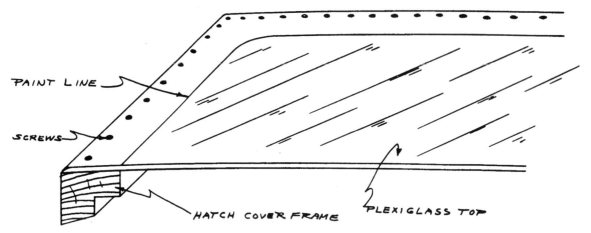

10-21   Hatch cover detail.

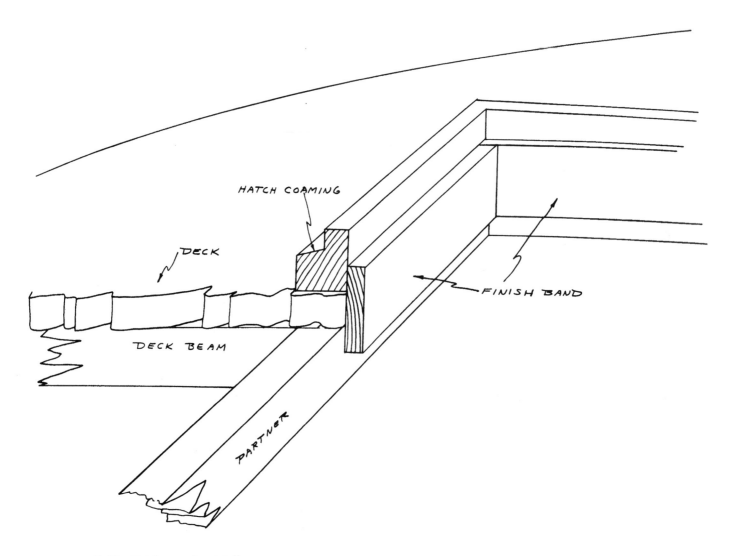

10-22   Hatch coaming detail.

Lowering the engine into place on its bed. Note how the ceiling in the cockpit runs parallel to the sheer and how the starboard support for the pilothouse is set inboard to provide a clear area for working the lobster traps.

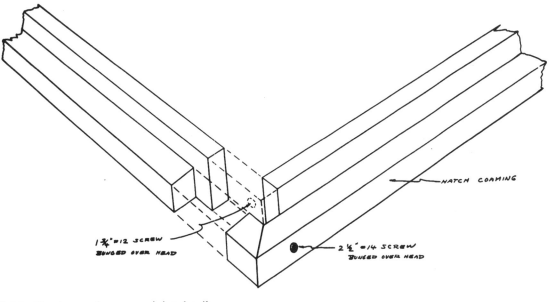

1 ¾" #12 SCREW BUNGED OVER HEAD

HATCH COAMING

2 ½" #14 SCREW BUNGED OVER HEAD

10-23 *Hatch coaming corner joint detail.*

Chapter 11

Interior Joinery

The cabin sole or floor is the first project in the cabin. Probably it will be laid directly on the floor timbers, but if any support framing or beams are necessary, they can be made up out of left over stock from the hull timbers. If you lay the sole, we'll say in 4 inch or 5 inch wide boards parallel to the centerline, you will have a series of long pointed ends on both sides of the sole. You will have to back up these points against the hull with pine or cedar blocks, or you will probably break some of them off even before you get the inboard work done. Another method of laying the sole, which I feel is better, is to fit the two outside pieces to the hull and then fill in the center area between them with tapered boards. This method does not produce any sharp points, and it will be stronger along the edges. The center board should be left loose unless you build in an access hatch. The edges of the outside pieces, where they fit against the timbers, will have an extreme under-bevel. This should be cut back so that the top corner has a face ⅜-inch thick that will fit against the ceiling. This will eliminate the sharp edge you would otherwise have.

It this is to be a working lobsterboat, you will probably ceil up the entire cabin from the bulkhead to the fourth or fifth timber aft of the stem, making sure to leave a 1-inch air space between the sheer clamp and the first strake of ceiling. Neither the bow area nor the corresponding one near the transom should be ceiled in any boat, so that plenty of air can get in and prevent dry rot. The fisherman usually wants only a couple of side seats in the cabin and that is about all.

However, if this is to be a pleasure boat and a cabin interior has to be built in, any joiner bulkheads will have to be made and installed next and the ceiling fitted around them afterward. To mark where the bulkheads land, you will need to set up a stiff straightedge about 1 inch by 4 inches, nailed athwartships to the underside of the deck carlins. This straightedge has to be squared across the boat.

Two vertical straightedges should then be run down from the cabin top or forward deck to the outboard edges of the cabin sole. These are to be tacked to the athwartship straightedge and also to the cabin sole using your spirit level to set them plumb. The aft edge of these vertical pieces should correspond with one side of your joiner bulkhead. Lastly, you will need a third straightedge, which should be as long as two-thirds of the boat's beam and will be used for marking. One end of it has to be cut so a pencil can be attached with its lead in line with the straightedge, as shown in Figure 11-4. These straightedges can all be made of pine.

The straightedge fitted with the pencil will be used for marking the inside of the hull, so the bulkhead and boundary cleats can be shaped and positioned. The mark should be on the small or under-bevelled side of the bulkhead, the forward side in this part of the boat. The use of the marking straightedge is shown in Figure 11-5 where it is held against the two vertical straightedges and slid up and down or crossways, marking the bulkhead line on the hull.

Now tack short blocks of wood about ¾ inch by 1½ inches by 4 inches temporarily around the hull, about a foot apart, on the cleat side of the line (forward in this case). These blocks give you something solid to fit your pattern against.

Rough mark and saber saw the pattern boundary pieces until they come within ⅜ inch or ½ inch of fitting the hull. Then scribe in the pattern pieces with your dividers for the final fit. Now cut and nail on a straight piece of pattern stock representing the inboard edge of the bulkhead and do the same with the top and bottom pieces that fit against the overhead or sole. Nail on a diagonal brace, and the bulkhead pattern is completed, but before removing it, take your bevel gauge and get the angles at

several points from the pattern to the hull and elsewhere as necessary. If the bulkhead at its boundary will have a standing bevel, you will have to allow for this when cutting out the bulkhead.

Remove the pattern and use its boundary edge to mark out oak cleats to be fastened to the hull in place of the temporary blocks, which can now be removed. Saw the cleats out to shape and also to the angles that you have taken with the bevel gauge. They should be the thickness of the boat's timbers and about 1¼ inches wide. Treat the cleats with Cuprinol and screw them into place against the hull planking. Also, make up and screw the overhead, sole, and cabin side cleats into place.

Now saw out the bulkhead or half bulkhead, as the case may be, and check it for fit in the hull. Trim with a plane or spoke shave if necessary, then treat the boundary edge with Cuprinol or paint and fasten the bulkhead in place against the cleats.

You will go through the same setup and motions for the rest of the interior athwartship bulkheads, which are usually of ½-inch plywood. The fore and aft partitions are relatively simple, as all vertical edges are straight, and the only fitting should be to the overhead. Even so, you still have to make patterns for them to assure a good fit. Unless these partitions are going between the bulkheads, you will have to mill corner posts, as all inboard joinery should be rounded so as to prevent injury in case people get thrown around in heavy seas.

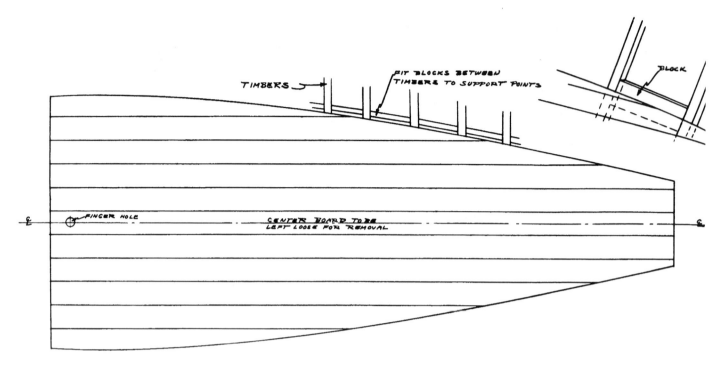

11-1 *Cabin sole—method 1.*

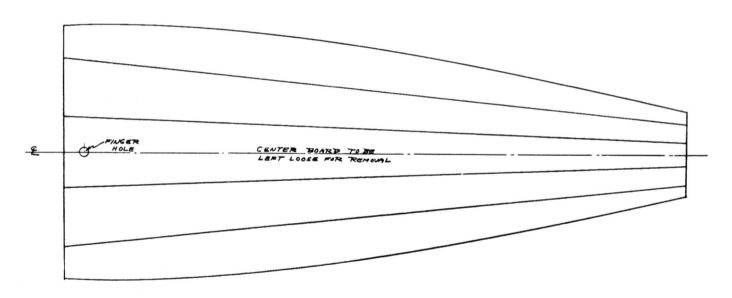

11-2 *Cabin sole—method 2.*

142

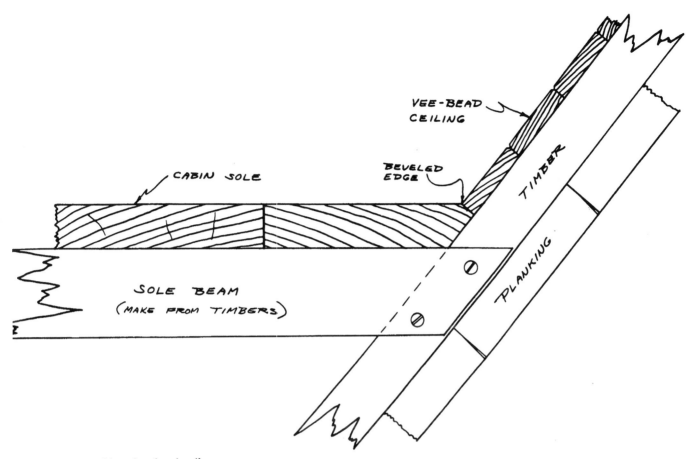

11-3 Cabin sole edge detail.

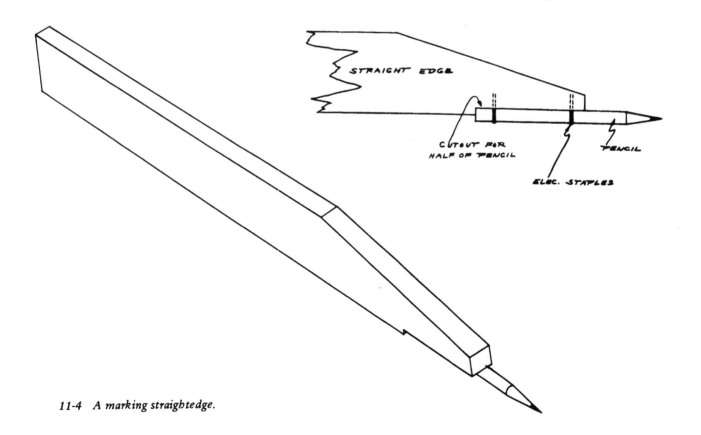

11-4 A marking straightedge.

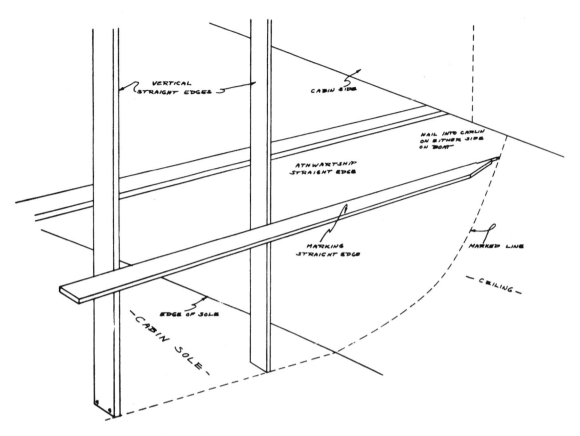

11-5 *Method of marking the location of the bulkhead boundary cleats.*

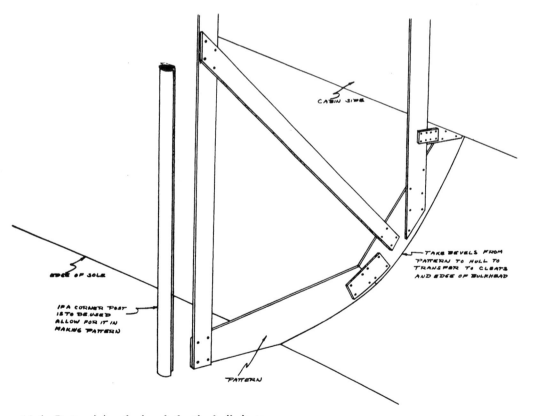

11-6 *Determining the bevels for the bull cleats.*

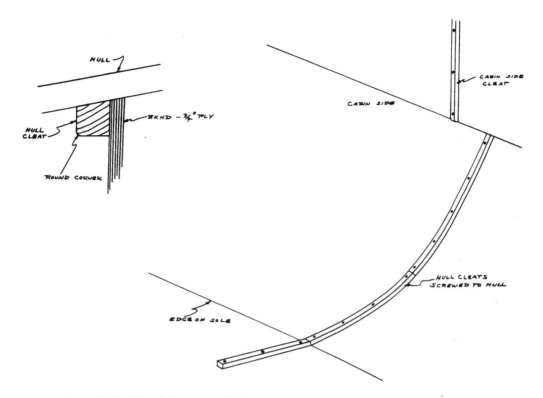

11-7 The cabin bulkhead cleats installed.

JAMBS, HEADERS, AND CAPS

Mill and install all of the interior door jambs and headers, using details shown in Figure 11-11. As mitered joints are not practical in boatbuilding, you should not rabbet the headers, but leave their undersides flat. This way the fitting of the door jambs will be square. Also, the header should be about ½ inch wider than the jambs so that it projects ¼ inch on either side. This makes a very neat job and is simple to do.

Door stools are not generally used in interiors where the door opening comes down to the cabin sole.

Cap the exposed edges of the half bulkheads and partitions. The caps should be made of mahogany and rabbeted to go down over the edge of the plywood about ⅜ inch. You will have to make corner knee caps of mahogany to fit the radius corners of the half bulkheads. Make them oversize, as you can trim and fair to the adjoining straight pieces after all the capping is in place. The corner knee caps should be installed first; tap them in place and hold them with glue and 4d galvanized finish nails. Then cut and fit the outboard end of the top cap, and, holding it in place with its inboard end lying on the knee cap, saw a slight undercut through both caps with a finish saw. The cap will probably fit a little tightly, and you may have to run the saw through the joint once or twice more. Glue and fasten the top cap on. Do the same on the vertical cap, and you have it made. Once you have gone through the motions, you will get the picture.

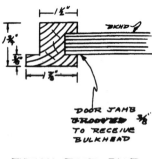

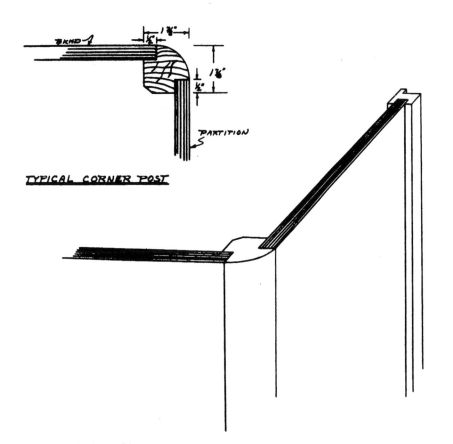

TYPICAL CORNER POST

PARTITION

TYPICAL DOOR JAMB

DOOR JAMB GROOVED 3/8" TO RECEIVE BULKHEAD

11-8 Cabin corner post and door jamb detail.

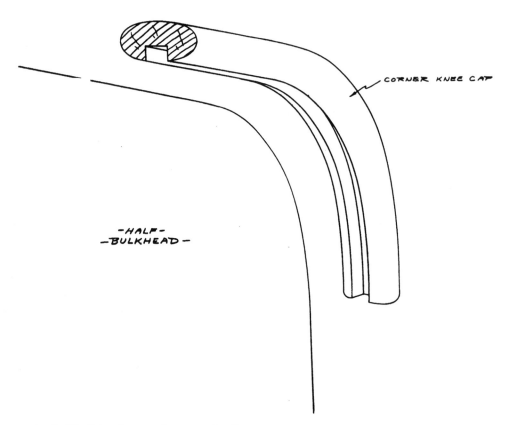

CORNER KNEE CAP

—HALF—
—BULKHEAD—

11-9 Half bulkhead corner knee cap detail.

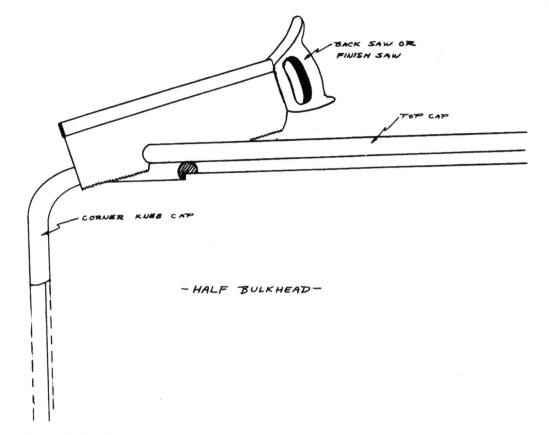

BACK SAW OR
FINISH SAW

TOP CAP

CORNER KNEE CAP

—HALF BULKHEAD—

11-10   Sawing the cap joints.

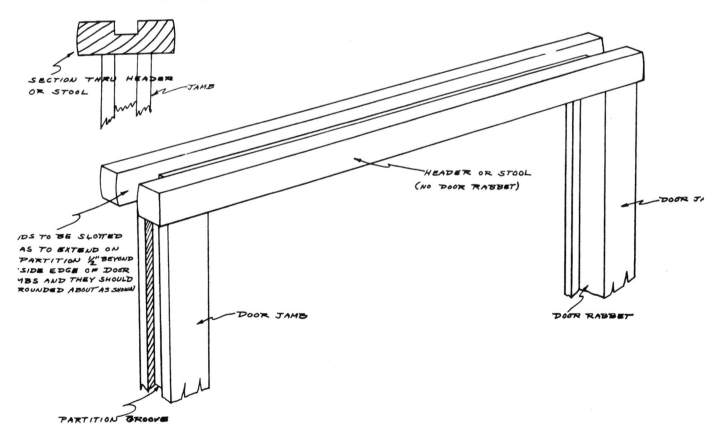

SECTION THRU HEADER
OR STOOL

JAMB

HEADER OR STOOL
(NO DOOR RABBET)

DOOR J

...DS TO BE SLOTTED
AS TO EXTEND ON
PARTITION ½" BEYOND
SIDE EDGE OF DOOR
...MBS AND THEY SHOULD
...ROUNDED ABOUT AS SHOWN

DOOR RABBET

DOOR JAMB

PARTITION GROOVE

11-11   Interior door jamb and header detail.

BERTH FRONTS

The berth fronts can be made up using plywood or you can mill pine or mahogany and connect the uprights with the top and bottom pieces by mortise and tenon joints. Cap the top edges as you did the half bulkheads. If you cap the top edges, be sure that the berth front extends 2 inches above the berth flat, so as to hold the mattress in place. If you should use a pine or mahogany drop center finish board, the berth front need only extend up to the underside of the flat.

DRAWERS AND DRAWER RUNNERS

Regular drawers, such as you would make for use in your house, will slide out and fall onto the sole when the boat rolls. Therefore, drawers in boats have to drop at the front to lock them in place. I once built a boat for a fellow who insisted that a Sears and Roebuck sink cabinet with doors and drawers in it would save a lot of building time. He seemed to feel that there was no need to take so much time custom building these items into the boat. So I kept quiet and let him get his mail order cabinets. During the boat's trial runs outside the harbor, it was fairly rough. The skipper was running the boat from the flying bridge, and all of a sudden he heard this gosh-awful crash-banging below. So he laid the boat to and went down to see what was going on. The drawers were all over the floor and the doors were banging back and forth. It isn't too often that your house rolls. Boats are different.

The drawer runs should be fastened in at least ⅛ inch below the bottom edge of the drawer opening. Excellent runs can be made from 1 inch by 4 inch pine with formica on top; 1 inch by 1 inch pine or mahogany guides can be fastened to these runs to keep the drawer from cocking and jamming.

The drawer fronts should be made of ⅞-inch pine or mahogany and face edges should be routed to a ⅜-inch radius. Drawers are about the easiest things to foul up on, so be very careful in measuring for them. If you were making drawers often, it would be no problem, but there is so little of this in boatbuilding one gets out of practice. The drawer lips, when the drawer is assembled, should be as follows: the top lip should be ½ inch, as the drawer will drop ⅛ inch when in place. The side lips should be ⅜ inch and the bottom lip ¼ inch, as again the drawer will drop ⅛ inch when in place. Don't forget that the bottom lip should be ¼ inch plus the thickness of the bottom. Plywood makes good material for the drawer sides, bottoms, and backs, as it won't swell and warp as much as pine or mahogany.

In assembling the drawer, apply glue to the rabbets on the side pieces that will attach to the drawer front and nail these three pieces together with 5d galvanized box nails. Apply glue to the rest of the rabbets and grooves, and insert the bottom panel first and then the back piece next. Now nail through the sides into the back piece with the 5d nails and turn the drawer bottom-side up to nail the bottom to the drawer front and back. It is a good idea to clamp the sides to the bottom with a door clamp about midway between the front and back. Then let the drawer set overnight or until the glue dries.

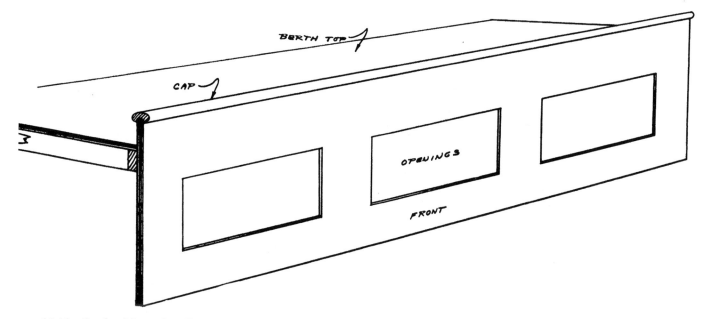

11-12 Berth with cap installed.

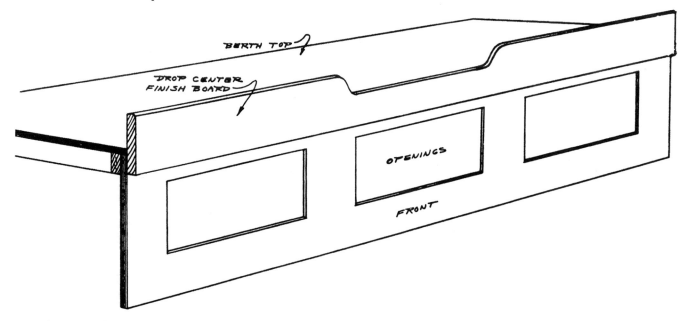

11-13 Berth with a drop center finish board.

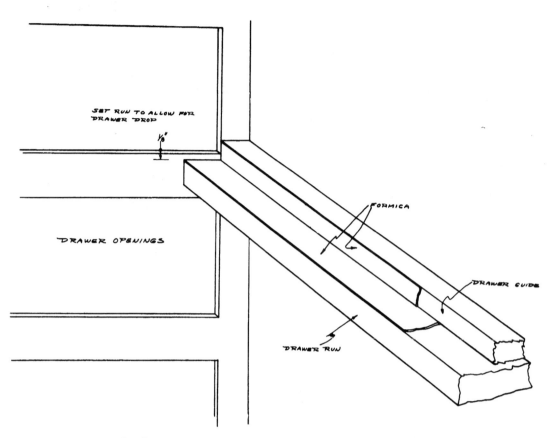

SET RUN TO ALLOW FOR
DRAWER DROP

⅛"

DRAWER OPENINGS

FORMICA

DRAWER GUIDE

DRAWER RUN

11-14   *Drawer run detail.*

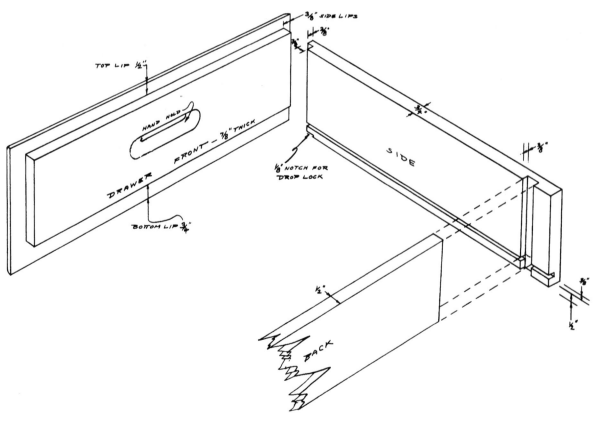

⅜" SIDE LIPS

⅜"

TOP LIP ½"

HAND HOLD

DRAWER FRONT — ⅞" THICK

⅛" NOTCH FOR
DROP LOCK

SIDE

⅜"

BOTTOM LIP ¾"

½"

BACK

⅜"

½"

11-15   *Drawer detail.*

CABIN CEILING

The cabin ceiling should have been milled out as described in Chapter 9 along with the cockpit ceiling. Only the exposed areas of the hull, such as above the berths and countertops and inside the head, should be ceiled. Remember that wood has to breathe, so the less you close off with the ceiling, the better. In some cases boundary cleats will have to be fastened to the hull for the ceiling to land on.

You should always start the ceiling at the sheer clamp and work down the hull. Cut yourself some spacer blocks of ceiling material about 1 inch wide and 4 inches long, place these up against the sheer clamp and tack them to the timbers. Then fit and fasten in the top piece of ceiling against the blocks. Use a 1½-inch chisel to pry up on the lower edge of the ceiling. Do this by tapping the chisel into the planking with your hammer and applying pressure to the ceiling piece with your left hand, while nailing it home with your hammer in your right hand. One-inch "Anchorfast" nails are excellent for this job.

After the ceiling work is completed, pull the nails from the 1-inch by 4-inch spacer blocks along the top of the ceiling, and you will have a 1-inch air space between the ceiling and the sheer clamp.

For a really fine ceiling job, the nailing can be set using your nail set and hammer and then filled with plastic body putty prior to sanding and painting. Also, for looks, don't plane too heavy a vee bead on the edges of the ceiling.

COMPANIONWAY

In most cases, the companionway will be to one side of the engine box or the hatch. Begin by trimming the door opening so it is ⅞ inch wider than the hatch opening on either side as shown in Figure 11-16. The companionway door jambs, usually of mahogany or dry oak, will be similar to the interior jambs, except that they will be a little larger in section—about 1⅞ inches square—or as large as you can mill from 2-inch stock. You will also have to mill out the door stool, companionway coamings, and their inside trim band as well as make up the cabin door and hatch. You will need a pattern for the forward piece of hatch coaming, so get this made first and then mill out all of the other pieces and sand them. Figure 11-21 shows how these pieces should look. Hatch coamings are made from 1¼-inch stock.

Make the door stool longer than the opening so that after milling you can cut off an end about 3 inches long. Take your door jambs and this 3-inch piece of door stool up into the boat. Set the door jambs in place with the hatch partners resting in the box that you cut in the top of each jamb (see Figure 11-12). Use a block and hammer to get the jambs well seated, then set your 3-inch piece of door stool into place at the bottom of the opening. Slide this piece over to one jamb and tick mark the jamb for cutting, then slide over to the other jamb and do the same to that one. Remove the door jambs and square these tick marks across the front and back of the jambs, and mark the rabbet angle as well. Saw off the heels of the jambs to the marks and clean out the rabbet with your sharp, 1½-inch chisel.

The door stool itself can now be fitted and glued in. The door jambs can also be glued and driven into place with your block and hammer. The next step is to cut out relief in the back sides of the door jamb tops to receive the aft ends of the companionway hatch coamings.

Now you can assemble the coaming. The

athwartship piece of coaming is let into each side piece about ½ inch. Cut out these grooves in the side pieces and shape their ends. Then get the proper length of the athwartship piece and cut it to fit. Glue and screw the three pieces of coaming together, driving 2-inch flat-head screws through the side pieces into the athwartship piece.

Fit the assembled coaming in place and measure and mark the length and angle of the aft ends. The length can be marked by measuring from the forward end of the hatch opening to the aft edge of the bulkhead on either side; the angle can be gotten with your bevel gauge. Saw the ends off and fit the coamings to the cutouts in the door jambs.

After fitting the coamings, apply glue and fasten through the door jambs into the coaming ends with 1½-inch #10 flat-head screws. Fasten the hatch coamings down to the beam at the forward end and to the partners at the sides with the proper length screws, which will vary, as the outboard piece is considerably higher than the inboard one. Don't forget to use bedding under the coaming and also to counterbore for the screws so bungs can be used.

The bungs should be glued and tapped in at this point; be careful to keep their grain lined up with that of the piece being bunged. Trim off the bungs with your chisel and sand the companionway for painting or varnishing. A well executed job on this installation is a beautiful sight to see.

Fit the inside finish bands, hollowing their backs for a tight fit and gluing behind their top edges. Fasten them with 1-inch escutcheon pins, setting their heads with your nail set and filling with Duratite wood dough. Keep the top edges of the band down from the top about 1 inch to allow room to lay in a screen.

The door will be a panel type, using ⅜-inch plywood, of mahogany if you prefer, for the panel. The header and stiles should be 1⅜ inches by 3 inches or 3½ inches, and the bottom piece will be 1⅜ inches by 4 inches or 4½ inches. Their inner edges are grooved to receive the panel, and they are connected to each other by mortise and tenon joints. A ¼-inch mahogany dowel, which you will have to make, should be driven through the stiles and tenons while the door is in the clamps drying after it has been glued. The dowels should be set in glue also. After the glue has set up, sand the door and hang it with the proper hinges.

The hatch cover can be made of plywood fitted with edge pieces that extend ⅜ inch below the underside of the hatch cover. Relieve the aft edge piece to allow the door to swing clear.

Edge molding should be made and attached to the bulkhead to cover the raw edge of the trunk cabin roof. This molding will have to be sawn from a wide board; mark it out with your trunk cabin beam mold. It should be about ⅝ inch thick and 2 inches wide. After milling, nose off both top corners and the outside bottom corner with sandpaper. Fit the pieces on either side of the companionway, keeping the top edges ¾ inch above the trunk cabin roof. Cut out dust reliefs at the outboard end of each molding. Then fasten them on with 1¼-inch #10 flat-head screws. The dust reliefs are cut down flush with the cabin roof in a scallop fashion and are about 1½ inches wide.

Bung the screw holes, trim the bungs with a chisel, and sand the molding for painting. This completes our interior joinery.

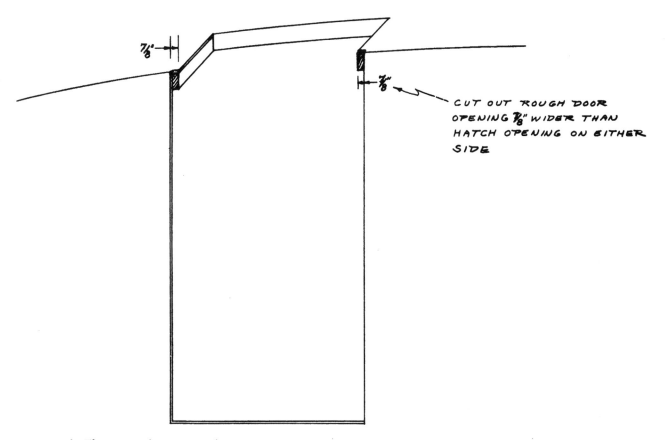

7/8"

CUT OUT ROUGH DOOR
OPENING 7/8" WIDER THAN
HATCH OPENING ON EITHER
SIDE

7/8"

11-16 *The companionway opening.*

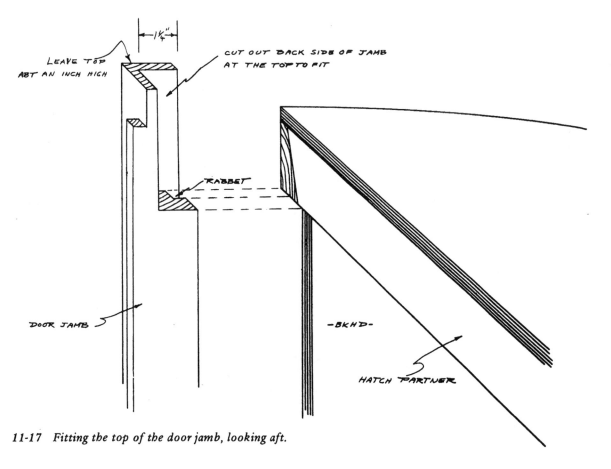

1 1/4"

LEAVE TOP
ABT AN INCH HIGH

CUT OUT BACK SIDE OF JAMB
AT THE TOP TO FIT

RABBET

DOOR JAMB

-BKHD-

HATCH PARTNER

11-17 *Fitting the top of the door jamb, looking aft.*

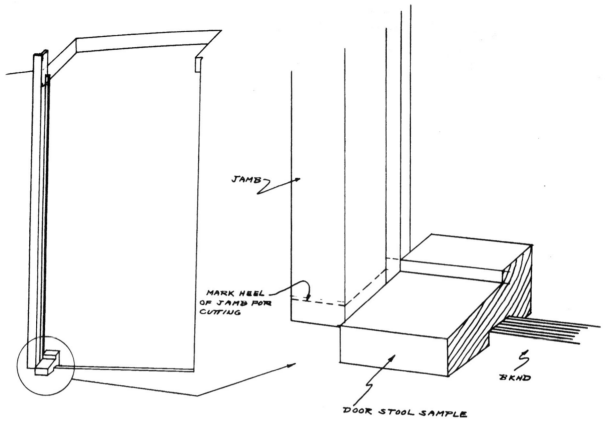

11-18 *Method of marking the heels of the jambs for cutting.*

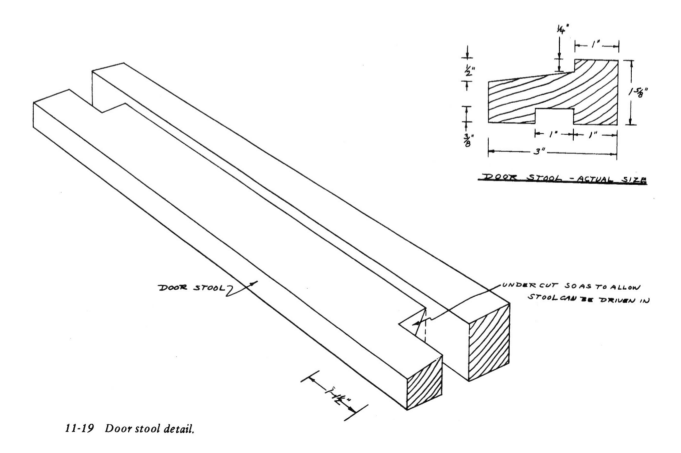

11-19 *Door stool detail.*

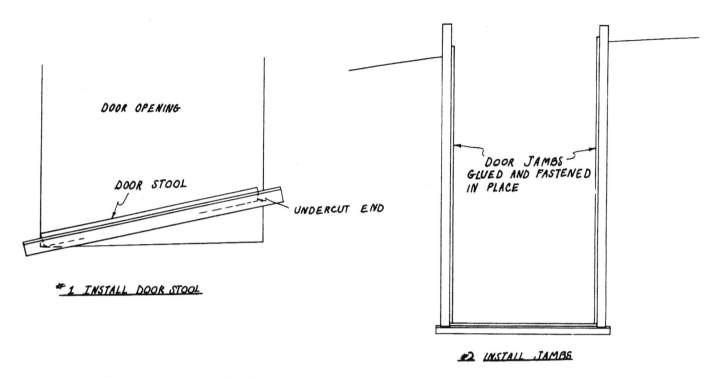

DOOR OPENING

DOOR STOOL

UNDERCUT END

#1 INSTALL DOOR STOOL

DOOR JAMBS
GLUED AND FASTENED
IN PLACE

#2 INSTALL JAMBS

11-20 Installing the door stool and jambs.

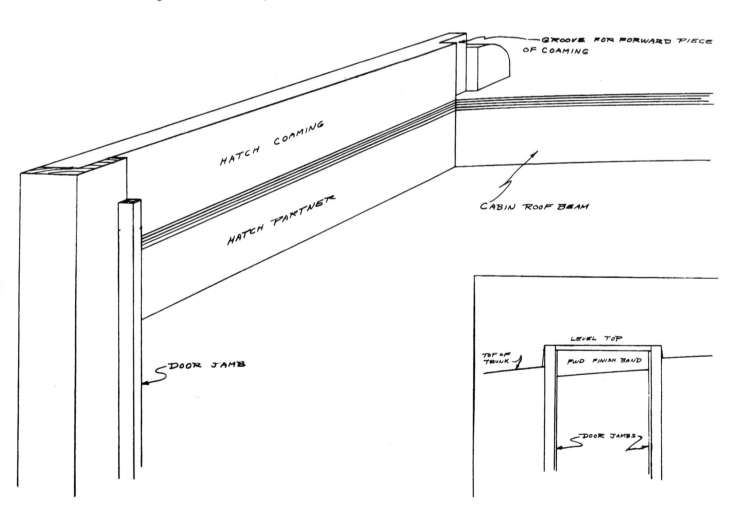

GROOVE FOR FORWARD PIECE
OF COAMING

HATCH COAMING

HATCH PARTNER

CABIN ROOF BEAM

DOOR JAMB

LEVEL TOP

TOP OF
TRUNK

FWD FINISH BAND

DOOR JAMBS

11-21 Companionway hatch coaming detail.

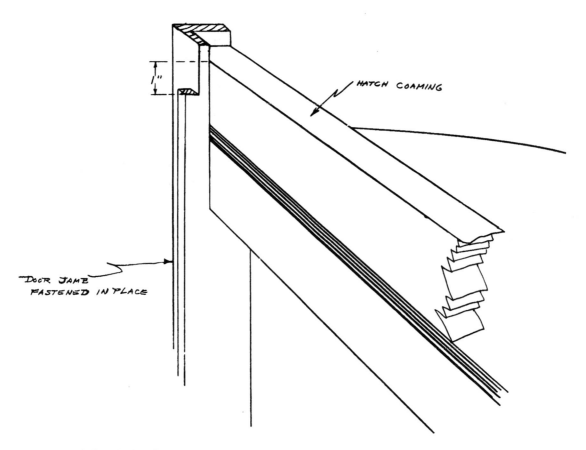

11-22 Fitting the hatch coaming to the door jamb.

HATCH COAMING

DOOR JAMB
FASTENED IN PLACE

1"

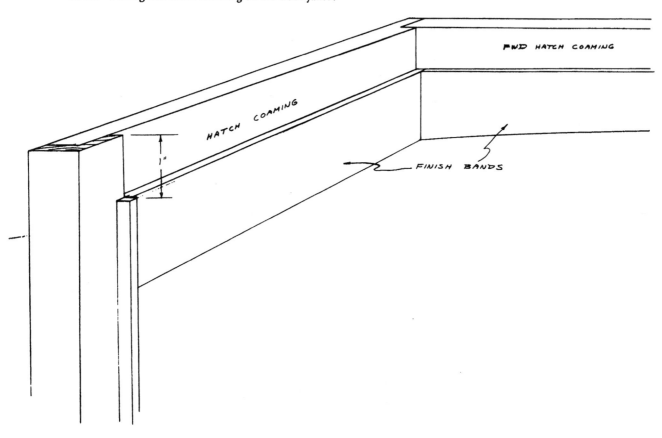

11-23 Companionway finish band detail.

FWD HATCH COAMING

HATCH COAMING

FINISH BANDS

1"

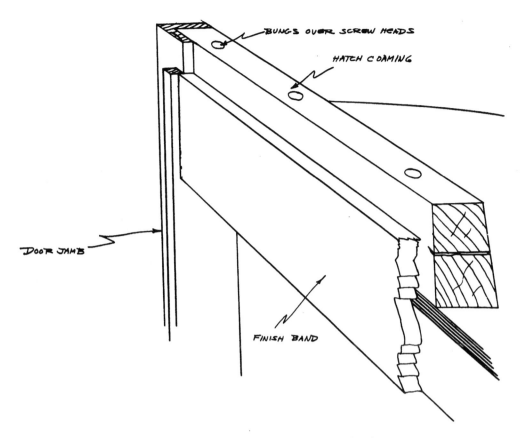

11-24   Fastening the aft end of the coaming to the partner and jamb.

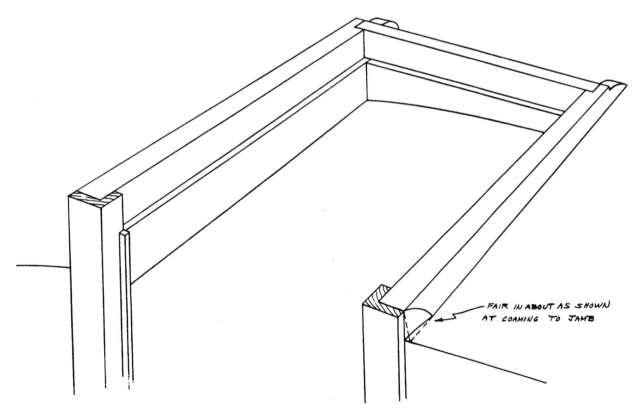

11-25   The finished companionway, ready for the door and hatch.

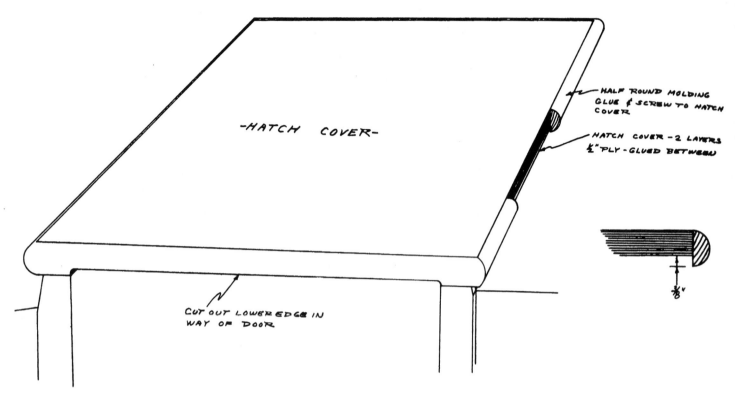

11-26 Companionway hatch detail.

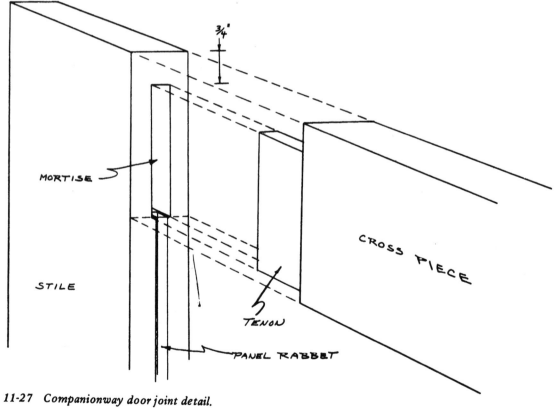

11-27 Companionway door joint detail.

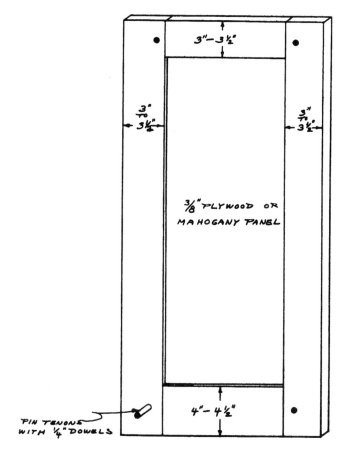

3"–3 ½"

3"
TO
3 ½"

3"
TO
3 ½"

⅜" PLYWOOD OR
MAHOGANY PANEL

PIN TENONS
WITH ¼" DOWELS

4"– 4 ½"

11-28   Approximate sizes for the parts of the panel door.

Chapter 12

Plumbing and Mechanical

The first plumbing project should be putting in the sea cocks and through-hull fittings. A through-hull fitting is used for drainage above the waterline and, together with a sea cock, is also used for hull penetrations below the waterline. We have to install a sea cock for the engine sea water intake, and both an intake and overboard sea cock for the toilet. Also, we have to install through-hull fittings for the sink drain and engine exhaust, both of which are usually above the waterline. If the boat should have a wash-down or fire pump hose arrangement, we will have still another sea cock to install for it.

All the sea cocks and through-hull fittings should be located and the hull bored for them. Before boring the holes, fasten oak backing blocks to the inside of the hull planking. These blocks should be as thick as the planking and about 1½ inches wider than the sea cock or through-hull flanges. They also are to be cut to fit tightly between the timbers.

You can bore the holes with an expansion bit and your bit brace, or, if you have a heavy duty drill and hole saws, you will find the job easier with them.

Once the holes are bored, screw the through-hull in until it bottoms in its sea cock. Measure between the two flanges, those of the sea cock and the through-hull fitting. Check this measurement on all the fittings as you go along installing them. This measurement should be about ⅛ inch shorter than the thickness of the planking, plus that of the backing block. If it is longer, you will have to cut the threaded shank of the through-hull fitting to the proper length with a hacksaw.

Before inserting the through-hull fittings, spread bedding compound under their flanges and wrap a single strand of soft cotton, two turns, around the flange as well. With the through-hull fittings in place, have your helper screw the sea cocks or lock nuts on them from the inside until they are hand tight. Most through-hull fittings have a pair of ears or dogs just inside the hole at the flange for tightening them. You can have a tightening tool made cheaply like the one shown in Figure 12-2. Using an adjustable wrench to turn the tool, it is an easy matter to tighten the through-hull fittings into their sea cocks. The tool will fit through-hull fittings from ¾ inch to 2 inches.

Note: The galley sink overboard line should have a check valve in it so that the sea water cannot enter when the boat is rolling, but the waste water will still drain.

When the sea cocks and through-hull fittings are all installed, you can bore out for the transom exhaust flange hole. You will go through the same motions in installing this piece of hardware as in the through-hull fittings, except for fastening it. The exhaust flange is much larger and does not usually have a lock nut, so, although you can screw fasten the flange to the transom, it is best to bolt it right through both the transom and the backing block. Buck Algonquin exhaust fittings are about the best I have seen other than those custom cast to your own pattern.

Nowadays you can order water-jacketed exhaust loops that fit the engine exhaust manifolds right along with your engine. So all you need to complete the exhaust is a wire-reinforced exhaust hose. Support this hose with a board running along under it and strap both the board and hose to the cockpit beams with leather straps or copper hangers made of flattened ½-inch copper

tubing. Both ends of the exhaust hose should be installed using double hose clamps.

Whenever you wish, the engine can be set into place on the engine beds and shimmed to an initial alignment with the propeller shaft coupling. Align it again after the boat has been in the water for 24 hours (48 hours would be even better) as the hull will swell and change any earlier alignment you might have made. A final alignment should be made about a month later. You can hire an engine mechanic to do the alignment or you can do it yourself by following instructions in the engine installation manual or in any one of a number of publications.

Morse cable controls, such as the twin "S" model, are very popular for engine controls. You will have to mount the control on a levelling pad on top of the trunk cabin roof, then attach the ends of the cables to the shifting lever on the reverse gear and to the throttle on the engine. The opposite ends are attached to the control levers at the control.

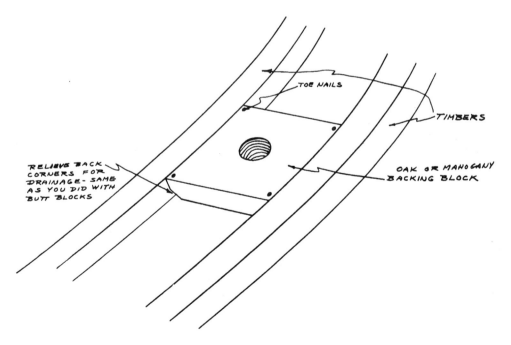

12-1 A through-hull backing block.

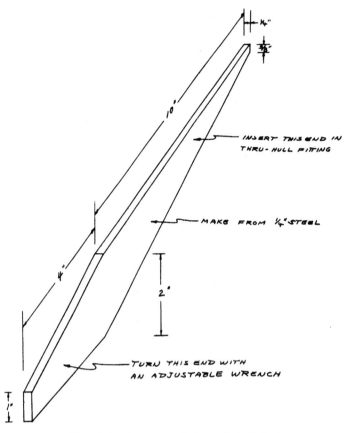

1/4"

3/8"

10"

INSERT THIS END IN
THRU-HULL FITTING

4"

MAKE FROM 1/4" STEEL

2"

TURN THIS END WITH
AN ADJUSTABLE WRENCH

1"

12-2   *A tool for tightening seacock through-hull fittings.*

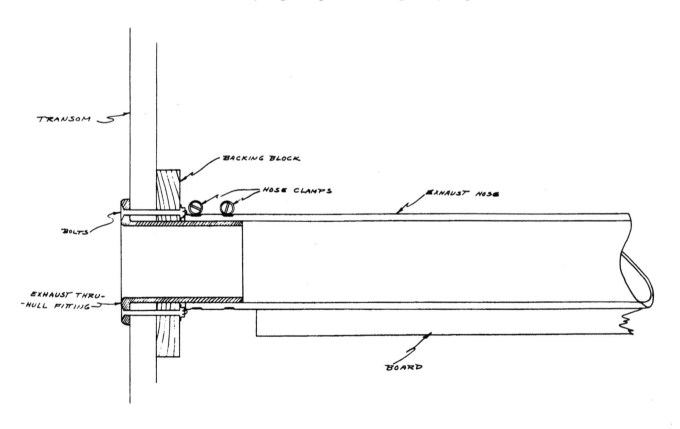

TRANSOM

BACKING BLOCK

HOSE CLAMPS

EXHAUST HOSE

BOLTS

EXHAUST THRU-
HULL FITTING

BOARD

12-3   *Exhaust detail.*

FUEL SYSTEM

Fuel tanks should be constructed to meet Coast Guard recommendations. They should be properly baffled and have a proper fuel feed arrangement. All fuel feed fittings should be on the top of the fuel tank. You can make a copper feed tube that reaches from the top fitting down to within 1 inch of the bottom of the tank. The bottom end of the tube should be fitted with a copper screen, and the upper end should be soldered into a bushing. Insert the tube into the tank and tighten down the bushing using gasket shellac on the threads. This tube should be located in the center of the tank so that when the boat is rolling, it won't lose suction so quickly if the tank is getting low on fuel. There must be a shutoff valve

and filter at the tank and another shutoff valve at the engine. Also, there must be a section of flexible fuel line at the engine. The rest of the fuel line can be copper tubing with double-flared ends for fittings. The fuel fill pipe should not be less than 1½-inch pipe. The fuel tank vent line should not be less than ½-inch tubing. If the tank is mounted under the transom deck, the vent fitting in the top of the tank should be in the center of the tank athwartships. The vent tubing should be coiled twice and go out through the transom as high as possible.

The fuel tank may be located under either the deck or the cockpit and should be mounted on chocks lined with neoprene or rubber straps. Then the tank should be anchored into place with securely fastened posts or braces.

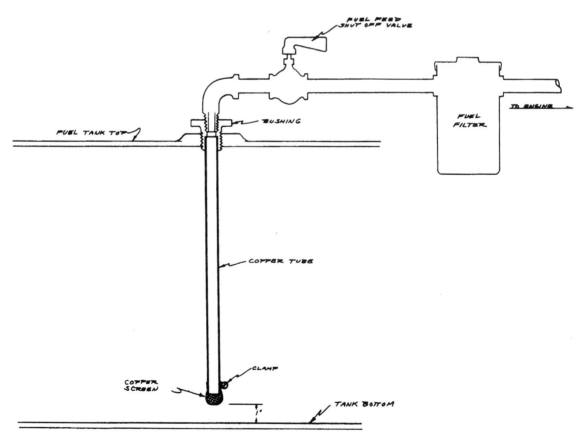

12-4 Fuel tank feed tube detail.

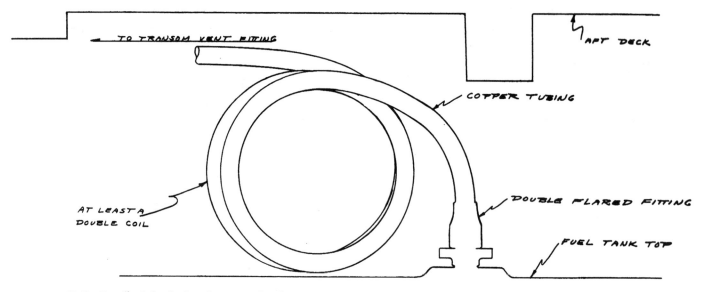

12-5   Detail of the fuel tank vent under the stern or side deck.

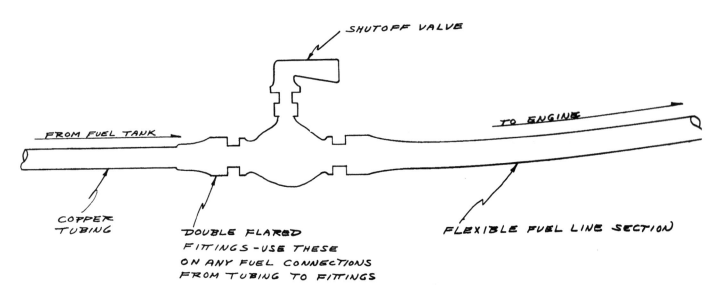

12-6   Detail of fuel feed line at the engine.

STEERING

While there are some boats still using cable or rod type steering, hydraulic steering cannot be equalled. Hydraulic steering is simple to install and has no bearings to maintain; the only mounting is for the helm unit and slave. Bolt the helm unit to the bulkhead and then make an oak block 3 inches thick and about 10 inches wide to mount the slave unit on. It should be long enough to span two floor timbers and can be located by setting the slave in place at the tiller. Lag or drift pin the block to the two floor timbers and bolt the slave to the block. Aeroquip hydraulic hose can be run from the helm to the slave. You can measure the lengths needed and the dealer will cut the fittings and attach them to the hose for you. The hose should be kept as straight as possible, rising as it goes forward from slave to helm. It is a good idea to run these hoses through PVC plastic pipe strapped to the cockpit beams, or clip the hoses on a board fastened to the cockpit beams. After the hydraulic system has been filled and bled, the steering system is ready for work.

Molded fiberglass or bronze rudders are easy to make or obtain. The rudder will have to be fitted with a tiller to suit the hydraulic slave, and the pintle of the rudder will be fitted into a bronze plate set into the skeg and fastened. If the pintle is 1 inch in diameter, it should be long enough to go through the plate and be bored for a ⁵⁄₁₆-inch bronze pin. The pin should be 1½ inches

long, so this means that the hole in the skeg under the bronze plate will also have to be 1½ inches in diameter. The plate should be about ½ inch thick, 2½ inches wide, and 3½ inches long, and be bored and countersunk for #14 screws on all four corners. It should be let into the skeg as shown in Figure 12-9. Put the plate on the pintle and insert the pin. Have your helper remove the nuts and lift the stuffing box up from the horn timber inside the boat. Now shove the rudder shaft up through the horn timber hole and set the bottom of the rudder and the bronze plate into the plate rabbet. Your helper can then replace the stuffing box and tighten the nuts down while you drive the screws into the heel plate. Attach the tiller, pack the stuffing box and pin the clevis from the hydraulic slave to the tiller to complete this hook-up.

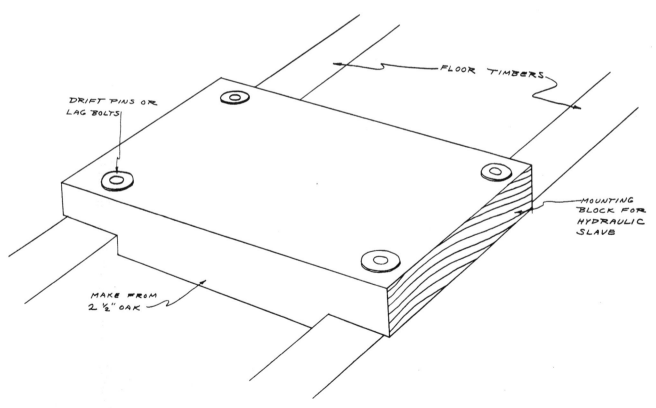

12-7 *Hydraulic slave mounting block.*

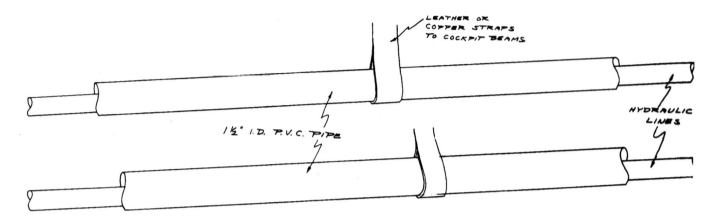

LEATHER OR COPPER STRAPS TO COCKPIT BEAMS

HYDRAULIC LINES

1½" I.D. P.V.C. PIPE

12-8   *Run hydraulic hose through PVC pipe to prevent sags.*

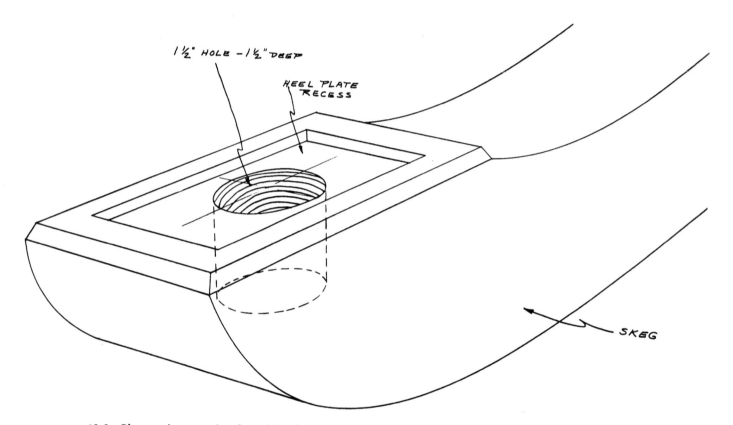

1½" HOLE — 1½" DEEP

HEEL PLATE RECESS

SKEG

12-9   *Skeg ready to receive the rudder pintle.*

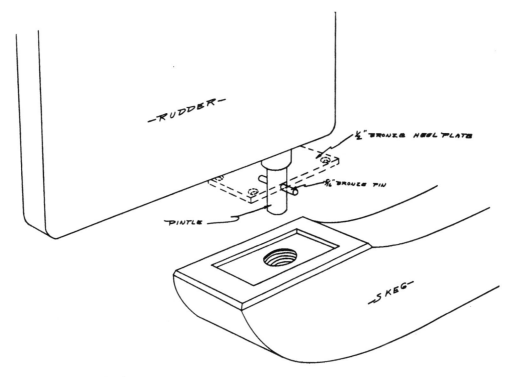

12-10 *Rudder heel plate assembly.*

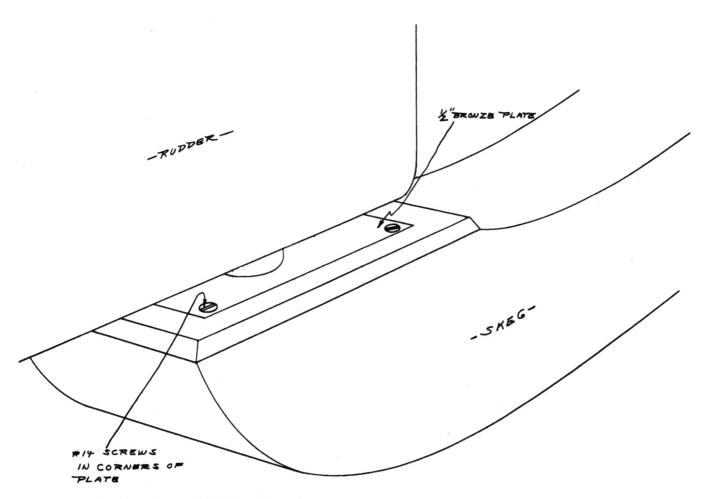

12-11 *Rudder in position and heel plate fastened.*

ELECTRICAL

The wiring should be of top quality and run throughout the boat in a neat manner, using proper clips and fittings. All end lugs should be soldered to the wire ends and the wire size should be sufficient for the service.

All units should be fused and incorporate a positive and ground bus bar system that is easily accessible. When mounting the running lights and horn, be sure to bed them well to prevent moisture from corroding the wires. The engine wiring should be installed as per the engine wiring diagram that will come with your engine handbook.

HARDWARE

Engine space ventilation has to be provided for. It consists of an exhaust vent line extending from low down in the bilge to the cowl vent fitting in the overhead or on the side of the trunk cabin and an intake vent running from an above-deck vent to the opposite side of the engine compartment. There are engine ventilation kits that you can purchase for this application.

Having been blown out of a boat because of the explosion of gasoline fumes, I can tell you that it is a terrible experience. I would strongly advise installing a bilge blower in the exhaust vent line. Also check your bilge often, as mechanical failure, such as leaking fuel lines and valves, is always possible.

The propeller shaft should be 1⅜ inches if it is of monel and 1½ inches if of bronze. Have an expert machinist check it for straightness and machine the taper and keyway outboard as well as fit up and face the coupling on the inboard end.

Metal fittings exposed to seawater, such as the stern bearing, rudder fittings, and shaft should be protected from electrolysis by applying zincs. Since this is covered in various books and articles, I will not go into detail here.

Lobstermen usually want a cage around the propeller to keep their potwarp out of the way. There are several boatyards and machine shops which regularly make them up. A cage is less necessary if the boat is used for pleasure.

Miscellaneous hardware that must be installed are the bow chocks to the buffaloes, quarter cleats or ring bolts aft, and hatch lifts in the cockpit hatches.

Another task is the installation of the brass or stainless steel half oval on the sheer guards and stem face. The half oval should be pre-drilled and countersunk for #10 oval-head screws. Drill and fasten the half oval to the guards and toe rails all around the boat and also to the quarter guards.

If the boat has a faired stemhead, the stem band will have to be looped over and fastened to the back of the stemhead first, then bent down over the stemhead. Pound it to shape with your hammer. When rounding over the forward point of the stemhead, have your helper hold a sledgehammer on the half oval at the top of the stem while you bend and pound the half oval in place against the front of the stem. Fasten off as you work down, and extend the half oval as far as the length will go onto the keel. The boat is now ready for finish painting and launching. As there has been much written on painting I'll only say here that it pays to paint as you go along while pieces are accessible and there isn't much lining off to do.

From the foregoing, you can see that wooden boatbuilding takes time because it is almost totally custom work. Some time ago I built a boat for a man who had a service business. He had stock bins with parts for anything his work force needed to do its work. He seemed to think that my crew was extremely slow and even went so far as to say we were dragging our feet. This stunned me for a moment, as we had a pretty good name for being fast, as well as being neat in our work.

I regained my senses soon enough and said to him, "Suppose you didn't have anything in your shop but iron ore and a foundry, and a customer came in and ordered a complicated piece of machinery with many parts. You would have to make patterns to cast these parts, then machine them all, and assemble them to build this piece of machinery.

"Then and only then, my dear man, could your operation compare with boatbuilding."

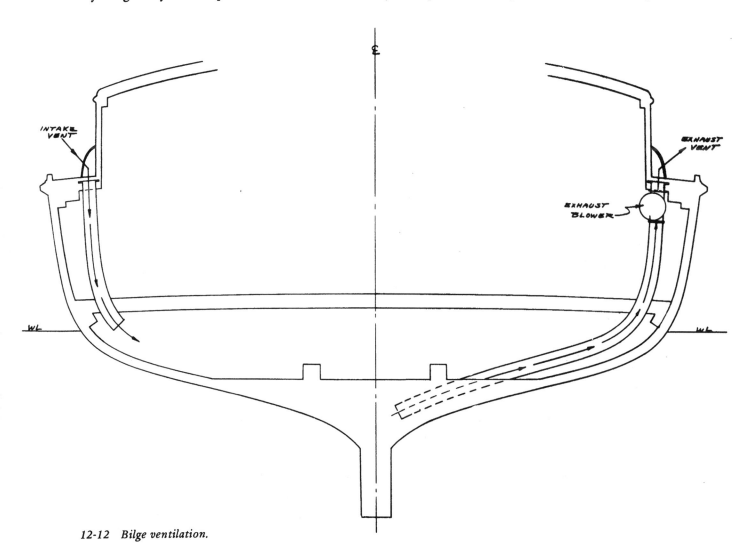

12-12 Bilge ventilation.

Appendix
Tools

Of all craftsmen, a boatbuilder undoubtedly has to have the most complete set of tools, a great many of which are common only to that trade. A number of them are expensive or hard to find, and are acquired over a long period of time. One even has to make many of his own tools. Because the boatbuilder sharpens his edge tools to suit himself, he is often reluctant to loan them. He takes pride in them and keeps them always at his reach, in most cases in a tool box that he has built himself. I have seen some boxes that were so meticulously made and finished that you would actually hesitate to put tools in them for fear they might be scratched. The following are the tools that the builder of wooden boats will find most useful.

LIPPED ADZE

The lipped adze is now one of the most cherished tools in the trade, as it is getting very difficult to find one of the old ones. The Saint John adze was my favorite. It was light in weight and when fitted with a handle made to suit only you, it was a beautifully balanced tool. In building lobsterboats, adzes are used for taking excess wood off the stem face and for fairing in the shaft log and stern post. In expert hands, it can be used to cut a rabbet. Even though you don't use it too often, it is a handy tool.

HAND PLANES

Jointer. You will need one of these iron jointers, which is 21 or 22 inches long. It is used mostly for jointing the edges of planks where its length helps get the edges absolutely straight. I can remember working with my grandfather, William Frost, when the keel pieces came through right off the saw and we would have to traverse plane the saw marks off with our jointers. It was a lot of work, but unnecessary now because these pieces come from the mill all planed.

Jack Plane. The jack plane is about 14 inches long, and is very useful in jointing the edges of curved planks when the jointer, because of its length, won't work. The jack is also used to smooth up cabin beams, and in facing off the guards and rails after sawing. I always prefer the Stanley jack plane for outboard jointing, rather than a wooden jack plane, because I like the weight of it. I'm not discrediting wooden planes in other applications, however, because they are invaluable.

Smooth Plane. The smooth plane is used a great deal for fitting and trimming short lengths of wood, such as in rounding the cabin corner posts. You can plane out an extreme curve with a smooth plane if it is held about 45 degrees to the working edge. And by grinding a curve in the blade, you can hollow or back out guard rails and moldings prior to putting them on the boat. This plane is useful in outboard jointing, because with it you can smooth up concave areas of planking.

Spoke Shaves and Draw Knives. Spoke shaves and draw knives, while not planes in the strict sense of the word, are used for planing and shaping small objects such as mooring bitts, structural knees, and corner molding knees. The draw knife is also useful in bevelling the top edge of the sheer strake, where a great deal of wood must be removed.

Rabbet Plane. The rabbet plane is indispensable, as you use it to smooth up planking rabbets, corner posts, etc., as well as for trimming the butts when planking.

Curved Bottom Wooden Hollowing Plane. This plane is used for backing out planks at the turn of the bilge and other areas where the plank must be hollowed for a good fit against the timbers. These planes are about 10 inches long with a blade width of about 1¾ to 2 inches. A wooden smooth plane of about the same dimensions can be reworked to make a hollowing plane. Some builders have a complete set of wooden planes from the jointer on down to smooth, rabbet, and molding planes. It would be very difficult to buy such a set today, as wooden planes have

become collectors' items.

Electric Jointer Hand Plane. The electric jointer hand plane has many uses in boatbuilding, and is a great time saver. If you get an extra set of blades, you can grind a curve in them for hollowing or backing out your planks. They are great for trimming off any excess wood, such as in chamfering, facing off the stem, and even in outboard jointing. They also come in handy for jointing the keel scarfs and other large splices and in trimming the sheer. My plane is a Skil, Model 100. I like its balance and feel, but it is not too different from the Stanley hand jointer.

CHISELS

The chisel most used is the 1½ to 2 inch butt chisel, with which the rabbet cutting is almost entirely done. It is also heavy enough to chip off bungs or to do light paring work, and is excellent for cutting out the timber boxes in the keel. However, you will still need a full set of butt chisels for other jobs on the boat. A 3- or 3½-inch slick is also desirable and very handy if one can be found.

SAWS

Portable Electric Hand Saw. These saws have been a Godsend since they first appeared on the scene. By nailing on a batten for the shoe to run against, or using the machine freehand, you can saw planking, sheer clamps, and rough-cut excess wood off any heavy piece so you can handle it on the bandsaw. Use a portable hand saw to saw out your timbers, and you can follow the grain so they will bend nicely after steaming. This saw takes the place of your hand rip saw, and does the work faster and easier.

Handsaws. You will need at least two handsaws, but three would be better. The D-23 Disston 26-inch, 10-point crosscut saw seems to be the most popular. It is good to have two of these, and when filing or having them filed, it is a good practice to rake the teeth a little more than normal, as they will then cut faster in oak or semi-dry wood. The third saw should be a 20-inch 11-point one for fine work. A backsaw is better for cutting molding or joiner bulkhead cap joints, but the work can be done with your 20-inch saw.

Saber Saw. A power saber saw is very handy as you can stab it through wood without drilling to saw holes; it is excellent for cutting out the instrument panel and window openings, and in making patterns for interior joinery. It is most amazing what this little tool can do, and with proper blades it is almost like having a portable bandsaw.

DRILLS

Electric Drill, ¼- or ⅜-inch. The electric drill plays a major role in boatbuilding. Counterboring or other light drilling is done with this size drill. It will even bore ⅜- or ½-inch holes through heavy oak, if barefoot ship augers are used. Some models are reversible and have variable speed control. Some are also made in a screwdriver version, which I use extensively. A ¼- or ⅜-inch drill can be used as a sander when fitted with the 3M 9-inch flexible sanding pad. A very smooth surface can be obtained by using fine sandpaper on such a pad if the machine is carefully held.

Electric Drill, ½-inch. The reversible ½-inch electric drill is the tool for any heavy boring jobs that you may have, such as boring for the keel bolts. It can be used with a boring bar for boring for the stern bearing and

inside stuffing box.

As far as boring goes, speed bits will do in most cases, and you will need a number of them in sizes from ¼ inch to 1½ inches. For the especially long bores, you will need ship augers (either spur or barefoot), or railroad bits, which if need be can be lengthened by welding an extension on their shanks.

Notes on Drilling

Fuller or Greenlee counterbores are used with electric drills to bore for screw fastenings in one operation. They come in various sizes and may be adjusted for length of the screw and depth of the counterbore. Best results are obtained if taper drills are used as then the hole closely matches the shape of the screw for its entire length.

In addition to the counterbores, a set of twist drills is useful. These are a standard "hardware store" item and a series graduated by 1/32-inch increments would not be too expensive. They are used in boring for untapered fastenings, such as small bolts, nails, and the shanks of screws. You can also grind these to a taper for use with counterbores if you hold your electric drill, with one of them spinning in it, against the wheel of your bench grinder. This gets the basic shape, after which you will need to individually relieve each flute a bit so it will cut. Taper drills made this way are of course cruder than store-bought ones, but they are much less expensive.

Notes on Boring

In boring with a ship auger you will have to keep pulling back on the drill every few inches to clear the auger of chips. If you draw the auger nearly out of the hole after it bores 4 to 6 inches of wood, it will usually stay free and cut well. You will get the feel of it after boring a couple of holes.

Ship augers are made both with spurs (lead screws) and without. Barefoot augers, as the latter type are called, are easier to control but need a certain amount of push to make them cut. They are used when the direction of the hole is critical, as without a lead screw they don't tend to take off and follow the grain.

Bit Braces. Even though electric screwdrivers are used extensively, you will still need your bit brace for a number of jobs. For example, in fastening a delicate piece of finish, you wouldn't dare use an electric screwdriver, because if you slipped, it would ruin your work. You will also need a bit brace when putting in shutter planks, so you can gradually work the plank into place by alternately hitting it and taking up on the screws.

SANDERS

Vibrator. The Porter-Cable (Rockwell Co.) has a dual action (orbital or straight line) vibrator sanding machine that has worked out well in boatbuilding. This machine sands around curves that you will encounter in sanding the hull. It also does a fine job on flat work.

Disc. In recent years, we have been using a flexible-back sanding disc pad in ¼-inch electric drills. This disc comes in 7 and 9 inch diameters and has a semi-stiff foam pad on its base. It does a remarkable job, and is used extensively around boatyards now.

SHARPENING TOOLS

Sharp tools are a pleasure to use, and are much more easily controlled than dull ones. There should never be a reason for using dull tools. They are the mark of the unskilled worker. The grinding of plane blades, chisels, and similar edge tools should be performed carefully, so they don't overheat and lose their temper. An electric bench grinder is usually used with a 40 to 50-grit wheel. Hold your blade at the proper angle and work it back and forth evenly until sparks from the grinding wheel flow over the top edge of your blade. When you see this happening, dip the blade into a can of water to cool it, and feel for a wire edge on the flat side of the blade edge. If you can feel this wire edge, you are ready for the whetstones. Be careful not to burn the blade when grinding it. If you have a lot to grind, dip the blade into the water often.

For whetting, you should have a fine India stone and a hard Arkansas stone. These should be about ¾ inch by 2 inches by 6 or 7 inches in size. I keep mine in a can of kerosene, as this keeps them clean and very effective. Starting with the India stone, grip the blade firmly in your right hand with your forefinger pressing down on the center of the blade near the edge. Now press down on your forefinger and the blade with the first three fingers of the left hand. Stroke the full length of stone, exerting pressure as you push away from you and easing up as you draw back. The downward pressure should be exerted by the left hand, and the back and forth motion by the right hand. Use five or six strokes on the bevel side, then turn the blade over and press it flat on the stone for a few strokes. Repeat this process until the wire edge disappears, then give the blade a few strokes on the hard Arkansas stone. You cannot get a better edge than this.

A note on sharpening plane blades: It is a good practice to either grind off their corners or whet them off on the India stone to prevent them from digging into your work when planing.

Remember to keep your tools sharp always. It not only reduces your work greatly, but I believe sharp tools are much safer than dull ones. I have never been cut with a sharp tool.

CAULKING WHEELS AND IRONS

As far as I know, these may still be purchased at marine supply houses, though I understand they are hard to find in some areas.

HAMMERS

I think each individual has his own feel for a hammer. Look for a 16- or 20-ounce model that hangs well in your hand.

A top maul or small sledge hammer of about five pounds is needed for driving through-bolts or drift pins.

A two pound striking or blacksmith's hammer is also very useful for certain operations, such as driving home the shutter plank.

Glossary

BATTEN

Usually a long flexible piece of wood used to draw a fair line around several points. Often called a fairing batten. There are also lining battens, which are used in planking a hull to help get the plank edges fair and "eye sweet." Battens are usually made from a uniform-grained softwood such as pine, mahogany, or fir, although green (unseasoned) oak may be used for really tight bends. There is also a spiling batten, so called, which is really a thin board wide enough so as not to bend or "edge set" when taking a spiling.

BEAM MOLD

A pattern, usually made of pine or mahogany and a little longer than the beam of the boat, for marking out the deck beams, trimming the sheer, and positioning the stud beams. Beam molds are also made for the cabin top and pilothouse roof beams.

BED

To set a piece of wood, metal, or glass in bedding compound before fastening it into place. Bedding compound is a non-drying pasty substance that prevents the entrance of water. Bed also refers to the foundation for the engine or any other major mechanical device.

BEVEL

The slant of a surface or line when it is not at right angles or square.

BEVEL GAUGE

A device for measuring the amount of bevel and for marking it onto a surface. It consists of a stock and a tongue, and may be of wood, metal, or a combination of the two.

BORE

To make a circular hole using an auger or bit. Boring usually applies to large holes, whereas drilling describes small ones.

BUNG

A wooden plug used to fill counterbored holes over the heads of fastenings. Although of the same shape as a dowel, its grain runs across, rather than with, the centerline, so that if put in correctly, the grain of the bung runs the same way as that of the piece it is driven into. To make them watertight and to hold them in place, bungs are usually set in glue, thick paint, or varnish. Bungs are sometimes driven into a bored hole to provide a center for the spur of a counterbore bit.

BUTT LOG

A log from the lower end, or butt, of a tree. Butt logs are generally free of branches and the clearest and best lumber comes from them.

GLOSSARY

CARLIN
A fore and aft piece of deck framing that runs along the inboard edge of the side decks. It is also the clamp to which trunk cabin roof beams are fastened.

CHALK LINE
A string covered with colored chalk that, when stretched taut between two points and snapped, marks a straight line in chalk dust.

COMPASS
A device having a pencil attached to one of its legs and a metal point to the other and used to draw circles or to measure and transfer distances from one surface to another. It is sometimes called a pencil compass to differentiate it from a magnetic one.

COUNTERBORE
A cylindrical hole in which the head of a bolt, screw, or other fastening is recessed and which is usually plugged with a bung. The tool used to make this hole is also called a counterbore, and the word is used as a verb to describe the operation of boring the hole.

CROSS SPALL
A board that ties the upper halves of a mold together.

CROWN
The convex curve of a deck or a cabin top that allows the water to run off. Also called camber.

DADO
A group of specially shaped blades for a circular saw that, when mounted together. will form a groove in a piece of wood as it is passed over them.

DECLIVITY BOARD
A wooden wedge that is made up and held against or glued onto a spirit level to produce a desired departure from plumb and level readings. The amount of tumblehome can be set by the use of a declivity board. This device is always needed if the boat is set up on an inclined launching ways so that the waterline slopes downhill.

DIVIDERS
Same as a compass but with metal points in both of its legs.

DRIFT OR DRIFT PIN
A length of round metal bar used as a nail to hold two pieces of wood together. A washer or clench ring is sometimes placed under its upper end to form a head.

DRILL
To make a hole using a twist drill; also short for the twist drill itself.

DOOR CLAMP
A sliding bar clamp (although sometimes a length of pipe is used in place of the bar) that is used to span and clamp wide pieces.

FLITCH
A board or timber that has been sided to thickness or sawn out on two sides only and has the bark still left on its edges. Oak and cedar usually come this way so that any natural sweep or curve can be used to advantage. Live edge, round edge, and through and through mean the same thing.

FLOOR
The floor of the mold loft where the boat's lines are laid down full size.

FLOOR TIMBER
A heavy plank on edge running athwartships and fitted to the bottom of the boat to strengthen it.

FRAME
The skeleton of the boat or a portion of it, such as the deck frame.

GREEN WOOD
Wood which is freshly cut and still has a high moisture content; unseasoned wood.

HEAD
A marine toilet.

HOOD END	The forward end of a plank where it fits into the rabbet.
HOUNDING	Sometimes called horning, it is the process of measuring used to square a member to the boat's centerline. The most common application is when diagonal measurements from the stem to the port and starboard sides of a mold are equalized, at which time the mold is said to be hounded or horned into position.
JOINING	The act of attaching one piece to another.
JOINT	The place where two pieces are joined.
JOINTING	The act of planing a straight edge on a piece of wood.
JOINTER	A long-soled hand-plane for truing up the edge of a piece of wood; also a stationary power tool with a long bed and revolving cutters for doing the same thing. There are also portable power planes, combining the features of the above tools, which are commonly called electric hand jointers.
LAYDOWN	The lofting; the full size lines of the boat that are drawn up and faired before construction commences. The molds and patterns are "picked off" the laydown.
LIVE EDGE	See flitch.
MORTISE	The socket or female part of a mortise and tenon joint.
PARTNER	A fore and aft piece of framing that makes up the boundary of a hatch. In sailing vessels, partner is that part of the deck which is penetrated by the mast.
RABBET	An incision in the stem, keel, or other member to allow an adjoining piece to lay flush against it.
RAKE	Inclination, usually aft, from vertical.
ROUND OF THE BILGE	Also called the turn of the bilge, it is the rounding area just below the waterline where the topsides join the bottom of a round-bilged boat.
SCRIBE	To scratch a line into a piece of wood as in scribing the waterline; also to mark one piece for fitting against another by the use of dividers. The latter is sometimes called scribing down or scribing in a piece, since the dividers are usually held either vertically or horizontally.
SHAFT LOG	A part of the boat's keel assembly that is put in with its grain lined up with that of the propeller shaft and with the shaft stuffing box attached to its inboard end. Often the shaft log is made up in two halves for ease in shaping the shaft hole.
SPILE	To determine the boundary shape of a piece by the use of an intermediate template called a spiling board or batten. Rather than fitting an exact pattern, the rough-fitting spiling batten is held in position and marked at a constant (normally an inch or less) distance in from the desired boundary, after which the batten is removed and placed on the piece to be cut. That piece is marked by measuring out from the line on the batten by the same amount as was measured in, or just reversing the procedure used to mark the batten. Spiling is used to determine the cutting lines for planking, and with practice it is about as accurate as making a pattern, although much faster and less wasteful of material. The technique for spiling planks is pretty much covered in this book,

but there are a number of variations, some of which are described in other boatbuilding texts.

SPIRIT LEVEL	A device for establishing a horizontal or vertical line by means of centering a bubble in a liquid-filled tube. It is often simply called a level.
SPLINE	A narrow strip of wood fitted in a groove between two pieces of wood to make the seam watertight. Splines are always used in split shaft logs.
SQUARE	At right angles; also an implement for drawing lines at 90 degrees to each other.
SPUR	The lead screw of a wood bit or ship auger.
STEM BAND	A protective strip of metal, half oval or half round in section, which is attached to the face of the stem.
STOP JOINT	The joint at the nib end of a scarf between two pieces of wood.
STOPWATER	A softwood dowel that is driven across the grain in the way of a joint to keep the water from leaking past it.
STRAKE	A hull plank that runs continuously from bow to stern.
STUD BEAM	One of the many short deck beams that support the side deck.
SWEEP	A piece of flitch-sawn wood having a natural curve to it.
STOCK	The unshaped wood from which the boat is built.
SOLE	The floor of the cabin.
TENON	The male part of a mortise and tenon joint.
TIMBER	A rib or a frame running from the keel to the rail to which the planking is fastened. Timbers in a boat are usually of oak, which holds fastenings well and bends into position with steaming.
TIMBER HEAD	The top or upper end of a timber.
TIMBER HEEL	The opposite end of a timber from its head.
TIMBER HEEL BOXES	The sockets cut into the keel into which the heels of the timbers are fitted and fastened.
WOOD END	The end of a planking strake at the extreme aft edge of the transom. The wood end is exposed on most powerboats and is trimmed and sanded to finish so it is flush with the transom planking.

A 36-Foot Lobster Boat

LOA	36'4½"	Designed by Royal Lowell	
DWL	34'8"	Built by Bruce Cunningham	
Beam	11'6"	Owned by Capt. Wyatt Albertson	
Draft	3'7"		

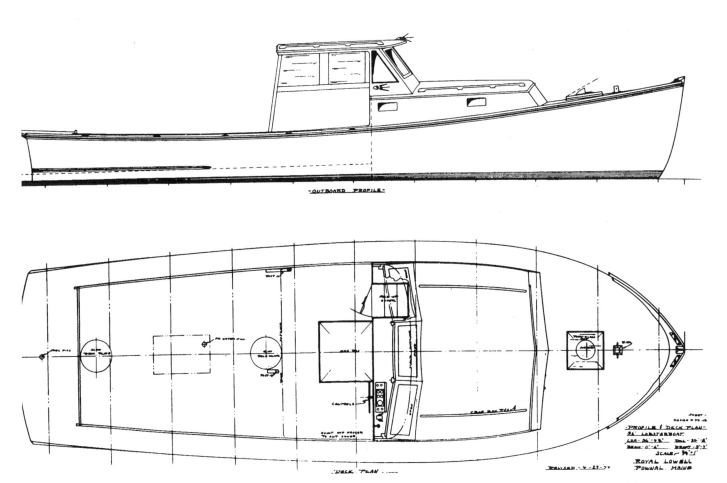

"OUTBOARD PROFILE"

"DECK PLAN"

PROFILE & DECK PLAN
36' LOBSTERBOAT
LOA - 36'-9½"   DEPTH - 5'-6"
BEAM - 11'-6"   DRAFT - 3'-3"
SCALE - ¾" = 1'
ROYAL LOWELL
POWNAL, MAINE

181

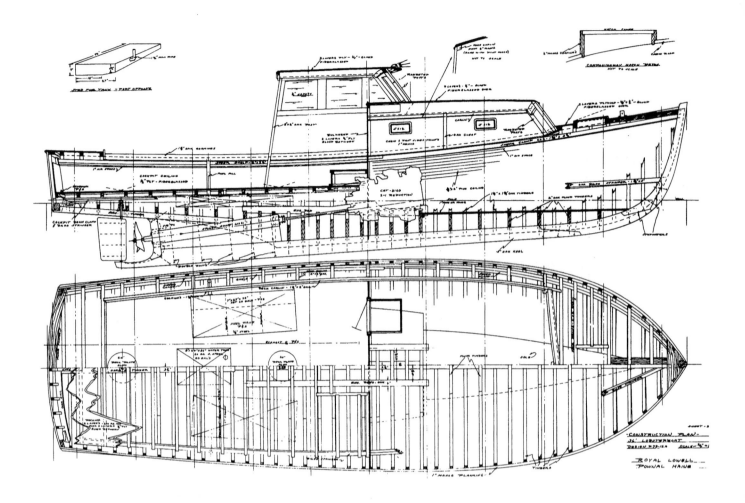

182

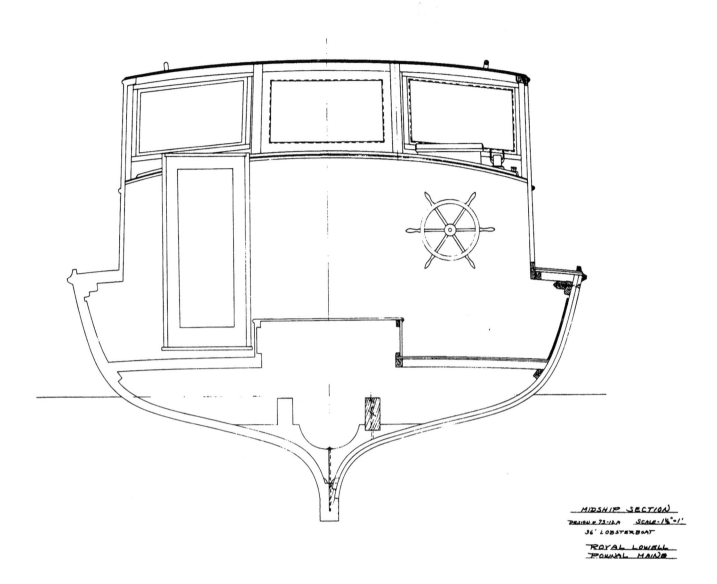

MIDSHIP SECTION

DESIGN # 73-12A   SCALE-1½"=1'
36' LOBSTERBOAT

ROYAL LOWELL
POWNAL MAINE

183

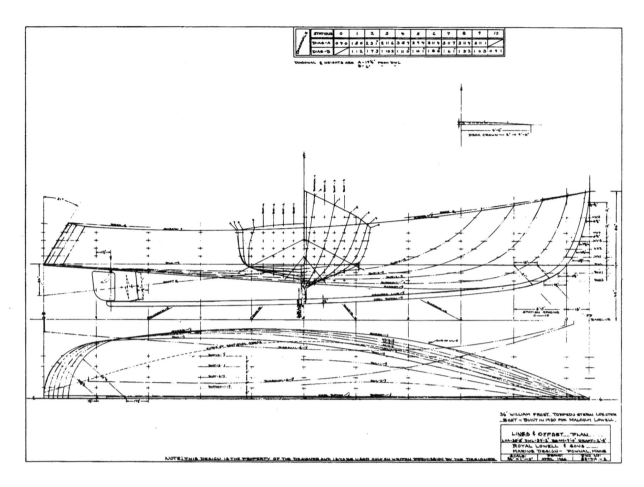

36-Foot Torpedo Stern Lobsterboat

L.O.A.	35'-8"
D.W.L.	34'-2"
Beam	9'-0"
Draft	2'-8"

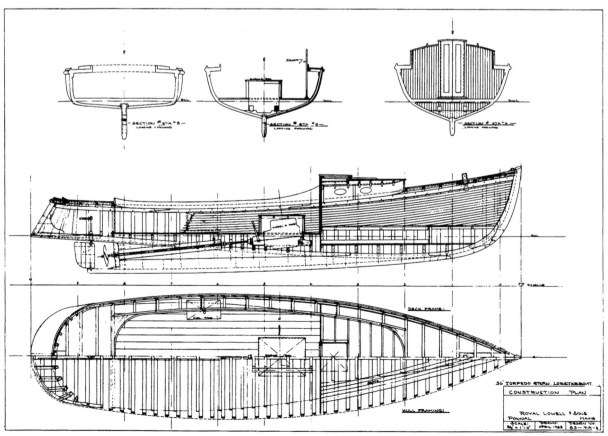

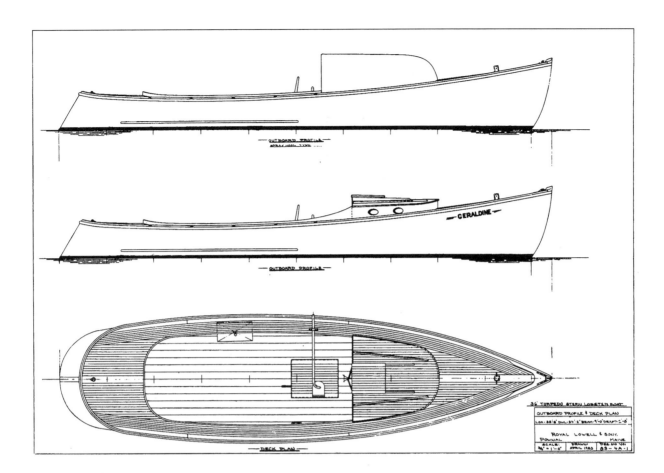

36' TORPEDO STERN LOBSTER BOAT

OUTBOARD PROFILE & DECK PLAN		
LOA·36'·8' DWL·34·2" BEAM·9'·0" DRAFT·2'·0"		
ROYAL LOWELL & SON.		
POWNAL		MAINE.
SCALE: ¾" = 1'-0"	DRAWN: APRIL 1983	DES. NO. 83-4A-1

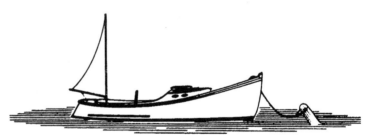

THE JONESPORT - BEALS ISLAND
Torpedo Stern Lobsterboat

These boats were built at a time when small engines were becoming more available, and the transition from small sailing workboats to power launches was taking effect.

This particular boat was designed, and built by William Frost for Malcolm Lowell in 1930. However, there were other versions of the Torpedo stern lobsterboats built by Maurice Dow, and George Brown. All of these boats were graceful of lines, and performed well with a small amount of power. Some of them were built with bent front trunk cabins, while others were open boats that were fitted with canvas spray hoods.

The Hartford five and ten single cylinder engine, and the Myannis, as well as a few other one lungers were used as the engines for these boats. The Model " A " Ford 4 cylinder and the Red Wing 4 cylinder engine were also used to power these boats.

Royal Lowell

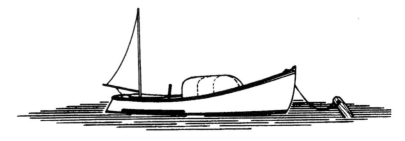

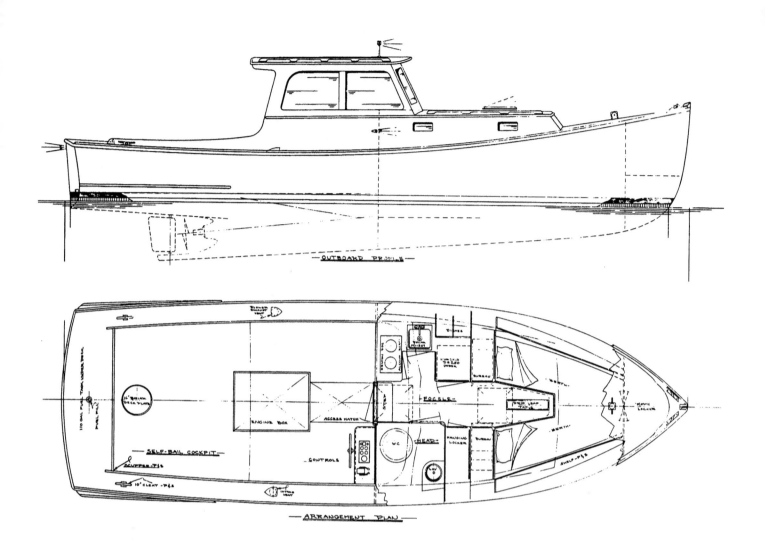

32-Foot Sport Cruiser
Design Based on Holland 32-Foot Fiberglas Model

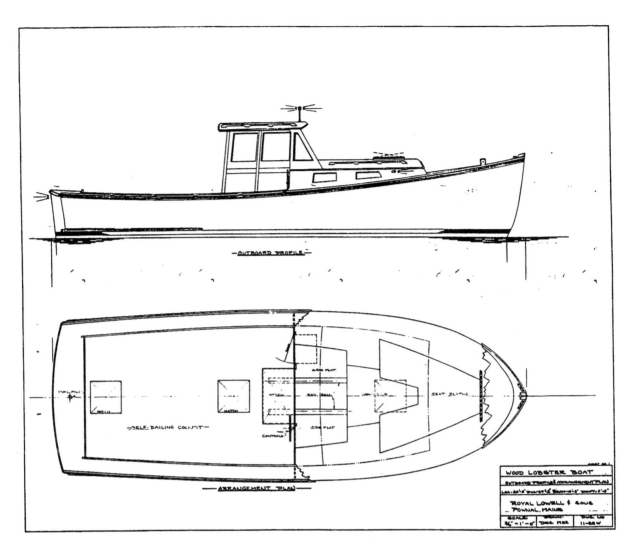

— ARRANGEMENT PLAN —

WOOD LOBSTER BOAT
OUTBOARD PROFILE & ARRANGEMENT PLAN
LOA 30'-8" DWL 29'-2" BEAM 10'-8" DRAFT 3'-5"
ROYAL LOWELL & SONS
POWNAL, MAINE
SCALE ¾"=1'-0" DEC 1982 DWG NO. 11-82W

30-Foot Lobster Boat
Last Model Designed and Built by Royal Lowell
in the Tradition of the Down East Masterbuilders

L.O.A.	30'-8"
D.W.L.	29'-2"
Beam	10'-8"
Draft	3'-5"

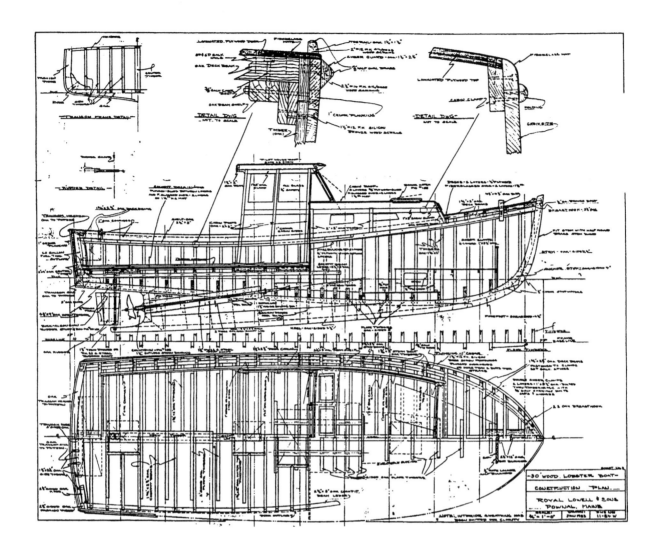

30' WOOD LOBSTER BOAT
CONSTRUCTION PLAN
ROYAL LOWELL & SONS
POWNAL, MAINE

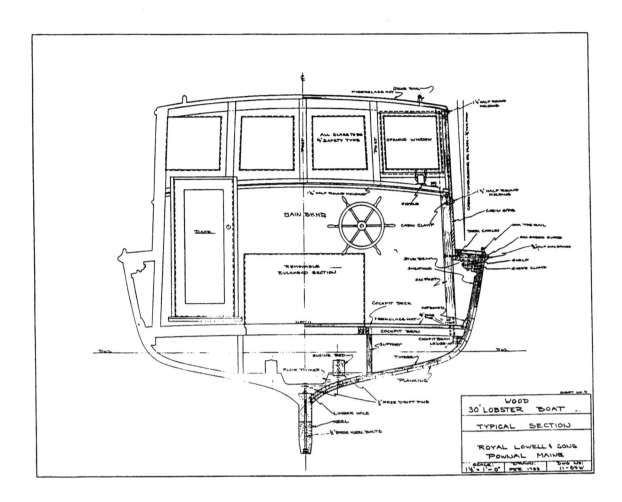

GRAB RAIL

FIBERGLASS MAT

1½" HALF ROUND MOLDING

ALL GLASS TO BE
¼" SAFETY TYPE

POST

OPENING WINDOW

1½" HALF ROUND MOLDING

MAIN BKHD

1½" HALF ROUND MOLDING

FIDDLE

CABIN CLAMP

CABIN SIDE

DOOR

DECK CARLIN

OAK THE RAIL

OAK CHEEK GUARD

½" HALF OAK BRASS

STUD BEAM

SHELF

SHEATHING

SHEER CLAMP

OAK POST

REMOVABLE
BULKHEAD SECTION

COCKPIT DECK

NIBBOARD

FIBERGLASS MAT

WIRE

COCKPIT BEAM

COCKPIT BEAM
LEDGE ½"

HATCH

DWL

ENGINE BED

SUPPORT

TIMBER

DWL

FLOOR TIMBER

PLANKING

½" WIRE DRIFT PINS

LIMBER HOLE

KEEL

½" BRASS KEEL BOLTS

	SHEET NO. 4
WOOD	
30' LOBSTER BOAT	
TYPICAL SECTION	
ROYAL LOWELL & SONS	
POWNAL MAINE	
SCALE: 1½"=1'-0"	DRAWN: FEB 1983	DWG NO: 11-84W

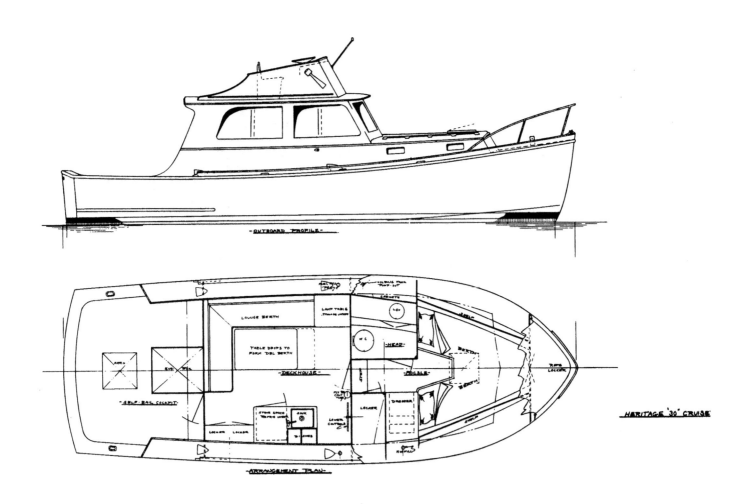

Cruiser Version of 30-Footer
Based on 30-Foot Fiberglas Hull Designed and
Built to Cruise New England Waters

L.O.A.	29'-9"
D.W.L.	28'-4"
Beam	10'-6"
Draft	2'-11"

Over Fifty Complete Full-sized Construction Plans are Available From:
William Lowell, 14 Osborn Street, Lisbon, Maine 04250-6643 207 353-9503

Designs of Royal Lowell

16' Peapod... LOA 16' - 1/2″ DWL 14' - 10″ Beam 4' - 6″ Draft 0' - 10 1/2″... Plan #40

18' Vee-Bottom... LOA 18' - 0″ DWL 16' - 8″ Beam 6' - 4 1/2″ Draft 1' - 6″... Plan #67

18' Round Bilge... LOA 18' - 3″ DWL 17' - 1 1/2″ Beam 6' - 6″ Draft 1' - 0″... Plan #58

18' Round Bilge Open Launch... LOA 18' - 5 1/2″ DWL 17' - 4″ Beam 7' - 10 1/2″ Draft 2' - 3″... Plan #38

22' Round Bilge Fiberglass Model... LOA 21' - 7 1/2″ DWL 20' - 2″ Beam 7' - 9 1/2″ Draft 1' - 4 1/2″... Plan #18

22' Round Bilge Wood Model... LOA 22' - 1 1/2″ DWL 20' - 2″ Beam 7' - 9 1/2″ Draft 1' - 9″... Plan #6

26' Round Bilge Fiberglass Model... LOA 25' - 5 1/2″ DWL 24' - 2″ Beam 9' - 8″ Draft 2' - 9″... Plan #57

26' Sportfisherman Vee-Bottom Wood I.O. Model... LOA 25' - 5 1/2″ DWL 22' - 6″ Beam 7' - 11″ Draft 2' - 1″... Plan #11

26' Vee-Bottom Fiberglass Model... LOA 25' - 7″ DWL 21' - 11 1/2″ Beam 8' - 0″ Draft 2' - 5″... Plan #32

26' Sportfisherman Vee-Bottom Fiberglass Model... LOA 25' - 7″ DWL 22' - 6″ Beam 8' - 6″ Draft 2'- 10″... Plan #36

27' Round Bilge Fiberglass Model... LOA 26' - 11″ DWL 25' - 0″ Beam 9' - 4″ Draft 3' - 0″... Plan #30

28' Round Bilge Fiberglass Model... LOA 27' - 10″ DWL 26' - 7 1/2″ Beam 10' - 1″ Draft 2' - 11″... Plan #60

29' Sport Cruiser - Bass Boat Vee-Bottom Wood Model... LOA 29' - 1″ DWL 26' - 8″ Beam 10' - 4″ Draft 2' - 8″... Plan #47

30' Round Bilge Fiberglass Model... LOA 29' - 9″ DWL 28' - 4″ Beam 10' - 6″ Draft 2' - 11″... Plan #4

30' Round Bilge Wood Lobsterboat, The Royal... LOA 30' - 8″ DWL 29' - 2″ Beam 10' - 8″ Draft 3' - 5″... Plan #35

30' Round Bilge Fiberglass Model... LOA 30' - 8″ DWL 29' - 2″ Beam 10' - 8″ Draft 3'- 5″... Plan #34

31' Round Bilge Fiberglass Model... LOA 30'- 8″ DWL 29' - 2″ Beam 11' - 6″ Draft 3' - 0″... Plan #70

31' Vee-Bottom Fiberglass Clamboat... LOA 31' - 0″ DWL 29' - 2″ Beam 10' - 0″ Draft 2' - 4″... Plan #A

31' Vee-Bottom Fiberglass Model... LOA 31' - 4 1/2″ DWL 29' - 2″ Beam 11' - 2″ Draft 3' - 4″... Plan #28

32' Round Bilge Fiberglass Model... LOA 30' - 4″ DWL 29' - 2″ Beam 10' - 3″ Draft 3' - 0″... Plan #43

32' Vee-Bottom Fiberglass Model... LOA 32' - 4 1/4″ DWL 30' - 0″ Beam 11' - 6″ Draft 2' - 11″... Plan #16

32' Round Bilge Fiberglass Model... LOA 32' - 7″ DWL 30' -10″ Beam 11' - 2″ Draft 3' - 0″... Plan #12

33' Round Bilge Fiberglass Model... LOA 33' - 0″ DWL 31' - 8″ Beam 11' - 8″ Draft 3' - 4″... Plan #48

34' Round Bilge Fiberglass Model... LOA 33' - 8″ DWL 32' - 1″ Beam 12' - 0″ Draft 3' - 6″... Plan #56

34' Vee-Bottom Fiberglass Model... LOA 33' - 11″ DWL 31' - 2″ Beam 11' - 9″ Draft 3' - 7″... Plan #29

34' Round Bilge Fiberglass Model... LOA 34' - 5 1/2″ DWL 32' - 6″ Beam 12' - 0″ Draft 4' - 9″... Plan #39

35' Round Bilge Fiberglass Cruiser & Quahog Model... LOA 35' - 1/2″ DWL 33' - 4″ Beam 11' - 6″ Draft 2' - 11″... Plan #2

35' Round Bilge Wood Model... LOA 35' - 9″ DWL 32' - 6″ Beam 12' - 1″ Draft 3' - 3″... Plan #46

36' Round Bilge Wood Torpedo Stern Lobsterboat... LOA 35' - 8″ DWL 34' - 2″ Beam 9' - 0″ Draft 2' - 8″... Plan #15

36' Round Bilge Fiberglass Model... LOA 36' - 0″ DWL 33' - 9″ Beam 11' - 0″ Draft 3' - 6″... Plan #63

36' Round Bilge Fiberglass Model... LOA 36' - 2″ DWL 34' - 4 1/2″ Beam 12' - 2″..Draft 3' - 1/2″... Plan #20

36' Round Bilge Wood Twin Screw Sportfisherman... LOA 36' - 3″ DWL 34' - 2″ Beam 12' - 0″ Draft 2' - 11″... Plan #7

36' Round Bilge Wood Downeast Lobsterboat... LOA 36' - 4 1/2″ DWL 34' - 8″ Beam 11' - 6″ Draft 3' - 7″... Plan #13

36' Round Bilge Lobsterboat... LOA 36' - 5 1/2" DWL 35' - 0" Beam 11' - 0" Draft 3' - 4 1/2"... Plan #53

37' Vee-Bottom Wood Sportfisherman The Scoot Too... LOA 37' - 2 1/2" DWL 34' - 1/2" Beam 12 – 0" Draft 3' - 4"... Plan #17

38' Round Bilge Fiberglass Model... LOA 37' - 8" DWL 35' - 10" Beam 13' - 4" Draft 5' - 8"... Plan #33

38' Round Bilge Model... LOA 38' - 1" DWL 36' - 8" Beam 12' - 8" Draft 4' - 0"... Plan #68

38' Vee-Bottom Wood Twin Screw Sportfisherman... LOA 38' - 2 1/2" DWL 35' - 0" Beam 13' - 0" Draft 2' - 10"... Plan #24

38' Round Bilge Model... LOA 38' - 3" DWL 36' - 8" Beam 12' - 0" Draft 3 - 10"... Plan #50

38' Sportfisherman... LOA 38' - 6" DWL 35' - 0" Beam 13' - 0" Draft 3' - 4"... Plan #55

38' Round Bilge Fiberglass Model... LOA 38' - 10 1/2" DWL 37' - 1" Beam 13' - 4 1/2" Draft 4' - 3"... Plan #54

39' Round Bilge Model... LOA 39' - 3" DWL 37' - 1" Beam 13' - 4 1/2" Draft 4' - 1"... Plan #37

39' Round Bilge Wood Model... LOA 39' - 6" DWL 36' - 8" Beam 13' - 3" Draft 3' - 6"... Plan #10

40' Round Bilge Fiberglass Model... LOA 39' - 11" DWL 37' - 11" Beam 13' - 9" Draft 4' - 0"... Plan #8

40' Vee-Bottom Fiberglass Model... LOA 40' - 1" DWL 37' - 6" Beam 13' - 2" Draft 4' - 4"... Plan #5

40' Round Bilge Wood Model... LOA 40' - 4" DWL 39' - 4" Beam 11' - 2" Draft 3' - 2"... Plan #64

42' Round Bilge Sportfisherman... LOA 41' - 10" DWL 38' - 4" Beam 13' - 1" Draft 3' - 1"... Plan #62

42' Vee-Bottom Wood Model... LOA 41' - 11 1/2" DWL 40' - 0" Beam 14' - 1" Draft 4' - 6"... Plan #45

42' Round Bilge Fiberglass Model... LOA 42' - 3 1/2" DWL 40' - 0" Beam 13' - 6" Draft 4' - 0"... Plan #14

42' Round Bilge Wood Fisherman... LOA 42' - 7 1/2" DWL 40' - 10" Beam 13' - 10" Draft 4' - 7"... Plan #31

44' Round Bilge Wood Sportfisherman, & Cruiser... LOA 43' - 8" DWL 40' - 0" Beam 14' - 0" Draft 4' - 3"... Plan #27

44' Vee-Bottom Fiberglass Model... LOA 43' - 8" DWL 40' - 5" Beam 15' - 1" Draft 5' - 2 1/2"... Plan #23

44' Round Bilge Cruiser... LOA 43' -11" DWL 41' - 8" Beam 14' - 0" Draft 4' - 7"... Plan #59

46' Round Bilge Fiberglass Model... LOA 46' - 2" DWL 44' - 0" Beam 15' - 0" Draft 4' - 6"... Plan #3

48' Round Bilge Fiberglass Model... LOA 47' - 9" DWL 45' - 0" Beam 16' - 6" Draft 7' - 2"... Plan #44

48' Vee-Bottom Wood Swordfisherman... LOA 48' - 5" DWL 44' - 0" Beam 16' - 1" Draft 4' - 2"... Plan #19

50' Round Bilge Model... LOA 50' - 4 1/2" DWL 47' - 0" Beam 16' - 0" Draft 5' - 9"... Plan #51

53' Multichine Steel Model... LOA 53' - 4" DWL 49' - 0" Beam 16' - 4" Draft 6' - 6"... Plan #25

55' Round Bilge Fiberglass Model... LOA 54' - 11" DWL 50' - 0" Beam 16' - 0" Draft 5' - 3"... Plan #49

55' Vee-Bottom Wood Lobsterboat... LOA 55' - 5 1/2" DWL 52' - 0" Beam 16' - 0" Draft 5' - 4"... Plan #61

56' Round Bilge Wood Model... LOA 56' - 4 1/2" DWL 52' - 0" Beam 17' - 1 1/2" Draft 6' - 7 1/4"... Plan #65

59' Round Bilge Wood Dragger... LOA 59' - 8" DWL 54' - 0" Beam 17' - 0" Draft 6 ' - 10 1/2"... Plan #9

60' Round Bilge Fiberglass Model... LOA 59' - 8" DWL 52' - 0" Beam 17' - 4" Draft 5' - 6"... Plan #22

64' Vee-Bottom Swordfisherman... LOA 64' - 0" DWL 58' - 4" Beam 18' - 0" Draft 8' - 0"... Plan #52

64' Round Bilge Wood Party Fishing Vessel... LOA 64' - 0" DWL 60' - 0" Beam 20' - 0" Draft 4' - 0"... Plan #21

65' Round Bilge Fiberglass... LOA 64' - 3 1/2" DWL 59' - 0" Beam 18' - 2" Draft 7' - 3"... Plan #26

65' Round Bilge Fiberglass... LOA 64' - 4" DWL 61' - 4" Beam 18 - 0" Draft 4' - 10 1/2"... Plan #42

70' Vee-Bottom Wood Research Vessel... LOA 70' - 1/2" DWL 66' - 0" Beam 18' - 6" Draft 7' - 0"... Plan #1

72' Multichine Steel Yacht... LOA 71' - 5" DWL 66' - 0" Beam 21' - 5" Draft 9' - 0"... Plan #66

Index

INDEX

194